Adjustment, Conditionality, and International Financing

Edited by
Joaquín Muns

Papers presented at the seminar on "The Role of the
International Monetary Fund in the Adjustment Process" held
in Viña del Mar, Chile, April 5–8, 1983

Sponsors

International Monetary Fund
Universidad Federico Santa María
Escuela de Negocios de Valparaíso
Fundación Adolfo Ibañez
Banco Central de Chile

International Monetary Fund • 1984

m.R.
ISBN: 0-939934-28-0

Foreword

This book is based on the papers and commentaries presented at the seminar on "The Role of the International Monetary Fund in the Adjustment Process" held in Viña del Mar, Chile, in April 1983. The seminar was jointly sponsored by the Central Bank of Chile, the Business School of Valparaíso—Adolfo Ibañez Foundation—Federico Santa María University, and the International Monetary Fund. The seminar was chaired by Professor Joaquín Muns of the University of Barcelona who has served as Executive Director in the Fund and the World Bank representing Spain and a number of countries in Latin America from 1978 to 1982. Participants were economists representing a wide range of views from universities, banks, and other nonofficial institutions in Argentina, Bolivia, Chile, Paraguay, Peru, and Uruguay. Participants, including members of the staff of the Fund, attended in a personal capacity and the emphasis was on informality and frankness.

The seminar was the first to be conducted in Spanish under the seminar program for nonofficials recently established by the External Relations Department of the Fund. The seminar program aims at promoting understanding of what the Fund has done and is doing to help members with their balance of payments problems. The seminars are also designed to improve the Fund's knowledge of thinking in academic, business, and other circles concerning the issues with which the Fund deals in order to find ways of enhancing the effectiveness of the Fund's work.

The book represents the continuation of the Fund's effort to publish a wide variety of views about its role and activities in the developing world. While the views are not necessarily shared by the Fund, it is our hope that their dissemination can contribute to a better discussion of the issues.

J. de Larosière
Managing Director
International Monetary Fund

Acknowledgement

I thank the three institutions which sponsored the seminar for requesting me to serve as seminar moderator and to compile and present its discussions and conclusions in book form. In particular, continuous contact with the International Monetary Fund—especially with Mr. Azizali F. Mohammed, Director of the External Relations Department, who conceived the seminar and worked tirelessly to ensure its success—provided the climate of mutual understanding that is so desirable in an effort of this kind. I also wish to make special note of the assistance I received at every step from the representatives of the Valparaíso Business School and the Central Bank of Chile, particularly Mr. Francisco Garcés and Mr. Rubén Azócar, as well as Mrs. Antonieta Bonet, who diligently handled the operational details of the seminar and thereby eased the work of all concerned.

Professor Fernando Ossa of the Catholic University of Chile, who served as Rapporteur, deserves special mention. I wish to emphasize and acknowledge his invaluable assistance, on which I relied throughout the sessions, while noting that this was but a portion of his outstanding work in support of the seminar.

I would like to acknowledge the devotion, effort, and enthusiasm brought to the seminar by Hernán Puentes of the Fund's External Relations Department, not only in the planning and execution stages but also in the subsequent drafting of this work, which owes a great debt to his efficient and patient efforts throughout the process from compilation of manuscripts to final publication of this book.

To conclude this note of appreciation, I would also like to thank other Fund staff members, including Juanita Roushdy, who coordinated the editing and production of the volume, and the Spanish and English Divisions of the Bureau of Language Services of the Fund, for translating papers from their original language.

Joaquín Muns
Washington

List of Participants

Moderator

Joaquín Muns
Universidad de Barcelona

Rapporteur

Fernando Ossa
Universidad Católica de Chile

Authors

John F. O. Bilson
University of Chicago and National Bureau of Economic Research

Mario I. Blejer
International Monetary Fund

Sebastian Edwards
University of California at Los Angeles

Jack D. Guenther
Citibank, N.A., New York

Linda M. Koenig
International Monetary Fund

Claudio M. Loser
International Monetary Fund

E. Walter Robichek
International Monetary Fund

Vito Tanzi
International Monetary Fund

Discussants and Other Participants

Argentina

Mario Brodersohn
Financiera Macro

*Guido di Tella
Saint Antony's College, University of Oxford and Universidad Católica de Argentina

*Armando P. Ribas
Bolsa de Valores

*Carlos Alfredo Rodríguez
Centro de Estudios Macroeconómicos de la Argentina

---

*Discussant

Bolivia

*Miguel A. Fabbri
Banco Nacional de Bolivia

*Gustavo Luna Uzquiano
Banco La Paz

Alfonso Revollo
Cámara Americana de Comercio

Luis Saavedra
Banco de Santa Cruz de la Sierra

Chile

José Pablo Arellano
Corporación de Investigaciones Económicas para América Latina (CIEPLAN)

Pedro Arriagada
Escuela de Negocios

*Sergio de la Cuadra
Universidad Católica de Chile

*Juan G. Espinosa
Centro Interamericano de Enseñanza de Estadística (CIENES)

Francisco Garcés
Banco Central de Chile

Jorge Selume
Universidad de Chile

Ramiro Urenda
Escuela de Negocios

Paraguay

*Julio Romero
Yaciretá Binacional

*José E. Páez
Petróleos Paraguayos, S.A.

Marcial Valiente
Econ Financiera, S.A.

Peru

*Carlos Amat y León
Universidad del Pacífico

*Carlos Boloña
Universidad del Pacífico

*Sergio Málaga
Banco Exterior de los Andes y de España

Alonso Polar
Banco Continental

---

*Discussant

Uruguay
  *Alberto Bensión
    Banco Comercial
  Alberto Tisnés
    Universidad de la República

United Nations, Economic Commission for Latin America (ECLA)
  *Carlos Massad

International Monetary Fund
  Azizali F. Mohammed
  Hernán P. Puentes

---

*Discussant

Contents

Foreword   iii

Acknowledgement   v

List of Participants vii

Summary of Conference . . . . *Joaquín Muns*   1

Recent Developments in the World Economy
and in Non-Oil Developing Countries
of the Western Hemisphere . . . . *Linda M. Koenig*   16
   Discussants
     Gustavo Luna Uzquiano
     José E. Páez and Julio Romero

The Process of Balance of Payments Adjustment . . *John F. O. Bilson*   34
   Discussant
     Armando P. Ribas

The IMF's Conditionality Re-Examined . . . . *E. Walter Robichek*   67
   Discussants
     Guido di Tella
     Miguel A. Fabbri

The Role of Economy-Wide Prices in
the Adjustment Process . . . . *Claudio M. Loser*   84
   Discussants
     Carlos Boloña
     Carlos Alfredo Rodríguez

Fiscal Deficits and Balance of Payments
Disequilibrium in
IMF Adjustment Programs . . . . *Vito Tanzi and Mario I. Blejer*   117
   Discussants
     Carlos Amat y León
     Sergio de la Cuadra

The Role of International Reserves and Foreign
Debt in the External Adjustment Process . . . . . *Sebastian Edwards*   143
   Discussants
     Juan Guillermo Espinosa
     Sergio Málaga

The Role of Commercial Banks in the
Adjustment Process . . . . *Jack D. Guenther*   184
   Discussants
     Carlos Massad
     Alberto Bensión

Summary of Conference

Joaquín Muns

In the summer of 1982, after a decade of uneven economic growth with an accumulation of significant imbalances and inflationary tensions which were difficult to control, the world economic situation entered a period of severe financial crisis when efforts were made to renegotiate the external debt of an increasing number of countries, especially in Latin America. The gravity of the situation has once again put to the test the role and operational capacity of the International Monetary Fund (IMF) and, in a broader context, the principles and instruments of international economic cooperation established at Bretton Woods after World War II.

In this situation, it seemed timely and advantageous to hold a conference on "The Role of the International Monetary Fund in the Adjustment Process," which took place April 5–8, 1983 in Viña del Mar, Chile.

The seven papers which appear in this volume are either original texts presented by the authors, or, in some cases, edited versions prepared for inclusion herein.

This summary seeks to fulfill three objectives. The first part offers an overview of the international economic situation which served as a framework for the conference and of the principal events which led up to it. The second part presents a summary of the discussions. Finally, the third part describes the major conclusions which could be drawn from the two and one-half days of sessions which made up the conference.

ECONOMIC ENVIRONMENT

The international economy over the last ten years has been characterized by a series of phenomena which have given it a very distinct shape and which have at the same time led to a series of problems culminating in the financial crisis of 1982.

The most notable characteristics of the period 1973–82 are the following: (a) extreme fluctuations in the rates of economic growth, but with slower overall growth than that of the postwar period, particularly from 1963 to 1972; (b) the continuation and aggravation of the inflationary pressures

1

which had started to develop in 1970–73; and (c) the appearance of severe current account imbalances in the balance of payments, with sharp variations in total amounts over relatively short periods of time (see Table 1).

The period under consideration can be divided into two cycles, both of which are characterized by a phase of substantial increase in petroleum prices and by the process whereby the various groups of countries adapted to the new circumstances. From this perspective, the first cycle covers the period 1973–78; the second begins in 1979 and actually has not ended, as we shall see.

The differences between the two cycles explain, to a great extent, the difficulties faced by numerous developing countries and which, for many of these countries, have led to a crisis in debt servicing. The basic element which differentiates the two cycles is that the adjustment process in the industrial nations when petroleum prices were first increased (1973–74) was largely completed by 1974–75, so that the growth of this group of countries as well as world trade development in 1976–78 reached levels comparable to those in the period immediately preceding 1973 (Table 1, Section A). In contrast, the industrial nations adjusted more slowly to the second increase in petroleum prices (1979–80), with a slower growth rate in output which continued through the three-year period 1980–82 and, despite the change in trend beginning in 1983, cannot yet be said to have ended.[1] On the other hand, in contrast with the preceding adjustment cycle, world trade in 1980–82 ceased to grow in volume, and the average dollar value of world trade decreased during the last two years of this three-year period (Table 1, Section C).

Faced with the situation which began in 1973–74, the overall strategy of the non-oil developing countries[2] was to maintain a maximum growth rate with the least possible fluctuations. Social, economic, and even political factors explain why this type of approach was taken. As can be seen from

---

[1]The most recent IMF projections estimate that the expected overall growth rate for the industrial nations in 1983 will be about 1.5 percent. The average annual rate for 1980–82 was 0.7 percent.

[2]The country classifications used by the IMF and in most of the papers discussed here are as follows: The industrial nations are Australia, Austria, Belgium, Canada, Denmark, Finland, France, Federal Republic of Germany, Iceland, Ireland, Italy, Japan, Luxembourg, the Netherlands, New Zealand, Norway, Spain, Sweden, Switzerland, the United Kingdom, and the United States. Oil exporting countries are those which meet the following two criteria (applied to the period 1977–79): petroleum exports (net of imports of crude oil) represent at least two thirds of the country's total exports and are at least 100 million barrels a year (equal to approximately 1 percent of annual world petroleum exports). The countries classified in this group are Algeria, Indonesia, the Islamic Republic of Iran, Iraq, Kuwait, Libya, Nigeria, Oman, Qatar, Saudi Arabia, United Arab Emirates, and Venezuela. The non-oil developing countries are the remaining developing countries. See *World Economic Outlook: A Survey by the Staff of the International Monetary Fund*, IMF Occasional Paper No. 9 (Washington, May 1982) pp. 140–41.

Table 1, Section A, here also there are two distinct phases in reaching this objective: one phase which extends to 1978, and another phase which begins in 1979.

In the first phase (1973–78), the average growth rate of the non-oil developing countries reached 5.2 percent—just slightly lower than the average for the preceding five-year period, during which it reached 6 percent a year. This effort led to an increase in the current account balance of payments deficit for this group of countries, from $11.3 billion in 1973 to $41.3 billion in 1978 (Table 1, Section B). The fundamental characteristic of this period—particularly up to 1977—from the perspective of financing this growing deficit, is that the cost represented by the additional debt taken on by this group of countries grew at a rate which on the average was equal to the value of exports of goods and services, so that the total burden of debt service, measured as a percentage of exports, showed little variation up to 1977 (Table 1, Sections C and D). On the other hand, although the level of reserves as compared with the value of imports of goods and services was lower in 1978 than the percentage in 1973 (25.9 percent compared with 31.4 percent), this ratio improved in the period 1975–78 (Table 1, Section E).

From 1978, the non-oil developing countries were affected by a substantial deterioration in the real terms of trade and by a significant increase in interest rates. This last factor combined with a debt composition in which short-term debt and debt to private financial institutions accounted for a growing share of total debt. This process substantially raised the cost of total active debt, but the importance and immediate impact of this fact were masked by the spectacular increase in exports of this group of countries during the two-year period 1979–80, which reached an annual average of 27.5 percent.

The increasing debt service of the developing countries made them very sensitive to any significant and continuous worsening in their export market situation. Unfortunately, as we have seen, this possibility started to become reality in 1980 with the beginning of the phase of slow growth in the industrial economies, a phase which continues today.

The financing mechanism of the current account deficit in the non-oil developing countries which prevailed since 1978 continued in 1981 and the first half of 1982. However, the increasing burden of debt service payments and the stagnation of exports reduced the ability to import and with it growth rates, which decreased significantly in the two-year period 1981–82. The failure of domestic policies to adapt to the new circumstances was translated into a drain on international reserves for many of these countries.

In mid-1982, the level of foreign reserves of several important debtor countries reached minimum levels. The reaction of private lenders, especially banks, was to reduce drastically the net flow of new funds.[3] This lack

---

[3]The data on this development are contained in the paper by Mr. Jack D. Guenther.

Evolution of Some Basic Economic Variables
During the Period 1973–82
for Principal Groups of Countries[1]

	Average 1963–72	1973	1974	1975	1976	1977	1978	1979	1980	1981	1982
A) *Growth of GNP*				(Percentage change over preceding year)							
Industrial nations	4.7	6.2	0.5	-0.6	5.0	4.0	4.1	3.4	1.3	1.2	-0.3
Oil exporting countries	9.0[2]	10.7	8.0	-0.3	12.3	6.1	2.0	3.1	-2.3	-4.3	-4.8
Non-oil developing countries	6.0[2]	6.1	5.4	3.3	6.0	5.2	5.4	4.6	4.3	2.4	0.9
B) *Current account balance of payments*				(In billions of U.S. dollars)							
Industrial nations		20.3	-10.8	19.8	0.5	-2.2	32.7	-5.6	-40.1	0.6	-1.2
Oil exporting countries		6.7	68.3	35.4	40.3	30.2	2.2	68.6	114.3	65.0	-2.2
Non-oil developing countries		-11.3	-37.0	-46.3	-32.6	-28.9	-41.3	-61.0	-89.0	-107.7	-86.8
C) *World Trade*				(Percentage change over preceding year)							
Volume	8.5	12.0	4.5	-3.5	11.0	5.0	5.5	6.5	2.0	0.5	-2.5
Value in U.S. dollars	3.0	23.5	40.0	9.5	1.5	8.5	10.0	18.5	20.0	-1.0	-4.0
Non-oil developing countries											
· Terms of trade	0.3	5.3	-5.9	-8.5	5.9	5.9	-3.7	-0.3	-6.2	-3.9	-2.7
· Value of exports of goods and services			37	—	18	19	-18	28	27	5	-2

(In percentage)

D) *External debt of non-oil developing countries*										
Long-term debt service as a percentage of exports of goods and services	15.9	14.4	16.1	15.3	15.4	19.0	19.0	17.6	20.4	23.9
Eurodollar rate of interest[3]	9.3	11.1	7.8	6.2	6.4	9.3	12.2	13.9	16.9	13.6
E) *Non-oil developing country reserves*										
As a percentage of imports of goods and services	31.4	21.6	19.1	23.6	25.2	25.9	22.3	17.5	16.2	16.3

Sources: International Monetary Fund, *World Economic Outlook: A Survey by the Staff of the International Monetary Fund*, IMF Occasional Paper No. 21 (Washington, 1983); Mr. Guenther's paper and Merrill Lynch & Company.
[1] For the criteria and composition of the groups, see note 1.
[2] Average for 1968–72.
[3] Rate of interest in the Eurodollar market for six-month offerings. Average of daily data.

of confidence was transferred to domestic sectors of the economy, and capital flight then aggravated the situation. The combination of these factors exhausted the maneuvering room of many of the economies affected and made it impossible for them to meet all debt service payments promptly. This situation was particularly severe in Latin America.[4]

The magnitude of the financial crisis brought on by this series of events and policies is far-reaching. In 1982, 18 countries were forced to renegotiate their external debt; this clearly indicated the widespread nature of the problem. Renegotiations affected 7 countries in 1980 and 13 in 1981. Moreover, the list of countries renegotiating their external debt has been growing in 1983, and most of the principal countries in Latin America are now being affected in one way or another. It can be said that through 1982 and up to April 1983, the international financial crisis has forced renegotiation upon countries whose debt represented between 45 and 50 percent of the external debt outstanding at the end of 1982.[5] In addition, since 1982, seven of the ten largest borrowers have been involved in renegotiating their debts.

On the other hand, the decrease in oil prices which began last year has extended the debt renegotiation problem to some oil exporting countries, so that the sequence of events described here is to a great extent also applicable to them.

SUMMARY OF DISCUSSIONS

The presentation of the seven papers which made up the conference led to a wide-ranging and interesting discussion on each of them. The following summary includes the most important points made in the initial remarks of the speakers and during the discussions which followed. The content is based on notes taken during the discussion and, to a great extent, upon the final summary which I presented, as conference moderator, at the final session. This summary is in no way intended to be an official, exhaustive report of everything discussed, in the sense of minutes of a meeting. It is basically an effort to organize the ideas and opinions expressed during the conference according to the author's perception of their interest and importance. The informal nature of the discussions and the grouping of remarks around different points of view make it advisable to omit the names of the individuals who took part in the discussion on each subject, which, at any rate, could not be faithfully recorded in what must of necessity be a very condensed summary of many hours of debate.

---

[4]The mechanics of this process in Latin America are reflected in the overall balance of payments for the region as shown by Ms. Linda M. Koenig in her presentation.

[5]Obviously, this does not mean that this amount was renegotiated. Renegotiation normally involves the short-term and part of the medium-term debt.

The first paper is entitled "Recent Developments in the World Economy and in Non-Oil Developing Countries of the Western Hemisphere" and was presented by Ms. Linda M. Koenig, Deputy Director of the Central Banking Department of the IMF. Its purpose was to provide background on recent developments in the international economy and in non-oil developing countries of the American continent. The author stressed first the general environment of slow economic growth, especially in the industrial nations, against a background of sluggish international trade and lessening inflationary pressures. The indicated decrease in petroleum prices has caused a noticeable improvement in the world outlook for a gradual recovery throughout 1983, a view which met with general agreement although it was stated that the effects of this renewed activity may be less in Latin America than in other areas.

With regard to the economies of non-oil developing countries in the Americas, Koenig emphasized in her paper the decrease in the region's total output in 1982, the increase in inflationary pressures, and the major changes in the various elements of the balance of payments for the period 1980–82. Particularly noteworthy were the decreases in capital inflows and exports, which forced a marked reduction in imports, the stagnation of the region's growth rate, and a loss of approximately $11 billion in the region's international reserves.

The gravity of the Latin American situation reflected in Koenig's presentation, about which there was no serious disagreement, led to an interesting discussion, revolving around three different subjects: the causes of the drastic deterioration of the economic situation in this area of the world; the nature of the adjustment made in 1982; and the outlook for the future.

Regarding causes, some of the participants were inclined to stress the role of exogenous factors; particular mention was made of the unfavorable developments in petroleum prices, high interest rates on debt, the worldwide recession, and the protectionist tendencies of the industrial nations. Another group of participants put more emphasis on internal factors—a lack of economic discipline, mismanagement of some basic elements such as the rate of exchange, and the maintenance of unmanageable levels of global demand based on a growing external debt. It was generally agreed that the two points of view were complementary rather than mutually exclusive, and that proper management of the domestic economy was essential in recent years, although it would have been difficult to avoid completely the negative effects of the international situation.

With regard to the second topic—the nature of the adjustment made in Latin America—emphasis was placed upon the abruptness and intensity of the adjustment in 1982 in response to the basic factor which arose in the region in that year: the crisis in the level of indebtedness. It was generally agreed that this adjustment was inevitable, and several participants stressed the role of the Fund in the effort to make the adjustment orderly.

The third topic discussed with reference to Koenig's paper involved the possibility of maintaining an adjustment of this size in the future, even while recognizing the necessity for it. Several participants expressed the fear that the drastic decrease in production could lead to serious social and political tensions in Latin America. Others expressed doubts as to the success of the effort unless there was a substantial drop in real interest rates on debt, a significant worldwide recovery, and a curbing of protectionist tendencies. There was even open reference to the specter of debt repudiation which hangs over the whole situation. It can be said in general that there was a belief the present situation could be overcome if everyone involved—governments, banks, and international organizations—made an effort to cooperate and continued to lend their support to the Latin American economies.

The second paper, "The Process of Balance of Payments Adjustment," was presented by Professor John F. O. Bilson of the University of Chicago. After making explicit the technical aspects of the monetary approach to the balance of payments, his paper developed the asset market approach to the balance of payments, which studies the transmission of financial disturbances in a world with integrated financial markets but segmented product markets. This transmission causes considerable instability in small countries when unstable conditions exist in the country which issues the reserve currency. If, in addition, the relationship among exchange rates in the industrial nations is extremely volatile, an even greater impact is felt in peripheral countries with regard to instability of real interest and exchange rates and of real prices for raw materials, partly because their residents have substantial debts denominated in various foreign currencies.

These difficulties inspire the author to seek a procedure which would permit small countries in particular to insulate their exchange rates as much as possible from disturbances emanating from the reserve currency countries. This is achieved by adjusting the exchange rate to maintain at all times the equality of central bank assets and liabilities computed in dollars (for example, in the absence of a change in the monetary base, the receipt of interest on the central bank's foreign assets would require an appreciation of the exchange rate in order to maintain this equality). The author believes that, through proper management of the asset portfolios of the central banks, two desirable objectives could be achieved: a greater stability in the exchange rate, on the one hand, and a lower cost of indebtedness, on the other.

Two different aspects of Bilson's presentation were discussed: first, the implications and technical consistency of the model, and, second, its usefulness in the real world in which we live.

With regard to the elements of the model, some participants disagreed with various aspects of the characterization of the monetary approach to the balance of payments. Others expressed reservations as to the credibility of the proposed exchange rate management. Doubts were also expressed as to the ultimate composition of the central bank assets which would support the proposed exchange rate policy.

The second group of questions was addressed in general to the practical difficulties of allowing variables such as exchange rates and money supply to be dependent upon the adjustment aimed at equalizing central bank assets and liabilities. For some this would establish relationships which cannot be realistically maintained in a world in which governments have assumed overall economic responsibilities.

In conclusion, Bilson's paper had the great merit of suggesting an instrument which, while admittedly still in the experimental stage, would improve exchange rate policies and lower the cost of indebtedness. His contribution is to look for logic and automatic procedures in areas which the author sees as being increasingly arbitrary and interventionist.

The third paper, entitled "The IMF's Conditionality Re-Examined," was presented by Mr. E. Walter Robichek, Advisor to the Managing Director of the IMF. The paper examined the conditionality of the Fund as one of the basic elements in its programs.

In the first section, Robichek analyzed the legal basis for the Fund's conditionality and justified and documented at length the institution's jurisdiction in this area. There was virtually unanimous acceptance of the Fund's legal right to establish some form of conditionality. The scarcity of resources and the need to discipline economies, as well as the Fund's statutory mandate, were the elements most frequently mentioned as justifications for its conditionality.

In the second section, Robichek analyzed the limitations which the Fund must face in its adjustment programs. In the author's opinion, the Fund's limited resources and the very nature of the magnitudes it deals with make greater flexibility in its programs impracticable. On this point, several participants expressed their judgment that the duration of Fund programs is exceedingly short under the present circumstances, but it was ultimately agreed that the Fund cannot avoid a difficult trade-off between resources and flexibility.

The third section of Robichek's presentation examined the policy instrumentation of the Fund's adjustment programs, concentrating on two aspects: the performance criteria and the supply and demand policies of the Fund's programs. In this section, several observations were made regarding issues such as: what some participants considered encroachment by these instruments on national autonomy, the acceptance in the Fund's programs of the automaticity of the market, and the priority given to objectives over the means of attaining them. Those who expressed these views generally felt that these problems hamper the full incorporation of the Fund's programs in the different and changing realities of individual countries. Other participants pointed out that the Fund has demonstrated its ability to use its influence and instruments pragmatically and flexibly.

In the fourth and final section of his paper, Robichek addressed the implications of the worldwide economic recession for the Fund's conditionality, particularly in light of the magnitude of the present difficulties. This section of the presentation led to observations regarding the adequacy of the Fund's capacity to face the present conditions. Some participants questioned whether the Fund was prepared or equipped for a world crisis like the present one; others stressed the importance of exogenous factors, such as the rate of interest of the debt, which are outside the Fund's control. It can be generally concluded that the majority agreed that the performance of the Fund would be strengthened by a widening of its capital base, which some believed could be obtained in the international markets, and through the Fund's close and continuing cooperation with governments and banks.

The fourth paper, "The Role of Economy-Wide Prices in the Adjustment Process," was presented by Mr. Claudio Loser, Division Chief in the Exchange and Trade Relations Department of the IMF. In the first section, Loser analyzed three basic aspects of the role of economy-wide prices in the adjustment process. He considered, first, the effects on the functioning of the economy in general; second, the need for coordination with other economic policy measures; and third, the practical rather than ideological desirability of using economy-wide prices in the Fund's programs. In this context, the following were considered economy-wide prices: exchange rates, interest rates, wages, and administered prices.

In the second part of his paper, Loser examined actual experience with economy-wide price policies in Fund programs. He stressed that the existence of price distortions was one of the most common problems in countries which undertook programs with the Fund and that, for this reason, measures to correct these distortions were characteristic of practically all of the programs. The author concluded that these pricing policies had generally been successful when accompanied by the prescribed policies which were necessary to support them.

In the final part of his presentation, Loser reviewed experiences with preannounced or fixed exchange rates which had been used in recent years in four Latin American countries (Argentina, Chile, Mexico, and Uruguay). Although the objectives of these policies were sound, the particular applications under study led to overvaluations of the exchange rate and had to be abandoned. A severe devaluation then occurred in all cases, giving reason to believe that the reaction was one of overshooting. The author concluded that this all happened principally because the exchange rate policy followed was not consistent with other governmental policies.

Loser's presentation led to a considerable number of remarks, which fall into several categories. First, several participants accused Loser of being excessively macroeconomic in his approach. They felt that it was important to know how prices affected the different sectors of the economy and how they were transmitted throughout the economy. It was their view that this aspect was so important that its effects could not be separated from the overall effect of macroeconomic policies.

Along the same lines, some participants emphasized the complexity of the relationship between prices and other economic variables. An example of this was the relationship between real exchange rates and real wages, regarding which there were several interpretations. Also, the fact that the Fund's programs seek to maintain a real exchange rate was a concern of some participants who felt that, given the difficulty of determining its equilibrium level, this policy could lead to competitive depreciations. It should be concluded from this discussion, for those who are of this opinion, that great care is required in dealing with economy-wide pricing policies at the global level.

A second group of participants included those who objected to the view of the markets involved in Fund programs. As an example, mention was made of the inflexibility existing in the labor market and of the incompatibility of this fact with the Fund's view of wages in its programs as a residual variable.

A third group of remarks referred to the increasingly difficult situation faced by the private sector in national economies and to the fact that the Fund's programs may not make sufficient allowance for this situation when they prescribe policies focusing more and more on problems in and of the public sector which, in many cases, cause serious difficulties for private sector financing.

There was general agreement regarding the significant negative effects which price distortions, particularly in exchange and interest rates, have had upon the economies of Latin America. It was felt that a price policy to correct these distortions was necessary, but that such a policy could be effective only if accompanied by parallel measures to support it. The need to coordinate the economy-wide price policies of Fund programs and national objectives and priorities was also mentioned.

The fifth paper, written by Mr. Vito Tanzi, Director of the Fiscal Affairs Department of the IMF, and Mr. Mario Blejer, economist in the same department, was presented by Mr. Blejer and entitled "Fiscal Deficits and Balance of Payments Disequilibrium in IMF Adjustment Programs." In the first section, the authors examined different views of fiscal deficits. In the second section, they reviewed the various sources of deficit financing, studying, in order, external sources, noninflationary internal sources, and, finally, inflationary sources. Under each of these categories, they examined existing arrangements and their specific impact on the deficit.

In the third section, Tanzi and Blejer considered the effects of expansionary fiscal policies on the balance of payments. They felt that the general effect of this type of policy was inflationary when it was not followed by an equal contraction in private sector financing. Next, they analyzed the financing of an expansionary fiscal policy, which could be achieved through monetary expansion, private sector loans, or external loans. They concluded that the first method was the most harmful because of its greater inflationary impact.

In the final section of the paper, the authors referred to the treatment of fiscal deficits under Fund programs. They justified the inclusion of these variables by reason of their effect on the balance of payments and concluded that the balance of payments had generally improved under those programs whose fiscal targets had been met.

The paper provoked several comments. Some referred to the political nature of budget deficits and, as a consequence, to the strong political impact which the Fund's actions could have in this area. Others commented that the Fund was concerned with the macroeconomic effect of the deficit and not its use, which could be beneficial, in their opinion, when it served to stimulate investment. Other participants expressed their conviction that private sector deficits could sometimes be equally harmful and could lead, as seemed to have been the case in Chile, to a crowding out of the public sector.

In general terms, it can be said that no one doubted the generally harmful effects of public sector deficits which, in the best of cases, were liable to cause serious difficulties for the private sector. The Latin American experience in this area was mentioned frequently as a case in point.

The sixth paper, entitled "The Role of International Reserves and External Debt in the External Adjustment Process," was prepared and presented by Professor Sebastian Edwards of the University of California at Los Angeles. He investigated various aspects of the external adjustment process in the developing countries by using theoretical models and a broad, complex system of interrelationships. The analysis, based on a sample of 19 countries, led the author to state that, during the period 1975–80, these countries used reserves and indebtedness as substitutes in the adjustment process, an aspect frequently ignored in economic literature on policies for overcoming external disequilibria. Again on the basis of an empirical analysis, the author concluded that the international community considered reserve and debt levels to be basic strategic variables in evaluating the level of risk faced by each country.

In his study, Edwards integrated a dynamic analysis of demand on reserves with that of conditions of equilibrium in the monetary sector of the economy. His conclusion, based on a study of an historical period, was that the reserve level was a function of the effort to eliminate discrepancies between desired and actual reserves and also of excess supply of money. According to this author, this made it necessary for economic authorities to give particular consideration to monetary aspects when managing international reserves.

With regard to recent external debt problems especially in the Southern Cone countries, this paper raised various topics of interest. Concerning the cases of excessive external borrowing, especially in those countries where there was a parallel process of financial liberalization, he suggested the need to improve the domestic system of banking supervision and to determine an optimum level of external indebtedness for the private sector based on the creation of a tax on foreign lending operations. The paper also alluded to the significance of recent Latin American experience with the failure of savings to respond favorably to the increasing level of external debt, which would indicate that it has to a great extent been directed toward the financing of consumption.

Finally, with regard to Latin America, Edwards concluded that future difficulties in increasing the debt would inevitably make it necessary to have a greater volume of international reserves if the confidence of the international community was to be maintained.

It was generally felt that Edwards's model and conclusions were very interesting. Some criticisms stressed possible deficiencies of the model. In this context, mention was made of the model's failure to include the demand on reserves by other economic agents or to distinguish among the various types of debt. Reference was also made to the fact that the relationship between the demand on reserves and that on money was not properly described in the model.

Other participants commented that the model was unrealistic in some ways or gave superficial treatment to some element which they considered essential, such as banking supervision. In this respect, several comments were made criticizing the disorderly process of borrowing in Latin America and the inability of the authorities to control it. The participants agreed that, although not designed to answer all these questions, Edwards's model was interesting and deserving of refinement in several areas, a task on which the author promised to follow through.

The final paper, "The Role of Commercial Banks in the Adjustment Process," was presented by Mr. Jack D. Guenther, Vice President of Citibank. The author's first section analyzed the borrowing rate of the developing countries during the 1970s and reached the conclusion that indebtedness grew parallel to the ability to service it. It was the author's opinion that, since 1980, the indebtedness of the developing countries had come to be of greater concern for three reasons: (1) their exports have stagnated; (2) interest rates have exploded and are very high in historical terms; and (3) the internal policies of the major countries have been inappropriate. The author concluded that these circumstances require that debt rise over the next five years by about three points below the rate of exports, which he estimated at about 10 percent. This led Guenther to propose, as reasonable and desirable, an annual increase over the next five years of 7 percent in net international bank commitments in the developing countries.

The second section discussed the balance of payments in the non-oil developing countries and considered the possibility that the period 1981–83 would produce an adjustment process that would reduce the overall current account balance of payments deficit from $102 billion to $65 billion. The author believed that this effort was possible, comparable with the effort achieved in 1975 and 1977, and compatible with the net increase in credit from the banks to these countries of 7 percent a year, which is proposed for the next five years.

In the final section, Guenther examined accusations that private banking was overexposed in the developing countries and had concentrated its lending on too few countries. The author provided data to refute these views.

All the participants' comments reflected the great interest with which Guenther's paper was received and, in general, discussions followed a number of lines of thought. Thus, some emphasized the fact that the study's predictions could not be realized without a worldwide expansion and a significant reduction in interest rates, aspects which in their opinion were not given sufficient emphasis in the paper. Others felt that the powerlessness of the debtors in the debt renegotiation process was the basic point to be made. For these individuals, the present situation obliged these countries to assume a very heavy burden, which, in their opinion, may have been underestimated by the optimism pervading Guenther's presentation. With respect to the events which led to the present situation, several participants pointed to the lack of coordination among all the parties involved in financing the developing countries and the insufficiency of the data utilized. In general, the Fund's work in renegotiating debt and its role as a catalyst for joint efforts were viewed favorably, but some of those who spoke demonstrated their concern over the risks which this relationship implies. Considering the gravity of the situation, some referred to the need to think about developing an emergency solution in case present arrangements failed. Finally, it was considered fundamental that banks not withdraw their confidence from Latin America, and Guenther's paper was considered to have made a very positive contribution to the reasoned attainment of this objective.

CONCLUSIONS

The conference did not propose to arrive at specific conclusions, but it seemed interesting to me to extract from all the discussions the more important points about which there were no serious differences of opinion and to incorporate them in the final report which I delivered as moderator of the sessions. In a sense, these points—of which there are five—can be considered the fundamental nuclei around which the ideas and opinions, developed during the two and one-half days of sessions, took shape.

First, there was a consensus that the economic situation in Latin America is very difficult. Koenig's paper illustrated perfectly the severity of the situation and described the international context in which this deterioration developed as well as the different specific ways in which this crisis has manifested itself in the context of Latin America.

Second, the adjustment needed in Latin America must seek to achieve simultaneously the recovery of financial solvency and the re-establishment of a balance of payments situation which is consistent with sustainable short-term and long-term debt levels and conducive to lasting growth.

Third, it was considered particularly important that the private international banking system continue to assist in the financial effort necessary to achieve the goals outlined by the adjustment programs. Should this source of financing become unavailable to any significant extent, it would pose a practically insurmountable obstacle.

Fourth, it was generally agreed that the efforts of the Fund in the adjustment process have been fundamental and would continue to be so. The examination of the fiscal and price policies which the Fund incorporates in its programs led to the conclusion that success depended on the consistency of these policies with other necessary supportive economic policy measures.

Fifth, the conference was clearly unanimous in the belief that the ultimate feasibility of the adjustment programs is intimately linked to two elements: an international economic recovery and a decrease in real rates of interest to levels more consistent with historical experience.

The underlying conviction throughout the conference was that just as endogenous and exogenous factors had necessarily combined to create the present state of affairs so too would the present adjustment require a combination of internal efforts and minimally favorable external circumstances.

Recent Developments in the World Economy and in Non-Oil Developing Countries of the Western Hemisphere

LINDA M. KOENIG

INTRODUCTION

This paper summarizes the major findings of the world economic outlook exercise carried out by the Fund staff in December 1982, with particular emphasis on developments in the non-oil developing countries of the Western Hemisphere. For purposes of the world economic outlook exercise, Fund members are divided into three groups: industrial countries, oil exporting countries, and non-oil developing countries; nonmembers constitute a fourth group. In the case of the Western Hemisphere, the group of non-oil developing countries includes five net oil exporters—Mexico, Ecuador, Bolivia, Peru, and Trinidad and Tobago—which do not satisfy the world economic outlook criteria for inclusion as oil exporters.[1] Only Venezuela satisfies these criteria.

The world economic outlook exercise is a comprehensive staff project involving a number of departments in the Fund. The exercise, carried out in full once a year and updated periodically, entails detailed country-by-country projections of growth, inflation, and the balance of payments based on a standard set of assumptions; these data are then aggregated for analytical purposes. The exercise draws on staff research and contacts with member countries and, particularly, on the consultations that the Fund conducts with member countries in the exercise of its responsibility for surveillance over exchange rate policies.

---

[1] The criteria used in the world economic outlook exercise to distinguish a country as an oil exporter are that oil exports (net of any imports of crude oil) account for at least two thirds of the country's total exports and that such net exports are at least 100 million barrels a year (roughly equivalent to 1 percent of annual world exports of oil). For a breakdown of the country groups see *World Economic Outlook: A Survey by the Staff of the International Monetary Fund*, IMF Occasional Paper No. 9 (Washington, May 1982), pp. 140–41.

16

As is described in the following sections, 1982 was a year of slow, in many cases negligible, real growth in most parts of the world. The growth performance of the non-oil developing countries of the Western Hemisphere was much worse than that of the other non-oil developing country regional groupings. Concurrently, the downward adjustment of real imports in the non-oil developing countries of the Western Hemisphere was much more severe than elsewhere. To some extent this was due to a slower adjustment to the second oil shock of 1979 than occurred in certain other areas of the world. However, the severity of the financial problems faced by Western Hemisphere countries in 1982 also reflected an extremely sharp reduction in net capital inflow—the counterpart of the enormous increase in the net inflow of capital of the preceding five years. The experience of these Western Hemisphere countries in 1982 raises questions concerning (1) how to arrive at a judgment regarding the sustainable current account deficit of a country or region in the present fragmented world monetary system, and (2) whether indeed the present system can provide for the balanced expansion of world trade over the medium run, and, if not, how it can be improved. These key questions recur with respect to many of the subjects discussed in the other papers of this volume.

RECENT DEVELOPMENTS IN THE WORLD ECONOMY AND PROSPECTS FOR 1983[2]

The world economy in 1982 was characterized by extremely weak economic activity and rising unemployment, declining inflation (but disappointingly small for the non-oil developing countries) and, for the first time since 1975, a shrinkage in the volume of world trade. Expectations of imminent economic recovery were repeatedly unfulfilled throughout the year. The recovery now apparently beginning is projected to bring year-on-year growth in gross national product (GNP) in the industrial countries of a little over 1 percent in 1983. In the second half of 1983, the real GNP of these countries is projected to expand at an annual rate of 2.5 percent. Inflation is expected to moderate further throughout the world in 1983 and the volume of trade to recover by 3 percent.

---

[2]The 1983 projections cited in this paper are those made by the Fund staff in February 1983. Subsequent estimates indicated, for the industrial countries, a somewhat faster recovery in output, a better current account balance, and a more rapid reduction in inflation than originally had been foreseen, linked to a lower than projected level of petroleum prices. However, the situation of the non-oil developing countries and, in particular, those of the Western Hemisphere was not materially altered by these changes.

Output

Output growth in the industrial countries, as measured by the change in real GNP, declined by 0.3 percent in 1982 (Table 1). Output declines were particularly pronounced in the United States and Canada, at 1.8 percent and 4.9 percent, respectively. Real GNP grew weakly in all other industrial countries except the Federal Republic of Germany, where it declined by slightly over 1 percent. However, whereas output tended to stabilize in the second half of the year in the United States and Canada, activity in most European countries was much weaker in the second semester than in the first. Economic recovery, which appears to be beginning in the United States and Canada, is expected to spread gradually to the European countries during 1983. The Japanese economy, which among those of the major industrial countries was relatively less affected by the slowdown in activity, is projected to expand in 1983 at the same 3 percent rate it registered in 1982.

The chief factors behind the poor output performance of the industrial economies in 1982 were the decline in fixed investment and inventory holdings and the contraction in real imports of the non-oil developing countries as a group. This decline in imports was the consequence of poor terms of trade and lower export volume for the non-oil developing countries; sharply higher interest payments; and a major decline in net long-term capital inflow.

In the non-oil developing countries, real output growth, while not actually declining, slowed substantially (Table 2). The only exceptions within this group were (1) major exporters of manufactures, whose real growth already had plunged to 0.4 percent in 1981 and remained at that rate in 1982, and (2) the so-called low-income countries—those whose output, as estimated by the World Bank, did not exceed the equivalent of $350 in 1978. On a regional

Table 1. Major Industrial Countries: Changes in Real Output[1]

(In percent)

	1979	1980	1981	1982	Proj. 1983
Canada	2.9	0.5	3.1	−4.9	0.9
United States	2.8	−0.4	1.9	−1.8	1.6
Japan	5.2	4.2	2.9	3.0	3.0
France	3.3	1.1	0.4	1.4	0.4
Germany, Federal Republic of	4.0	1.8	−0.2	−1.2	−0.3
Italy	4.9	3.9	−0.2	0.4	0.9
United Kingdom	2.0	−2.1	−2.2	0.6	1.0

[1] GNP, excepting gross domestic product (GDP) at market prices for France, Italy, and the United Kingdom.

basis, real output of non-oil developing countries in the Western Hemisphere contracted by 0.7 percent, while the output growth of other regional groupings except the non-oil developing countries in Europe slowed very substantially (Appendix, Table 11).

In 1983, the rate of real output growth of non-oil developing countries is projected to recover to 2.4 percent, still very far below their growth rate in the 1960s and 1970s. The recovery will be spread among most analytical and regional subgroupings with the exception of the non-oil developing countries in the Western Hemisphere, whose combined output is projected to decline by a further 0.3 percent.

Real output of the oil exporting countries fell in 1982, for the third consecutive year, but is expected to recover in 1983.

Inflation

The rise in the combined GNP deflator of the seven major industrial countries decelerated progressively during 1982, a trend that is projected to continue in 1983. Most of the decline in inflation from 1981 to 1982 reflected the sharp drop in the rate of price increase in the United States and Canada. In 1983, a pronounced decline in inflation is expected to be more widespread. As a great deal of the progress in reducing inflation has been made in countries whose inflation rates were above the industrial countries average, the dispersion of inflation rates across countries is expected generally to moderate in 1983 (Table 3).

Progress toward reducing inflation in the rest of the world was less marked in 1982 than in the industrial countries. While the average inflation rate for oil exporting countries declined from 13 percent to 10 percent, it rose from 31 percent to 36 percent for non-oil developing countries; however, this increase reflected an acceleration of inflation in a few large countries; the median inflation rate for non-oil developing countries dropped from 13.4 percent to 11.8 percent, the second consecutive year of decline from the 1980

Table 2. Major Country Groupings: Changes in Real Output

(In percent)

	1979	1980	1981	1982	Proj. 1983
Industrial countries[1]	3.4	1.2	1.2	−0.3	1.3
Oil exporting countries[2]	3.1	−2.3	−4.3	−4.7	4.5
Non-oil developing countries[2]	5.0	4.9	2.8	1.8	2.4

[1] Mainly GNP. See footnote 1 of Table1.
[2] GDP at market prices.

peak of 15 percent. Continued weakness in demand management, particularly in the fiscal area, and the need, in many countries, for corrective price increases (Table 4 and Appendix, Table 12) impeded any further progress in reducing inflation.

Throughout the world, the decline in nominal interest rates lagged behind the decline in inflation, a development that to a significant extent reflected trends in the United States. However, during the second half of 1982, as the rate of inflation in the U.S. leveled off and, at the same time, inflationary expectations began to decline, real interest rates in the United States did decline substantially, although remaining far above their historical levels. This decline in real U.S. interest rates exceeded that of other industrial countries and virtually did away with the substantial yield differentials among industrial countries that had prevailed earlier in the year. At the end of 1982, real short-term interest rates of the major industrial countries were all around 4 percent, still far above historical levels.

International Trade and Payments

The volume of world trade, which had grown by very little in 1980 and not at all in 1981, contracted by 1.5 percent in 1982, the first such contraction since 1975. Imports of oil exporting countries grew much more slowly than in previous years, those of the industrial countries were flat and those of the non-oil developing countries contracted by an estimated 4 percent. As noted above, the import capacity of these countries was reduced by a variety of factors including a deterioration in the terms of trade (for the fifth consecutive year), a fall in export volume, sharply rising interest payments, and a substantial contraction in net external financing.

There was a major realignment in the current account positions of the different groups of countries, as the combined current account surplus of oil

Table 3. Major Industrial Countries: Changes in GNP Deflators

(In percent)

	1979	1980	1981	1982	Proj. 1983
Canada	10.3	11.0	10.1	10.4	7.0
United States	8.7	9.3	9.4	6.0	4.6
Japan	2.6	3.0	2.9	2.4	2.7
France[1]	10.3	11.8	12.0	12.5	9.0
Germany, Federal Republic of	4.1	4.4	4.2	4.4	4.0
Italy[1]	15.9	20.7	17.6	17.1	17.2
United Kingdom[1]	15.0	19.2	12.1	8.3	5.6

[1] GDP deflator.

exporters virtually disappeared while, as noted above, the combined deficit of non-oil developing countries contracted (Table 5). In some countries, this contraction reflected successful adjustment efforts undertaken in the recent past but, in many others, it was a development imposed by the drop in external financing and the exhaustion of gross international reserves. Countries in the latter category had to effect an especially large compression in import volume, and in many cases suffered declines in real output.

It is worth noting that between 1979 and 1982 the overall export volume of non-oil developing countries expanded cumulatively by 21 percent, whereas their import volume rose by only 2 percent.

For 1983, the combined current account position of the industrial countries is expected to move more strongly into deficit, a consequence of the emergence of a large current account deficit in the United States and a reduced surplus in the United Kingdom, and to be offset by a rise in the current account surpluses of Japan, the Federal Republic of Germany, and other European countries. The combined current account surplus of the oil exporting countries is projected to remain negligible, while the combined deficit of the non-oil developing countries is projected to contract further. This further narrowing of the non-oil developing countries' current account deficit assumes the successful pursuit of major adjustment programs in Brazil, Mexico, Argentina, and a number of smaller Western Hemisphere countries. It is interesting to note that the improvement in the combined current account position of Western Hemisphere countries was responsible for one third of the fall in the aggregate current account deficit of the non-oil developing countries in 1982 and for over two thirds of the further contraction forecast for 1983.

Notwithstanding the improvement in their combined current account position, the non-oil developing countries, which as a group had accumulated net international reserves over the preceding six years, lost reserves in the amount of $11 billion in 1982, as their net borrowing from private sources declined even more sharply than the fall in the current

Table 4. Major Country Groupings: Inflation Rates

(In percent)

	1979	1980	1981	1982	Proj. 1983
Industrial countries[1]	8.0	9.1	8.6	7.2	6.0
Oil exporting countries[2]	10.9	12.7	12.9	10.0	9.5
Non-oil developing countries[2]	24.7	32.2	31.3	35.5	31.6

[1] Mainly GNP deflators. See footnote 1 of Table 1.
[2] Cost of living indices.

account deficit. For 1983 it is projected that this group of countries will regain a little under half of the reserves lost in 1982 thanks to the continued reduction in their current account deficit and an estimated doubling in their reserve-related borrowing (mainly use of Fund credit).

DEVELOPMENTS IN THE NON-OIL DEVELOPING COUNTRIES OF THE WESTERN HEMISPHERE

The trends of slow growth and curtailed foreign borrowing that have been described for the non-oil developing countries as a group characterize, in a much more pronounced fashion, the non-oil developing countries of the Western Hemisphere. In part this is true because developments in the Western Hemisphere group as a whole are strongly influenced by trends in Mexico, Brazil, and Argentina. However, a great many other countries in the region heavily dependent on net inflows of capital from private lenders also suffered a curtailment of net lending which, coming on top of weak export demand and the rise in interest rates, seriously affected their overall performance.

Output

The Western Hemisphere countries constitute the only regional group among the non-oil developing countries to have suffered an absolute decline in their combined output in 1982—their combined gross domestic product (GDP) contracted by 0.7 percent, whereas for all non-oil developing countries together it rose by 1.8 percent.

This contraction in output obviously was influenced to a significant extent by trends in the three largest countries of the region. The real GDP of

Table 5. World Payments Balances on Current Account
(In billions of U.S. dollars)

	1979	1980	1981	1982	Proj. 1983
Industrial countries	−6	−41	−1	−4	−10
Oil exporting countries	69	114	65	1	3
Non-oil developing countries	−61	−89	−103	−90	−70
Other countries	−6	−5	−6	—	—
Memo: asymmetry[1]	−4	−21	−45	−93	−77

[1]Corresponds mainly to flows between industrial and oil exporting countries.

Argentina contracted by 4 percent; that of Brazil was stagnant; and that of Mexico grew by only 2 percent—well below the 8 percent average annual expansion of the four preceding years (Table 6). Real output declines were, however, common throughout the region. Altogether, 12 countries out of the 26 Western Hemisphere countries covered by this survey experienced a contraction in the level of real output. Countries suffering particularly large output declines included Chile, Bolivia, Uruguay, the Dominican Republic, and Guyana—all of which faced major financial crises during the year. Apart from the 12 countries whose real GDP contracted, another three—Brazil, Bahamas, and the Netherlands Antilles—experienced zero real growth and more than half of those whose economies grew did so at a slower rate than in 1981. In no other regional grouping was the falling off in economic activity so severe, or so widespread. It also is worth noting that the weak growth performance of the Latin American economies continued the trend begun a year earlier when output in Argentina, Brazil, Paraguay, and several other countries fell in absolute terms while growth in certain others—notably Mexico and Chile—remained buoyant only because of large and ultimately unsustainable capital inflows.

A look at trends in median, as opposed to average, non-oil developing country growth rates by region conclusively demonstrates that the poor performance of the Western Hemisphere countries was not merely the consequence of what happened in a few large countries. The median GDP growth rate of non-oil developing countries in the Western Hemisphere dropped from 2 percent in 1981 to zero in 1982 but that of African non-oil developing countries remained stable, and that of European non-oil ones rose marginally. Median growth rates took a substantial dip in Asian and Middle Eastern countries, but these declines occurred from very satisfactory rates in the preceding two years. This was not so for the Western Hemisphere group of countries, whose median growth rate had been dropping steadily from its 1978 peak.

**Table 6. Major Western Hemisphere Non-Oil Developing Countries:
Changes in Real GDP**

(In percent)

	1979	1980	1981	1982
Argentina	7.1	0.7	−6.0	−4.3
Brazil	6.8	7.9	−3.5	—
Chile	8.3	7.5	5.3	−12.8
Colombia	5.1	4.0	2.5	1.5
Mexico	9.2	8.3	8.1	2.0
Peru	3.8	3.1	3.2	0.7

Inflation

The average inflation rate for non-oil developing countries of the Western Hemisphere accelerated sharply, whereas for many other country groupings it declined. However, in the case of inflation, unlike that of real output, this was the product of developments in a few countries. The median inflation rate for the region contracted sharply, from 14.8 percent to 9.4 percent. Inflation moved from two digits to one in 12 countries of the region and declined substantially in several others. Across the region inflation was influenced by the appreciation of the U.S. dollar, which contributed to a real effective appreciation of the currencies of most Western Hemisphere countries against the weighted average of trading partner currencies. The decline in the median inflation rate also reflected the adoption, in certain of the larger countries—notably Brazil and Chile—of economic strategies geared to the reduction of price increase (Table 7). The largest relative declines were experienced in the more open economies of Central America and the Caribbean.

In contrast, the rate of price increase accelerated markedly in Argentina and Mexico, where expansionary fiscal policies and an exhaustion of foreign exchange reserves combined to greatly intensify pressures on the domestic economies. Another country in this category was Bolivia, where major corrective price increases combined with expansionary demand policies to drive the rate of inflation up sharply.

The taking of corrective price action in many countries of the region is likely to preclude any significant progress on inflation in 1983. Although the adjustment programs for Brazil and Mexico do indeed aim for some reduction in the rate of price increase, in many others inflation, as measured by the rise in average consumer prices, is projected to intensify or merely stabilize.

Table 7. Major Western Hemisphere Non-Oil Developing Countries: Average Consumer Price Changes

(In percent)

	1979	1980	1981	1982
Argentina	159.5	100.8	104.5	164.8
Brazil	52.7	82.8	105.6	98.0
Chile	33.4	35.4	20.2	9.4
Colombia	29.8	26.5	26.7	23.9
Mexico	18.2	26.3	27.9	58.9
Peru	67.7	59.2	75.4	64.5

International Trade and Payments

As noted above, a major part of the compression in the current account deficit of the non-oil developing countries is accounted for by the countries of the Western Hemisphere. And this external adjustment occurred despite an extremely weak export performance and a major increase in the net outflow on account of services and transfers.

In U.S. dollar terms, the combined exports of the non-oil developing countries of the Western Hemisphere are estimated to have contracted from $87 billion in 1981 to $80 billion in 1982, slightly below the 1980 level (Table 8). This fall in export earnings was principally the consequence of a 7 percent contraction in the unit value of exports, but it also subsumed a 1 percent decline in export volume. Almost every country in the Western Hemisphere suffered a fall in the U.S. dollar value of exports in 1982, with major declines occurring in Argentina (from $9 billion to $8 billion), Uruguay (from $1.2 billion to $0.9 billion), Brazil (from $23 billion to $20 billion), and the Dominican Republic (from $1.2 billion to $0.8 billion). Mexico's exports were stable at $21 billion.

With net capital inflow to the Western Hemisphere group dropping sharply and investment income payments (that is, interest payments on the external debt) claiming a much larger share of export earnings than in the preceding year, the region's imports contracted by nearly $20 billion. Virtually all of

Table 8. Western Hemisphere Non-Oil Developing Countries: Summary Balance of Payments

(In billions of U.S. dollars)

	1978	1979	1980	1981	1982	Proj. 1983
Current account[1]	−13.3	−21.4	−33.2	−43.3	−36.8	−22.7
Merchandise	−1.2	−4.1	−9.1	−8.4	3.7	13.5
Exports	(48.0)	(62.1)	(80.8)	(87.2)	(80.1)	(88.3)
Imports	(−49.3)	(−66.2)	(−90.0)	(−95.6)	(−76.4)	(−74.8)
Services and private transfers	−12.1	−17.3	−24.1	−34.9	−40.5	−36.2
(Of which interest on indirect investment)	(−9.9)	(−14.7)	(−22.2)	(−31.4)	(−36.9)	(−36.0)
Capital account[2]	22.0	27.4	31.7	40.8	21.6	20.6
Other[3]	0.5	1.6	0.4	—	—	—
Overall balance	9.2	7.6	−1.1	−2.5	−15.2	−2.1

[1] Excluding official transfers.
[2] Including official transfers and errors and omissions.
[3] SDR allocation and valuation adjustment.

this represented a fall in the real import level, as the unit value of imports decreased by less than 1 percent.

This abrupt contraction in imports put an end to the substantial and accelerating rise in regional imports that had taken place over the preceding five years. Notably, in 1979 and 1980 the growth in the value of the region's imports had averaged 35 percent. Over this two-year period the combined current account deficit of the non-oil developing countries of the Western Hemisphere rose from $13 billion to $33 billion; the increase was financed by a $10 billion rise in the net inflow of long-term and short-term private capital and by a $10 billion deterioration in the overall balance of payments position of the region. As a consequence, in 1980 the combined net international reserves of these countries contracted after four years of steady increase.

In 1981, as the world recession took hold, the combined imports of the non-oil developing countries of the Western Hemisphere expanded by only 6 percent. This diminution in the growth of imports incorporated absolute declines in the import levels of Brazil and Argentina, two countries that were already facing financial constraints. Even though the combined trade balance of the Western Hemisphere countries stabilized in 1981, their current account deficit moved upward from $33 billion to $43 billion as the rise in the level of their external debt and the sharp increase in interest rates combined to produce a $9 billion increase in investment income payments. In retrospect, the diminution in the rate of import growth during this period must be seen as insufficient, as a large increase in the current account deficit was covered by higher borrowing from private financial intermediaries (as well as by a $2.5 billion loss of net international reserves, incorporating a $1.7 billion fall in gross reserve holdings). It is clear, however, that many countries of the region expected the decline in export growth to be short-lived, an expectation shared by a large part of the international financial community (Table 9).

Disappearing hopes of a strong economic recovery in 1982 caused private lenders to reassess their exposure to major Latin American borrowers early in the year and with growing intensity after the second quarter. As a consequence, the net inflow of long-term private funds to the region was cut back by nearly $17 billion and—despite several emergency debt rollovers—there appears to have been an increase in the outflow of short-term capital as well. Despite the sharp cutback in imports in 1982 and the actual decline in the current account deficit, the non-oil developing countries of the Western Hemisphere experienced a combined balance of payments deficit amounting to $15 billion and lost gross international reserves in the amount of nearly $11 billion. In many instances, gross official reserve positions were virtually exhausted.

In absolute terms, the largest cutbacks in current account deficits occurred in Mexico (from $13 billion to $6.5 billion), Argentina (from $4.5 billion to

$2 billion), and Chile (from $4.5 billion to $2.5 billion) (Table 10). Monetary authorities in the first two countries were forced to suspend the sale of exchange not only for capital remittances but also for a wide range of current transactions, and sizable arrears were incurred. In Chile, a comfortable international reserve position enabled the authorities to maintain free access to exchange for current transactions, but they were forced to abandon the fixed exchange rate policy which was the cornerstone of the authorities' economic strategy.

An even more drastic curtailment of capital inflows to the region was avoided by action on the part of national monetary authorities, the Bank for International Settlements (BIS), and the International Monetary Fund, which undertook to convince private banks that any abrupt cutoff of credit to countries in severe financial straits would lead to extremely serious difficulties in these countries and might, possibly, precipitate an international financial crisis. In the context of negotiations of medium-term adjustment programs in Mexico, Argentina, and Brazil, private lenders agreed to increase their overall exposure, although at a much slower pace than that of previous years.

Notwithstanding the slower rate of net borrowing in 1982, the debt service burden of the non-oil developing countries of the Western Hemisphere— which increased very sharply in 1982—will decline only moderately in 1983. Interest payments on long-term and short-term debt together are projected to absorb 27 percent of exports of goods and services and amortization on the

Table 9. Western Hemisphere Non-Oil Developing Countries: Current Account Financing

(In billions of U.S. dollars)

	1979	1980	1981	1982	Proj. 1983
Current account deficit	21.4	33.2	43.3	36.8	22.7
Use of reserves	−7.9	0.7	1.7	10.6	−1.8
Non-debt-creating flows, net	6.8	5.6	6.8	5.6	5.9
Net external borrowing	22.5	26.9	34.8	20.6	18.6
Long-term borrowing	18.4	22.7	39.3	22.1	28.2
From official sources	2.5	3.1	5.0	4.5	4.6
From private sources	15.9	19.6	34.3	17.6	23.7
Reserve-related liabilities	0.3	0.4	0.8	4.6	3.9
(Of which use of Fund credit)	(0.2)	(−0.2)	(0.3)	(1.3)	(6.8)
Other short-term borrowing	3.9	3.8	−5.3	−6.1	−13.6

long-term debt only, 25 percent. By comparison, the same ratios in 1982 were 32 percent and 24 percent, respectively.

A forecast incorporating the adjustment targets of the countries that have entered into Fund-supported stabilization programs and the staff's broad assumptions regarding the policies which other Western Hemisphere countries will follow in 1983 (subject to the constraints of capital availability and international reserve positions) points to a continued contraction in the combined current account deficit of the region—to approximately $23 billion—with a further small contraction, of 2 percent, in total import value. This is based on the assumption of a 10 percent recovery in the value of exports (3 percent on account of unit values and 7 percent on account of volume), which is consistent with the 1.5 percent recovery in real output of the industrial countries. The implicit further 5 percent contraction in total import volume is, of course, predicated on the pursuit of adjustment policies in a number of large countries. This forecast incorporates a greater net use of Fund credit than at any time in the past ($6.8 billion compared with $1.3 billion in 1982 and $0.3 billion in 1981) but, on the other side, a $2.7 billion net repayment of emergency short-term lines of credit from the BIS and national lenders and a small ($1.8 billion) buildup of gross reserve assets, which is viewed as the minimum to restore such assets to a minimum working level in a number of countries.

**Table 10. Major Western Hemisphere Non-Oil Developing Countries:
Current Account Balances**

(In billions of U.S. dollars)

	1979	1980	1981	1982
Argentina	−0.5	−4.8	−4.6	−2.2
Brazil	−10.7	−12.9	−11.7	−15.9
Chile	−1.2	−2.0	−4.7	−2.5
Colombia	0.6	−0.2	−1.7	−1.8
Mexico	−5.6	−7.7	−13.0	−6.6
Peru	0.7	−0.1	−1.5	−1.4

APPENDIX

Table 11. Non-Oil Developing Countries: Changes in Real GDP

(In percent)

	1979	1980	1981	1982	Proj. 1983
Weighted Averages	5.0	4.9	2.8	1.8	2.4
Africa	2.5	4.4	2.9	1.3	1.4
Asia	4.6	5.1	4.8	4.1	5.3
Europe	4.1	1.6	2.2	2.3	1.5
Middle East	4.5	6.7	4.2	2.5	5.4
Western Hemisphere	6.7	5.9	0.5	−0.7	−0.3
Medians	4.4	3.4	3.2	2.4	3.0
Africa	4.0	2.4	3.0	3.0	3.4
Asia	6.1	5.4	5.4	3.8	4.5
Europe	5.7	2.6	2.2	2.3	0.6
Middle East	4.5	5.3	4.8	3.5	4.7
Western Hemisphere	4.7	3.5	2.0	—	2.0

Table 12. Non-Oil Developing Countries: Changes in Consumer Prices

(In percent)

	1979	1980	1981	1982	Proj. 1983
Weighted Averages	24.7	32.2	31.3	35.5	31.6
Africa	18.9	19.9	22.1	18.5	21.2
Asia	6.6	12.7	9.8	5.6	5.8
Europe	27.5	40.5	26.1	25.7	18.3
Middle East	25.9	42.4	34.7	38.4	35.1
Western Hemisphere	49.6	58.3	65.5	86.3	73.8
Medians	12.0	15.1	13.4	11.8	10.0
Africa	11.7	13.6	13.0	14.1	12.0
Asia	7.9	15.0	13.0	8.0	7.5
Europe	14.3	16.2	15.7	19.6	14.2
Middle East	14.0	15.2	11.2	11.8	13.0
Western Hemisphere	15.6	18.1	14.8	9.4	9.0

Commentary*

GUSTAVO LUNA UZQUIANO

Linda Koenig's paper discusses the development prospects of the non-oil developing countries of the Western Hemisphere against the background of the world economic recession. The analysis concerns the performance over the last few years of economic growth, inflation, trade, and international payments. Focusing on the short term, Koenig leaves aside the major questions of economic policy—which will be discussed later during the seminar.

I would like to make the following points with respect to the paper.

1. Economic Growth

In 1982 the world economic recession and the declining output of the industrial countries in terms of gross domestic product (GDP), especially that of the United States (which decreased by 2 percent), depressed the growth rates of the non-oil developing countries, and meant that most commodity prices were at their lowest levels in three decades and that the volume of international trade had ceased to grow. Many developing countries, already struggling with large debt repayments, were thus seeing their problems exacerbated by the rise in interest payments, adverse trends in the terms of trade, and depressed export volumes, not to mention a sharp decline in per capita income, aggravated by a high level of unemployment.[1]

The foregoing shows the large extent of economic interdependence among our countries, strikingly evident in a situation of increasingly overwhelming crisis, as at present.

In her analysis of the outlook, Koenig states that the recovery of the industrial countries "assumes" a recovery of the real output growth rate to 2 percent in 1983, which assumes, in this relationship of interdependence, a rise in economic growth of 2.4 percent for the non-oil developing countries. This is definitely inadequate. But more serious is the exception made for the non-oil developing countries of the Western Hemisphere, whose combined production is expected to decrease again, by 0.3 percent. An initial conclusion we might draw from what has been said is that a recovery of output and a slight improvement in demand in the industrial countries would mean an adjustment in world trade, enabling the non-oil developing countries to expand their exports and thus improve their balances of payments.

---

*The original version of this paper was written in Spanish.
[1]See, World Bank, *World Development Report 1982.*

In the non-oil developing countries of the Western Hemisphere, however, inflation apparently accelerated in 1981–82, though countries fared differently in this respect. While it is desirable to stabilize inflation, inflationary expansion in a large number of developing countries is possible in 1983. This is said given the unfortunate structural constraints on a number of our economies and because immediate, drastic anti-inflationary policies could aggravate unemployment and depress the income of the public. This sociopolitical reality leads us to prefer the alternative of a gradual, progressive, medium-term anti-inflationary policy for certain countries in the region. From the standpoint of our countries, it is difficult for me to understand how economic growth can be stimulated and the planned targets met if we assume that the instruments of anti-inflationary policy mean reducing expenditure, restricting credit, and curbing domestic demand.

2. International Trade and Payments

In general terms, it is confirmed that the growth rate of world trade fell significantly in 1982. While the current account deficit of the industrial countries will be much higher in 1983, that of the non-oil developing countries is expected to contract even more.

In the past, many of the non-oil developing countries of the Western Hemisphere have financed their chronic current account deficits by steadily expanding their external borrowing, largely from private international banks, and by drawing down their international reserves. This state of affairs has become unsustainable because, while international trade has been contracting, commodity prices have fallen in an unprecedented manner, the terms of trade have deteriorated, and interest payments have reached impossible levels, revealing the vulnerability of the international financial system. In general terms, therefore, the adjustment process implies adoption of anti-inflationary policies, improvement of international trading conditions, and the inducement of more accessible credit policies on the part of international banks (Mexico, Brazil, Argentina).

In this framework we note the prospect that the debt service burden of the non-oil developing countries of the Western Hemisphere will decline moderately in 1983. Interest payments should not exceed 27 percent of exports of goods and services, reducing the region's overall current account deficit to some $23 million. All this depends on the industrial countries' achieving a real output increase on the order of 2 percent, otherwise, as another paper points out, there will be serious consequences for the trade and growth of the developing countries and a further reduction in lending to those countries by private banks.

Commentary*

JOSÉ PAEZ AND JULIO ROMERO

Ms. Koenig's paper raises a number of issues. Members of the International Monetary Fund are classified for the purpose of this paper as industrial countries, oil-exporting countries, and non-oil developing countries. The classification itself suggests the prevalent ranking by order of importance in the world economic order, with the non-oil developing countries at present being of little significance in its composition. The analysis focuses basically on three issues: first, output as measured by the change in gross domestic product; second, inflation; and third, the balance of payments. The paper presents a study that is a sort of diagnosis of the world economy, and of Latin America in particular; it proves what we all know, namely, that the slowdown in the pace of economic activity throughout the world has been such that in Latin America there was a significant decline in the combined gross domestic product. In addition, there has been an increase in inflation in Latin America as a product of the sharp price increases in the major countries of the region. Finally, the projections for 1983 present what might be termed an optimistic vision in that they predict a reactivation of the world economy, a decline in the rate of inflation, and a general improvement in the world economy as a consequence of the reduction in the price of oil.

Koenig's paper suggests that the considerable increase in the importance of the oil factor has contributed to all the economic problems facing the world economic order. Furthermore, there would appear to be some suggestion that the analysis of the behavior of the Latin American region stems largely from an examination of events in Mexico, Brazil, and Argentina, while the remaining countries other than Venezuela—which is classified as an oil exporting country—remain on the periphery. Therefore, their behavior is reflexive. One might well ask how long oil and its derivatives will continue to set the pace for world events. Given the challenge implied by our current situation with regard to world trade, and, fundamentally, the behavior of oil prices, would it be possible to achieve successfully a new economic order, the outgrowth of a new strategy, in the short or medium term?

The Fund seeks to maintain stability throughout the world by making recommendations to its members; however, it is finding that its prescriptions cannot be implemented in many countries of our region simply because the actual situation does not correspond to the criteria sketched out by the Fund.

---

*The original version of this paper was written in Spanish.

On some occasions, this may include the prevailing ideology in a country, which can make it impossible to follow up on some Fund recommendations. It would thus seem that there are factors affecting the international economic order that are outside the scope of action or the influence of the Fund. It is obvious that few relationships have changed in the developed world, or shall we say industrial world, and that the developing countries, as noted earlier, behave reflexively. Koenig's paper appears to suggest that there are some countries in the developed world, such as the United States, Canada, Japan, which set the pace for the rest of the world.

The paper shows clearly that increasing net investment can still validly be considered a necessary condition for growth and development. Consequently, the role of external financing in the countries that receive capital remains and will continue to be significant. The information provided by Koenig shows the high degree of correlation between dynamism in the developing world and the flow of external financing. Accordingly, when it is posited that some of the major countries in the world are not in a position to sustain greater growth than at present, this underlines the fundamental importance to us of a limiting factor, namely, the flow of external resources into the developing countries. The prospects should not be assessed too optimistically because from the outset there is a limiting factor, the scant growth in the developed or industrial countries today. The possibilities for improving the financial and economic positions of all countries, increasing their rates of growth, decreasing their balance of payments shortfalls, all depend on the price of oil and petroleum derivatives remaining at their present levels or declining. The mere fact that a drop in the price of oil is announced causes us to change our projections, meaning that oil prices will continue to be a factor of great importance to our economic development in the medium term.

The Process of Balance of Payments Adjustment

JOHN F. O. BILSON

INTRODUCTION

The term "balance of payments" may be defined in a number of ways. In the narrowest definition, the term refers to changes in the international reserve position of a central bank. When a central bank follows a policy of fixing the exchange rate between its currency and a reserve currency, it does so by offering an infinitely elastic supply of the reserve currency in exchange for the domestic currency at a price equal to the established par value. When domestic currency is exchanged for the foreign currency, the central bank is said to be running a balance of payments deficit. The main issues relating to the process of balance of payments adjustment, under this definition, are concerned with the factors that induce a balance of payments deficit and the adjustment mechanism through which a balance of payments deficit restores equilibrium in the local financial markets. Throughout most of this paper, the narrow definition of the balance of payments will be taken to be the appropriate one.

At the other end of the spectrum, a wide definition would refer to the balance of payments as the change in the net foreign assets of the economy as a whole. From the national accounts, this definition may be equivalently interpreted as the current account balance or as the difference between national income and expenditure. The economics of the determination of the current account balance are quite different from the economics of the determination of the narrow definition of the balance of payments. The two are not, however, completely unrelated because the financial policies of the central bank may influence the income and expenditure decisions of the public and private sectors. Although the determinants of the current account balance will not be addressed in the paper, some thoughts on the relationship between recent current account difficulties and the central bank policy of fixed exchange rates are presented in the last section.

The plan of the paper is as follows. In the first section, certain institutional and accounting features of a fixed exchange rate regime are discussed.

Although the topic appears elementary, one intention is to demonstrate that many contemporary balance of payments problems can be traced to the institutional and accounting structure of the system. To illustrate this point, the conventional system is compared with an alternative system in the fourth section of the paper. The adjustment dynamics of the two systems is compared, and some macroeconomic implications described.

In the second section, the traditional "monetary" approach to the balance of payments is restated in a way that recognizes some of the features of the current international monetary system. In contrast to the expositions of this approach that were common in the 1960s, the approach is more concerned with the effects of financial instability in the reserve currency country than with the balance of payments implications of domestic policy. These issues are further discussed in the third section, where a modern "asset market" approach to the balance of payments is adopted. This approach, which is based upon the model developed in Dornbusch (1976), considers the transmission of financial disturbances in a world in which financial markets are integrated but in which commodity markets are segmented.

In the fourth section, the discussion centers on *how* to fix the exchange rate and *what* to fix it to. Given the extreme volatility in both exchange rates and interest rates during the past few years, the standard approach of fixing to the U.S. dollar may not be appropriate. The natural alternative of fixing to a basket of currencies—and the procedures for doing so—is considered; then some alternative strategies are examined. In each case, the choice of the reserve asset is linked to the procedures by which the choice is implemented. In every type of fixed exchange rate regime, it is necessary to follow certain rules if the system is to be successful. The purpose of an economic analysis is to describe the constraints and the implications of the fixed exchange rate system.

In the final section, the process of adjustment to economy-wide balance of payments difficulties is addressed. Each of the preceding systems describing central bank operations influences this process of adjustment, and each has associated costs and benefits for the economy as a whole. The paper contains no magic cure for the problems that have arisen in the past year in many countries whose exchange rates have been tied to the dollar, but it is hoped that some suggestions can be made which will limit similar problems in the future.

1. INSTITUTIONAL AND ACCOUNTING FEATURES

In its institutional and accounting structure, a central bank operating under a fixed exchange rate regime is very similar to an ordinary commercial bank. The commercial bank's liabilities consist of its stock of deposits, and its assets consist of its holdings of debt and liquid reserve assets. The balance sheet of a commercial bank, in its simplest form, is as follows.

Assets	*Liabilities*
Reserves	Deposits
Debt	

The operational rules of commercial banks and central banks under fixed exchange rates are also similar. Under the simplifying assumption that all of the deposits are sight deposits, the commercial bank is obligated to exchange deposits for reserves on demand. The bank meets this obligation by holding a sufficient quantity of reserves to meet the flow of deposits and withdrawals, and by holding a sufficient base of assets to guarantee its pledge. In the central bank case, the reserves are reserves denominated in the reserve currency, the deposits are the monetary base, and the debt represents central bank holdings of government securities and (sometimes) private debt. The central bank is obligated to exchange the reserve currency for the monetary base at the established par value. To meet its commitments, the central bank must also hold a sufficient quantity of liquid reserves and must also preserve the capital value of its assets.

Under normal conditions, both commercial banking and central banking are profitable and socially productive activities. The profitability arises because the debt typically bears an interest rate that exceeds the interest rates paid on the liabilities. The social productivity arises because the depositor, or money holder, is not forced to hold the deposit so that, by revealed preference, the liquidity of the deposit exceeds the interest forgone on directly holding debt.

The concept of forgoing interest in exchange for liquidity is a fundamental consequence of this type of banking system, and it has influenced the way in which economists have developed their theories and empirical tests of the demand for money. The basic idea is that of a trade-off between the demand for liquidity, as represented by income or the volume of transactions, and the opportunity cost of money, as represented by interest forgone. In both the commercial bank and central bank cases, the equilibrium is reached by an adjustment in the quantity of liquid assets issued.

This concept has led to specifications of the demand for money which are purely determined by the demand for liquidity. The standard specification states that the real value of a currency depends upon real income or wealth and the nominal rate of interest. Within this specification, the real value of the assets backing the money has no influence on its real value. The reason for this result is that the bank is assumed to have enough capital to ensure that variations in the real value of the portfolio are absorbed by owner's equity rather than by the depositors. There has been, however, a recent resurgence of interest in giving value to money through its asset backing, rather than through its usefulness as a medium of exchange. The discussions of a return to the gold standard, or of the adoption of other commodity-based moneys, are examples of this trend.

These are important questions in the discussion of a fixed exchange rate system because this system is a method for giving a value backing to a currency. In this regard, it is important to distinguish between two problems that the system faces: liquidity and bankruptcy. Until recently, most discussions of both domestic and international banking have been concerned with the liquidity problem; that is, the assets of the bank are sufficient to cover the liabilities but the immediate reserve assets are insufficient to cover the demand for them. In order to ensure liquidity, governments typically require that banks hold a certain proportion of their assets in reserve assets and, internationally, the ratio of international reserves to domestic credit is considered an important indicator of the ability of a central bank to defend its parity. The problem of bankruptcy, on the other hand, arises when the value of the debt, expressed in terms of the reserve asset, falls below the level required to maintain the commitment to the par value. In a fixed exchange rate system, bankruptcy may arise either because of increases in interest rates on the reserve asset or because fears of depreciation cause local debt to sell at a discount related to reserve asset denominated debt. Both factors have been important in recent cases of balance of payments difficulties.

Of the two problems, the bankruptcy problem is certainly the most serious. If a bank has sufficient assets to cover its deposits, it should not have difficulty borrowing funds to cover its liquidity requirements. On the other hand, if the value of assets falls below the value of liabilities, then depositors will have an incentive to withdraw their deposit while its value is still guaranteed. This situation leads to a run on the bank culminating in a depreciation of the value of the deposit. Seen in this light, the role of a depreciation is to restore the balance between the value of assets and the value of liabilities in the bank portfolio. The bankruptcy problem also illustrates the inherent instability of the system when the value of the bank's equity approaches zero. Even though deposit insurance has helped to mitigate this instability for commercial banks, it nonetheless still remains a major concern on the national level because the government itself may not have sufficient assets to cover losses on the central bank portfolio.

The obvious solution to the bankruptcy problem is to have sufficient equity so that any conceivable swing in the market value of the portfolio can be covered. In the case of the private bank, bankers would require a large spread between loan rates and deposit rates in order to bear this risk. From a national point of view, the nation's taxpayers would, in effect, be pledging their taxes to the support of the value of the money supply. In both cases, there would be a tendency to trade off the security of the equity base for a smaller commitment cost. Many small countries have such obvious alternative needs for capital that the support of a fixed exchange rate regime cannot be given the highest priority in the budget.

There are alternatives to the established institutional and accounting structures of present day banking systems, and these alternatives will be discussed in the fourth section of the paper. Before moving on to these topics, however, we shall first explore the adjustment dynamics of the conventional fixed exchange rate system. This shall first be done within the context of the traditional monetary model of the balance of payments and then within the more recent asset market approach.

2. MONETARY APPROACH TO THE BALANCE OF PAYMENTS

The monetary approach to the balance of payments[1] offered a simple and empirically appealing model of the determinants of the stock of foreign assets held by a central bank under a fixed exchange rate regime. By the end of the 1960s, this approach had become a standard model that was widely accepted within both the academic and policy communities. Its successor, the monetary approach to the exchange rate,[2] has recently been subject to widespread criticism for its failure to predict the evolution of exchange rates and interest rates during the current episode with floating exchange rates. It is therefore interesting to look at the monetary theory of the 1960s from the perspective of the 1980s. Two questions are of primary interest. First, why did the theory gain wide acceptance in the 1960s when our experience in the 1970s illustrated its serious deficiencies. Second, what are the implications of the new "asset market" theories (Dornbusch (1976)) of the exchange rate for balance of payments analysis.

The specific model that I will consider is contained in the following equations.

$$m = k + p + y - \epsilon i \qquad (1)$$
$$m = \theta r + (1-\theta) d \qquad (2)$$
$$p = p^* \qquad (3)$$
$$i = i^* \qquad (4)$$
$$m^* = k^* + p^* + y^* - \epsilon i^* \qquad (5)$$

All variables, except interest rates, are expressed in logarithms. The notation is as follows:

m = the monetary base
k = a shift factor in the demand-for-money function

---

[1] See Frenkel and Johnson (1976).
[2] See Frenkel and Johnson (1978).

p = the price level
y = the level of real national income
i = the nominal rate of interest
r = the stock of international reserves
d = the stock of domestic debt
ϵ = the interest rate semi-elasticity of the demand for money
θ = the ratio of international reserves to the monetary base.

Equation (1) represents the Cagan semi-elastic form of the demand-for-money function. The income elasticity of the demand for money has been set equal to unity, and the interest rate semi-elasticity has been assumed to be the same in both countries, but these assumptions will be of little consequence in what follows. Equation (2) is a log-linear expression for the central bank balance sheet identity. Equation (3) represents the purchasing power parity condition, with the log of the exchange rate normalized to zero. Finally, equation (4) represents the interest rate parity condition. Normally, this equation would also include a term representing the expected change in the exchange rate, but this term is unnecessary if we restrict our attention to a system with a rigidly fixed exchange rate and no political risk premium.

The virtue of the monetary approach is its straightforward solution for the international reserves held by the central bank. For the particular model given above, this solution is given in equation (6).

$$\theta r = m^* + (k-k^*) + (y-y^*) - (1-\theta) d \qquad (6)$$

In this equation, there is only one variable, the stock of domestic debt held by the central bank, that is directly under the control of the local government. Within the terms of the model, the domestic monetary authority can only influence the composition of the base; it cannot influence its total quantity. Consider, for example, an expansionary domestic credit policy whereby the central bank purchases domestic debt in exchange for currency. If the economy were closed, this action would put upward pressure on prices and downward pressure on interest rates. However, given the openness of the economy, as expressed in the purchasing power and interest rate parity conditions, the policy would give rise to current account and capital account deficits that would lead to a loss of international reserves. This process would continue until the loss in reserves was exactly equal to the initial expansion in the holdings of domestic debt.

For a given stock of domestic debt, the main influences on the stock of reserves are the reserve currency money supply and the factors influencing the demand for the domestic currency relative to the reserve currency. A contraction in the world money supply would lead to downward pressure on prices, and upward pressure on interest rates, in the reserve currency country. These developments would tend to decrease the demand for local exports, increase the local demand for imports, and lead to a capital flow toward the reserve currency country. Hence reserves would decrease, leading to a decrease in the local money supply which would continue until the monetary contraction in the center had been fully transmitted to the local economy.

The main criticism of the monetary approach has been directed toward its assumption of complete price flexibility and integrated world commodity markets. The issues relating to the failure of these conditions in the "real world" will be taken up in the next section. Even on its own terms, however, the model neglects some important aspects relating to the process of balance of payments adjustment.

The first point that we will consider are the issues relating to the demand for international reserve assets. In the monetary approach literature, it is standard practice to treat the stock of domestic debt as an exogenous policy instrument. However, the discussion of the liquidity problem in the previous section demonstrated that a properly functioning fixed exchange rate system requires that domestic credit policy be directed toward the maintenance of sufficient international liquidity. Furthermore, studies of the demand for international reserves demonstrate that countries do have a well-specified demand in international reserve assets and that deviations of actual reserves from the desired level predicted by the demand function do trigger an adjustment in actual reserves.[3]

It is consequently inaccurate to view domestic credit as an exogenous policy instrument. The rules of a fixed exchange rate system imply the following dynamic adjustment process. As suggested by the monetary approach, the central bank offers an infinitely elastic supply of international reserve assets to the market in order to maintain the par value. Hence the stock of reserves in the short run is determined by the demand for money and world monetary conditions. However, central banks use their domestic credit policies to ensure an adequate long-run level of international reserve assets. Thus, in the long-run the stock of reserves is determined by the central bank's demand for international liquidity.

Assume, for example, that the central bank's policy is to maintain a target ratio of international reserves to the monetary base.

$$H = R/(R + D) \tag{7}$$

In this equation, R represents the level of reserves, D the level of domestic

---

[3]See Bilson and Frenkel (1979).

debt held, and H is the target liquidity ratio. In log-linear form, this relationship may be expressed as

$$r = h + d \qquad (8)$$

where $h = \log(H/(1-H))$. Since the central bank does not directly control the stock of reserves in the short run, equation (8) will not tend to hold exactly at each point in time. Instead, one could envisage the central bank adjusting domestic credit in order to maintain the target ratio in the long run. One plausible rule is represented in equation (9).

$$Dd = \phi \, (r - h - d) \qquad (9)$$

Equation (9) assumes that the rate of growth of the domestic credit component of the base, Dd, is proportional to the difference between actual and desired stocks of international reserve assets. If a transitory shock causes a loss of reserves, the bank will undertake a contractionary domestic monetary policy to regain the lost reserves.

The dynamics of this system are illustrated in Chart 1. The MM locus represents the combinations of domestic credit and international reserves that are consistent with equilibrium in the money market. The Dd locus represents the reaction function of the central bank. The noticeable feature of the diagram is that the stock of reserves tends to "overshoot" its equilibrium value in response to a money market disturbance. In the long run, an increase in the demand for money will have a roughly proportional effect on both domestic credit and international reserves. The long-run reserve adjustment equation is consequently not equation (6) but equation (10).

$$r = m^* + (k - k^*) + (y - y^*) + (1 - \theta)h \qquad (10)$$

In this formulation, the stock of reserves is proportional to the reserve currency monetary base in the long run. Increases in the demand for the domestic currency relative to the reserve currency will increase the factor of proportionality, as will the central bank's desired liquidity ratio.

Another problem with the monetary approach is its failure to consider the capital gains and losses that occur when interest rates change. These capital transfers were not very important in the 1960s, when interest rates were relatively low and stable, but they have come to be of paramount importance in more recent analyses of balance of payments difficulties. A number of cases can be enumerated. With long-term fixed rate debt, an increase in the interest rate lowers the present discounted value of the interest and capital payments and transfers a real capital gain from the borrower to the lender. With floating rate debt, higher nominal interest rates—due to correctly

Chart 1.   Dynamic Adjustment to a World Monetary Expansion

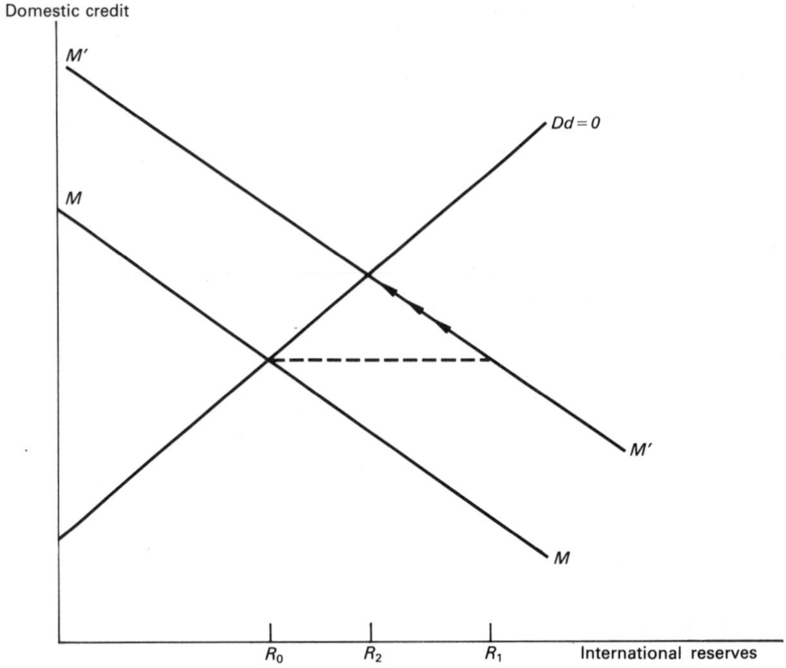

An expansion in the world money supply shifts the domestic money market equilibrium locus from *MM* to *M′M′*. Initially, central bank holdings of international reserve assets expand from R_0 to R_1. To regain portfolio balance, the central bank expands the money supply by purchasing domestic credit instruments, and its holdings of international reserves decline from R_1 to R_2.

perceived changes in the rate of inflation—have no real economic conse-quences as the increase in interest payments is offset by a decline in the real value of the debt. In this case, the higher interest payments may be considered as a prepayment of the debt. Finally, higher real interest rates on floating rate debt transfers a capital gain from the borrower to the lender.

Within the traditional monetary approach, the only role for interest rates was to influence the demand for money, but now, with many countries having large amounts of floating rate debt, the macroeconomic consequences of higher world interest rates are mainly felt in the form of higher debt service payments. Within the framework of the monetary approach, the debt issue is best handled by relating the level of real income in the home country to the interest rate. Higher interest rates depress real income both by increasing debt service payments and by the business cycle effects. If the local economy business cycle is more sensitive to interest rates than the reserve currency country business cycle, then increases in interest rates could induce a far larger balance of payments deficit than would be suggested by the money demand effect taken in isolation. Indeed, since the high interest rates should influence the demand for money in both countries, the money demand effect should not be of particular importance.

When the reserve currency money supply is reduced and the country is a net debtor with floating rate debt, private and public sector income declines because of the increase in interest rates. The decline in income will create an excess supply of money and a balance of payments deficit. Because of the fact that money is a liquid asset, it is likely that the initial reduction in money balances will exceed the long-run reduction. This fact, in combination with the overshooting dynamics arising out of the central bank's portfolio management strategy, will lead to a sharp short-run fall in international reserves.

This deficit may be complicated by capital losses on the central bank portfolio. If the domestic credit component of the monetary base comprises fixed rate government obligations, higher interest rates would lower the market value of these obligations and this fact could hinder central bank efforts to sterilize the reserve outflow. To maintain the long-run viability of the fixed rate system, the central bank should sell its domestic debt in order to absorb the reduction in the demand for money. In doing so, however, it will realize a capital loss on the transactions and hence lower the asset backing of the monetary base.

This process, then, has a potential for a vicious circle leading to a breakdown in the fixed exchange rate system. When interest rates rise, the central bank realizes a loss on its holdings of domestic debt instruments. This loss could reduce confidence in the ability of the central bank to maintain the parity and create a further drain on reserves and a further increase in interest rates. In fact, the fixed exchange rate system is inherently unstable whenever the dollar value of the assets backing the monetary base falls short of the dollar value of the base. In this case, it is either necessary to devalue the currency, so that the dollar value of assets and liabilities are brought back into line, or to obtain additional assets from the government.

The instability of a fixed rate system was not a serious problem when reserve currency interest rates were stable. However, the recent volatility of U.S. interest rates, in conjunction with unstable exchange rates between the major reserve currencies, has given this problem a central place in the analysis of fixed exchange rate systems. It is a problem that we shall return to in Section 4.

3. ASSET MARKET APPROACH TO THE BALANCE OF PAYMENTS

Seen from a recent perspective, the most obvious weakness of the monetary approach to the balance of payments lies in its reliance on the assumption of purchasing power parity. Indeed, it is difficult to understand how this assumption survived in the 1960s when the experience of the 1970s provided so much contrary evidence. However, the facts of the matter are that inflation rates were very similar in the 1960s. In addition, the relatively low and stable rates of inflation were associated with equally low and stable interest rates. Was the experience of the 1960s an accident, or can this performance be attributed to the system of fixed exchange rates?

In this section of the paper, this question will be answered through a reliance on an unusual source, Professor Dornbusch's model of exchange rate dynamics (Dornbusch (1976)). The source is unusual because one of the purposes of Dornbusch's model was to demonstrate that a flexible exchange rate system induces volatility in real exchange rates through the differential speed of adjustment between asset markets and commodity markets. We shall see, however, that the differential speed of adjustment, while a source of volatility in a flexible exchange rate system, is consonant with the maintenance of purchasing power parity in a fixed rate system. It is consequently possible to develop a standard model that is consistent with both exchange rate systems.

A fixed rate model based on Dornbusch's model is specified in the following equations.

$$m = k + p + y - \epsilon i \tag{11}$$
$$m = \theta r + (1 - \theta) d \tag{12}$$
$$Dp = \phi(m - k - p - y) + \Delta(p^* - p) \tag{13}$$
$$Dp^* = \phi(m^* - k^* - p^* - y^*) \tag{14}$$
$$i = i^* \tag{15}$$

The notation is the same as in Section 2. The main difference between this model and the monetary approach is that inflation is specified as a partial adjustment mechanism. In the local economy, the inflation rate responds to both the domestic monetary conditions and to the deviation from purchasing power parity. In the reserve currency country, the inflation rate purely responds to domestic monetary conditions. Although an expansion of the money supply does not have any immediate impact on prices, it does lead to a fall in interest rates which leads to an expansion in aggregate demand, a reduction in inventories, and an increase in the rate of inflation. This model of inflation, with its emphasis on adjustment to domestic monetary conditions, is quite different from the open economy, flexible price, model used in the traditional monetary approach. In fact, the only concession to the open economy in this model is the retention of the interest rate parity condition. As we shall see, this single element is enough to give the model a strong monetary flavor.

Although the inflation rate is determined by a partial adjustment mechanism, this is not a disequilibrium model. In the large country, the interest rate adjusts to clear the money market in the short run. Since the interest rate in the local economy is fixed to the world interest rate through the interest rate parity condition, the local money supply must adjust, through induced changes in central bank holdings of foreign assets, to maintain equilibrium in the local financial market. In all of this analysis, it should be emphasized that we are considering the consequences of an unanticipated change in domestic or foreign monetary policy. Consequently, the previous level of expected inflation is netted out of the model. It would be possible to incorporate rational expectations of future inflation resulting from the shock, but this would not really change any of the conclusions to be drawn from the model and so this complication is dropped from the model.

The short-run dynamics of this model are best illustrated by an example. Suppose that the reserve currency country undertakes a contractionary monetary policy. In order to clear the money market, the nominal rate of interest must increase. (To the extent that the policy lowers inflationary expectations, real interest rates will increase by more than the nominal rate increase.) In the absence of capital flows, local interest rates would then be below the interest rates on the reserve currency, and local currency would be exchanged for the reserve currency in order to obtain a higher yield. This balance of payments deficit would decrease the local money supply until local interest rates are once again equal to world interest rates. During the subsequent period of adjustment, the inflation rates in both countries would become negative and interest rates would gradually return to their long-run level as real liquidity is restored.

This description of the adjustment process is certainly more consistent with the informal evidence relating to the expansionary policy of the United States in the late 1960s and to the contractionary policies of the early 1980s. Within the monetary approach, a contractionary monetary policy is assumed to immediately lead to a decline in commodity prices, thereby leading to a fall in world commodity prices through the purchasing power parity arbitrage arguments and to a balance of payments deficit as the lower prices decrease the demand for money. At best, the model posits that the inflation rate and the rate of growth in the money supply will be contemporaneously correlated under a fixed exchange rate regime, whereas evidence suggests that the expansion in the money supply tends to lead the increase in the inflation rate.

Despite these important differences between the two models, it would be impossible for standard tests of the monetary approach to distinguish between the two models. For example, if the model presented above is solved for the reserve flow equation, the solution will be found to be that given in equation (16).

$$\theta\, r = m^* + (k - k^*) + (p - p^*) + (y - y^*) - (1 - \theta)\, d \quad (16)$$

This formulation differs from the earlier one only in the presence of the relative price term. However, successive substitutions into the price adjustment equations lead to the following relationship between the two inflation rates.

$$Dp = Dp^* + \Delta(p^* - p) \tag{17}$$

In words, if the economies start from a position in which purchasing power parity holds, there is nothing within the model that will induce a divergence from purchasing power parity. Although this result relies on the assumption that the adjustment velocities are the same, the general point that fixed exchange rate regimes lead to correlated inflation rates independently of the degree of commodity arbitrage will continue to hold. In essence, the fixed exchange rate correlates the monetary policies of the two countries through the interest rate parity condition, and it is the coordinated monetary policies that lead to the coordinated inflation rates.

In retrospect, it is possible to devise tests that distinguish between the monetary approach and the asset market approach. Although the reserve flow equation, the purchasing power parity condition, and the interest rate parity condition are common to the two models, the monetary approach implies a contemporaneous correlation between inflation and monetary expansion, while the asset market approach suggests that unanticipated changes in the money supply will tend to lead unanticipated changes in the inflation rate. The Granger-Sims causality analysis is consequently a natural starting point for a comparative testing of the two models.

Another method would be to analyse the response of an economy to a devaluation of its currency. Within the assumptions of the monetary approach, a devaluation would cause an instantaneous increase in domestic prices, leading to an increase in the nominal demand for money, and hence leading to a balance of payments surplus. Within the asset market approach, a devaluation has no immediate effect. Over time, however, the prices will increase because of increases in the price of imported intermediate and final goods and because of increased world demand for local exports. As prices increase, the demand for money will increase and there will be a tendency for local interest rates to increase. This tendency will result in an inflow of funds, a balance of payments surplus, and an increase in the money supply.

In the same way that the monetary approach may be criticized for its reliance on purchasing power parity, the asset market approach may be inappropriate because of its excessive reliance on the interest rate parity condition. Nominal interest rates may not be held equal to world interest rates for a number of reasons. First, the probability of a devaluation may be positive so that expectations of the probable change in the exchange rate should be factored into the interest rate differential. Within an extended model of this type, dynamic instability is a real possibility if the probability of a devaluation is related to the level of reserves held by the central bank. Consider, for example, a decrease in the demand for money that leads to a balance of payments deficit. The deficit lowers confidence in the currency, and the expectations of a depreciation cause the local interest rate to rise above the world interest rate. The increase in interest rates decreases the demand for money and lowers the local currency value of fixed rate long-term government debt held by the central bank. We consequently have an additional balance of payments deficit and a reduction in the bank's ability to defend the parity. This leads to a further increase in interest rates and so on.

The other case in which the interest parity condition is invalid is when capital controls effectively prevent the arbitrage from taking place for small differences in nominal interest rates. In this case, there is effectively a combination of two models. For modest interest rate differentials, the local interest rate adjusts to clear the domestic money market and the money supply is an exogenous policy instrument because the government effectively controls access to the central bank's holdings of international reserves. However, if the interest rate diverges by too great a magnitude from the world rate, then the economic incentives to avoid the controls on capital flows become large and further attempts to control the flow of capital become ineffective. The system consequently resembles a closed economy that is interrupted, on occasion, by immersion in the cold waters of international arbitrage. The instability of this system is assured unless the government remains aware of the international constraints on its actions. Capital controls may be a solution to the importation of very short-run financial instability from the rest of the world, but in the long run they are unlikely to be productive.

4. CHOICE OF A PARITY

In the preceding section, we have assumed the existence of a fixed exchange rate system and have analysed the process of adjustment under that system. The fixed exchange rate system is basically a combination of two policies; first, the choice of a reserve currency, and second, the policies adopted to maintain the par value. For most of the past century, the choice of a reserve currency was not a particularly important decision as all of the prospective currencies were themselves tied through a fixed exchange rate system; however, at the present time, when the exchange rates between the major currencies do vary over a wide range, the choice of a reserve currency is an important and difficult decision. As far as the policies required to maintain the par value are concerned, relatively little has been said on the topic. The model adopted in Section 2, in which the central bank adjusted domestic credit to achieve a target ratio of international reserves to the monetary base, appears to be the standard prescription. There are, however, alternatives to this approach and some of these alternatives may reduce the economic costs of the fixed exchange rate system.

In the discussion of the viability of a fixed exchange rate system, a great deal of emphasis has been placed on the reserve currency value of the assets backing the monetary base. There are, in fact, two views of the determinants of the value of a currency. Within the traditional monetary theory, money attains its real value because of its productivity as a medium of exchange. Within this approach, the real value of a unit of currency is increased by reducing the supply of the currency available. At the other end of the scale, there are those who argue that the value of a currency is determined by fixing its price in terms of some other asset, typically gold or foreign currency. In emphasizing the value of the assets backing the monetary base, the point is being made that a commitment to fix a par value is of doubtful value if the central bank does not have the financial resources to back the commitment. While maintaining a constant ratio of international reserves to the monetary base may help to preserve international liquidity, it does not solve the fundamental problem of capital losses on the domestic debt component of the base.

There is, of course, a great deal that can be done to limit these capital losses. Because of the recent volatility of interest rates, many financial managers have had to resort to hedging interest earnings and interest expense in forward and futures markets. To the extent that the central bank holds assets denominated in nonreserve currency currencies, hedging of the associated foreign exchange exposure may also be called for. It is indeed unfortunate that countries with a great deal of exposure to U.S. interest rate movements because of floating rate debt have not engaged in this type of hedging, nor have they encouraged private borrowers to do so. It is certainly true that much of the disruption caused by recent developments in international financial markets could have been avoided had financial hedging strategies been adopted.

There has, however, been another response to recent financial uncertainty, which is even more relevant to central bank financial policy. This development relates to the growth of money market funds as an alternative to traditional banking institutions. Money market funds differ from banks in their operating procedures: Whereas a bank promises to exchange dollars for deposits at a fixed exchange rate of unity, money market funds adjust the number of shares so that the dollar value of the shares is always equal to the dollar value of the portfolio. Most money market funds only hold short-term paper so that capital gains and losses are small, but the interest paid on money market funds varies with the rate of interest.

With money market funds, the general practice has been to adjust the number of shares owned by the depositor rather than to adjust the dollar value of a fixed number of shares. This is a reasonable practice since the money market fund retains complete control over the ownership of the shares in the fund. It would, for example, be more difficult to adopt this procedure if money market fund shares were bearer certificates whose ownership could be transferred without the knowledge of the fund management. In the case of bearer certificates, a procedure through which the price of the share is adjusted to reflect changes in the value of the portfolio would be preferable to the standard procedure. Currencies are, of course, the most widely used form of bearer certificate; equities and bearer bonds are other examples.

The procedure for fixing the exchange rate in the money market fund model is simplicity itself. At each point in time, the exchange rate is set such that the dollar value of the assets in the fund is equal to the dollar value of the shares issued. In symbols, we have

$$S(L/\$) \ V(\$) \ = \ M(L) \tag{18}$$

or

$$S(L/\$) \ = \ M(L)/V(\$) \tag{19}$$

where $S(L/\$)$ is the exchange rate, expressed as the number of units of local currency, (L), required to purchase one dollar, $(\$)$, $V(\$)$ is the dollar value of the portfolio, and $M(L)$ is the number of shares issued. The exchange rate is set at this level by the commitment of the fund to exchange shares for dollars at the current market price.

This model has a number of important implications for the economy. First, assume that the portfolio pays an instantaneous dollar rate of interest, i^*. For a given number of shares, the evolution of the exchange rate over time is described by equation (20).

$$S(t) \ = \ M/(V \ \exp(i^* \ t)) \tag{20}$$

The rate of change in the exchange rate is consequently

$$Ds \ = \ - \ i^* \tag{21}$$

where Ds represents the rate of change in the exchange rate and i^* is the short-term interest rate on dollar-denominated assets. In words, the local currency will appreciate against the dollar at the rate of interest. This appreciation is feasible because it results from the increase in the dollar value of the assets held by the fund.

An immediate consequence of equation (21) is the result that interest rate parity will cause local interest rates to be zero. The uncovered interest rate parity condition may be expressed as

$$i \ = \ i^* \ + \ Ds \tag{22}$$

where i is the interest rate on assets denominated in local currency. Substituting equation (21) into this condition leads to the result that the local currency nominal interest rate is zero. It should be stressed that this is purely an arbitrage argument. Assume, for example, that the local interest rate was not zero. Then an investor who currently holds dollar-denominated assets could transfer these assets into local currency. Since all of the dollar interest is paid through the appreciation of the local currency, and since the local currency also pays interest, the investor would be unambiguously better off. It is reasonable to suppose that enough investors would be willing to take advantage of this opportunity to drive the local interest rate to zero.

Another characteristic of the model is that the money supply is infinitely elastic at the established exchange rate. An expansion of the money supply would not cause a depreciation because both the assets and the liabilities would rise in the same proportion. The rapid rise, and subsequent decline, in the assets of U.S. money market funds would not have any effect on the dollar value of the remaining shares. The only determinant of the exchange rate in this model is the dollar value of the assets backing each unit of currency issued.

The money market fund model also offers stable world commodity prices, when expressed in local currency, if interest rates are forecasts of inflation rates. The local currency price of world-traded goods may be expressed as

$$S(t)P^*(t) \ = \ S \ \exp(- \ i \ t) \ P^* \ \exp(i \ - \ r) \ t \qquad\qquad (23)$$

where r now represents the real rate of interest. This expression may be simplified to equation (24).

$$S(t)P^*(t) \ = \ S \ P^* \ \exp \ (-r \ t) \qquad\qquad (24)$$

In other words, the local currency price of tradables will decline at the real rate of interest. This is, of course, the condition required by Milton Friedman for the optimum quantity of money. There is, however, an important difference between the mechanism for reaching this optimum. Friedman argues that the central bank should achieve the optimum by setting a certain target growth rate for the money supply. If the demand for money was stable, this money growth rate would eventually result in the optimum being reached. In contrast, the money market fund model achieves the optimum as an arbitrage condition, and it does not require any assumptions concerning the stability of the demand for money or a prolonged contraction in the monetary base. In fact, it is likely that the base would expand rapidly when the money market fund model was adopted.

The model implies that the long-run rate of inflation will be equal to the negative of the real rate of interest. Since negative inflation may not be desirable on macroeconomic grounds, it would be possible to modify the model by including a tax on the monetary base equal to the real rate of interest. This modification would provide some goverment revenue from the creation of money, and it would also lead to longer-run price stability. Higher taxation rates would, of course, lead to higher steady state inflation rates.

The stability of the rate of inflation obviously depends upon the stability of the real interest rate. When real interest rates are high, the appreciation of the local currency will exceed the rate of increase in world prices, so that the prices of goods traded in local currency will fall. This characteristic of the model should correctly be of concern to exporters, who would find the world price of their goods, calculated as the product of a fixed local currency price and an appreciating exchange rate, rising when high real interest rates are depressing world demand. However, it is also important to note that the price of imported traded goods, many of which are intermediate inputs, would also be falling and this would tend to increase aggregate supply. In the modern world, it is not at all clear that currency depreciation helps to maintain employment since the consequent increase in the local currency price of imported inputs tends to depress aggregate supply.

It may, however, still be the case that a system that ties the appreciation of the currency to the reserve currency interest rate results in an unacceptable level of exchange rate instability. There is nothing within the money market fund model that restricts the assets to be either local or reserve currency debt, and there may be good reasons, both from the viewpoint of financial management and economic policy, for holding a more diversified portfolio. In the remaining part of this section, two such alternative standards will be considered, a multicurrency asset fund and a fund comprised in part of domestic equities.

Let us first consider the multicurrency fund. In this case, the dollar value of the assets can be expressed as

$$V(\$) = V_0 + S_1 V_1 + S_2 V_2 + \ldots + S_n V_n \qquad (25)$$

where S_n is the dollar price of the n'th currency and V_n is the n'th currency value of the assets denominated in that currency. The evolution over time for each currency can be described as

$$S_n(t) V_n(t) = S_n(0) \exp(Ds_n t) V_n(0) \exp(i_n t) \qquad (26)$$

where Ds_n represents the ex post rate of change in the n'th currency exchange rate relative to the dollar, and i_n represents the interest rate on n'th currency assets. V_0 represents the value of dollar-denominated assets in the portfolio.

If uncovered interest rate parity held, there would be little advantage to be gained from multicurrency diversification. The evidence suggests, however,

that uncovered interest rate differentials have been very large during the
current floating rate period. If the other ex post yields are below the yield on
U.S. dollar-denominated assets, it is because the exchange rates on the other
currencies have depreciated by an amount that exceeds the interest rate
differential. It may be reasonable to suppose that if the major currencies have
depreciated against the dollar, then it is probably correct for small currencies
to also depreciate against the dollar. This, then, is the major argument for
diversification of a central bank portfolio.

The effects of this diversification can be substantial. Consider, for
example, when U.S. interest rates reached their peak in September 1981.
The ex post yields on the major currencies for one-year money market
certificates from September 1981 to September 1982 were as follows.

	Percent
U.S. dollar	17.58
Canadian dollar	17.75
Japanese yen	-7.18
French franc	-7.04
Deutsche mark	4.33
Swiss franc	-1.19
British pound	-0.31
Average	3.42
Standard Deviation	10.51

The lesson to be drawn from these results is that while a fund consisting
solely of U.S. instruments would have appreciated in value by 17.58 percent
over this period, a fund with an equally weighted portfolio of these
currencies would actually have only appreciated by 3.42 percent. The
difference constitutes a foreign exchange translation loss on the holdings of
foreign currency denominated instruments.

It is important to note that domestic interest rates would still be zero with
multicurrency portfolios. This result again follows from an arbitrage
argument. An investor could hedge the foreign exchange risk of the fund
portfolio by selling the foreign exchange in the forward market. The cost of
this hedging would, from the covered interest parity condition, be equal to
the interest rate differential. Hence the covered return on the portfolio, ex
ante, would remain equal to the interest rate on the reserve currency.

The purpose of a multicurrency portfolio is, then, to create unanticipated
movements in the exchange rate that would act as a stabilizing force in the
economy. Although it is difficult to specify the characteristics of this
portfolio without delving into special cases, the general idea would be to hold
assets denominated in currencies in proportion to the need for a stable
exchange rate with that currency. In making this decision, the weakness or
strength of a particular currency is not of great importance because

anticipated changes in value will be discounted into the interest rate paid on assets denominated in that currency.

It may, however, be possible to extend the case to consider holdings of domestic equity in the portfolio. There are two reasons why this approach, possibly in conjunction with a multicurrency portfolio, may be valuable. First, domestic equities could lead to a direct countercyclical exchange rate policy. For example, if the demand for a country's exports falls, the effect of this development could be mitigated by a depreciation of the exchange rate. If the central bank held the stock of companies engaged in exporting in its portfolio, then a decrease in the demand for exports would lower the value of the companies' stock, hence lower the dollar value of the portfolio, and hence automatically create the required depreciation. Second, the inclusion of local equity in the central bank portfolio may act as a substitute for international borrowing by the companies concerned and may spread the ownership of the national capital stock over a larger number of citizens. The extreme version of this model, in which the money supply is backed solely by equity holdings, is discussed in Bilson (1982). Engels (1981) also suggests a monetary standard in which the value of the currency is tied to the value of equity.

This has been a relatively long discussion, and it is now time to summarize the arguments presented. We have seen that the traditional mechanism for fixing an exchange rate relies on variations in the quantity of money, interacting with the demand for money, to bring about adjustment in the economy. We have noted that this mechanism may lead to substantial instability if financial conditions in the reserve currency country are unstable, and that it effectively ignores the value of the assets backing the monetary base. At the same time, we have seen that the central bank faces a bankruptcy problem when the value of the assets backing the base falls short of the value of the liabilities. In this section, we have explored an alternative adjustment mechanism that avoids most of these problems by continually adjusting the exchange rate so that the value of assets and liabilities are always equal. The consequences of this system are zero nominal interest rates, an infinitely elastic quantity of money, and a rate of inflation that is approximately equal to the negative of the real rate of interest. Furthermore, we have found that it is possible to build in an automatic countercyclical exchange rate policy by a judicious choice of the assets backing the money supply. In the final section of the paper, the various models of balance of payments adjustment from an economy-wide viewpoint are considered.

5. CURRENT ACCOUNT IMPLICATIONS

The current account deficits experienced by many countries in the past few years may be traced to both external and internal forces. Externally, the high level of U.S. nominal and real interest rates, the appreciation of the dollar, and the rise and fall of oil prices have all played a part. Internally, the present difficulties may be traced to an excessive use of external debt during an earlier period when real rates of interest were low and to the funding of projects whose economic viability was uncertain. Although it is not possible to go back into the past and correct the mistakes that were made, it is worthwhile to consider how the structure of the exchange rate system might prevent these types of problems from arising again. In this regard, two developments are of particular importance: the stability of real interest rates and the growth of domestic savings.

Within a conventional system of fixed exchange rates, we have seen that the real rate of interest on domestic debt is basically determined by the real rate of interest on the reserve currency. This fact, by itself, is of little importance, since most developing country debt is denominated in dollars. However, we have shown that the high real interest rates experienced during the past two years have been almost entirely a North American phenomenon. Ex post real interest rates on the major European currencies have been low and, in some cases, negative. Although it is not possible to predict that these conditions will continue during the next few years, elementary principles of financial diversification do suggest that debt should be issued in a variety of currencies, rather than being restricted to U.S. dollars.

In choosing the currency composition of the debt portfolio, an economy-wide perspective should be taken. The country should be considered as an entity generating a cash flow, and the object of the diversification is to choose a borrowing currency whose real value is positively correlated with the real value of local income. Thus, if income declines, the value of the debt will decline, while if income increases, the value of the debt will increase. As a simple example of these principles, an oil exporting country like Mexico or Venezuela should borrow in British pounds, since the value of the pound is likely to decline when oil prices fall. On the other hand, an oil importing country would be better off borrowing in Japanese yen or deutsche mark. In terms of its diversification characteristics, the U.S. dollar is not a particularly suitable currency for international lending because the United States is simply so different from other countries that predictable correlations cannot be established.

The correlations between developing country income and the exchange rates of the major currencies are also quite weak and unpredictable. This fact leads to the equity standard model whereby the value of debt would be linked to the performance of local equity. For example, a central bank could purchase domestic equity in exchange for currency. The exchange rate could again be set such that the dollar value of the assets is equal to the dollar value of the liabilities. As dividends were paid to the central bank, either the money supply would expand or the currency would appreciate. By reducing the paperwork required to own equity, such a system would encourage savings and reduce the need for external borrowing. To the extent that foreign borrowing was required, the government would encourage participants to denominate the debt in the local currency.

It has often been suggested that this type of equity debt would bear a high interest cost because of the riskiness of equity stocks in developing countries. It is true that the variance of the equity return is large, but this variance may not be of great concern to lenders in the developed world. Modern financial theory suggests that risk is not measured by variance, but by the covariance of the return with the return on the lender's portfolio. Seen in this light, the use of the U.S. dollar for foreign borrowing has probably not served the U.S. banks as well as some foreign currency borrowing. What the banks typically call currency risk is what their shareholders call international portfolio diversification. Hence, although debt tied to local indicators may be initially difficult to sell, it does offer a mechanism for reducing the problems associated with volatile dollar interest rates.

Mention was made above of the role of the financial system in encouraging private savings, but it may be worthwhile to stress this point again. The outstanding recent success stories in the national economic sweepstakes— Hong Kong, Japan, Korea, and Singapore, for example—have all experienced very high savings rates in comparison with other countries. One role for a financial system is to ensure that citizens do have an incentive to save and that the savings are used efficiently and productively. Any policy which leads to large and unstable inflation rates invariably encourages unproductive savings in real goods. An effective monetary system must be able to assure those who hold money that its real value will be preserved. Furthermore, the real assets sacrificed in exchange for money should also be used effectively to promote development, particularly of small businesses that are likely to be the most important sources of employment and growth in income.

The current account is, by definition, the difference between national income and national expenditure. Current account problems arise in the short term because of unpredictable changes in income and expenditure. During the past few years, instability in real exchange rates, real raw materials prices, and real interest rates have been the dominant causes of current account instability. The financial system, including the choice of an exchange rate regime, has an important role to play in insulating the economy from these external factors. Unfortunately, the traditional methods of operating a fixed exchange rate regime do not provide any insulating properties, and the choice of a purely flexible exchange rate is often not appropriate for a small country. This is the reason why so much time has been spent discussing alternative systems in the main body of this paper.

6. CONCLUSION

This paper began with a traditional definition of the balance of payments as the change in the international reserve holdings of a central bank. Within the confines of this definition, balance of payments theory has been concerned with the determinants of the balance of payments and with the implications of a fixed exchange rate regime for the economy as a whole. These issues have been explored on a number of levels. First, the traditional monetary approach to the balance of payments was re-examined from a perspective that recognized the importance of developments in the reserve currency country on the local economy. Emphasis was also placed upon the policies and conditions required for the central bank to maintain the parity. In the following section, the same issues were examined from the perspective of the more recent asset market approach to international finance. Although the asset market approach differs from the monetary approach when the exchange rate is flexible, the analysis demonstrated that the two models produce very similar behavior in aggregate economic time series when the exchange rate is fixed. In particular, similar reserve flow equations and the approximate maintenance of purchasing power parity are shared by the two models.

While fixed exchange rate systems may be appropriate for a small country when there is a stable reserve currency to fix to, these systems do have adverse consequences when financial conditions in the reserve currency country are unstable. These problems are increased by the adoption of flexible exchange rates between the major currencies and by the sharp changes in raw materials prices experienced during the last decade. As a result, developing countries have experienced unprecedented instability in real interest rates, real exchange rates, and real raw materials prices.

It is unlikely that this instability will disappear in the near future. Although inflation rates and interest rates are declining, the large deficits of the major developed countries have not yet been brought under control, and there is a prospect for problems arising in some major international banks. Given these considerations, it is important for small countries to adopt financial policies that insulate the economy from developments in the rest of the world. In a wide sense, this implies less reliance on external financing through the growing use of internally generated savings and it may imply the adoption of an exchange rate system that insulates the economy and interest rate movements. In Section 3, one system of this type was described in which money is directly tied to a real standard by defining money as an equity claim over the assets held in the central bank portfolio. The theory behind these types of equity standards is still in its developmental phase. Even so, the results so far obtained are of sufficient interest to provide a base for policy discussion.

BIBLIOGRAPHY

Bilson, John F.O., and Jacob A. Frenkel, "Dynamic Adjustment and the Demand for International Reserves," NBER Working Paper, No. 407 (Cambridge, Massachusetts: National Bureau of Economic Research, November 1979).

Dornbusch, Rudiger, "Expectations and Exchange Rate Dynamics," *Journal of Political Economy*, Vol. 84, No. 6 (December 1976), pp. 1161–76.

Engels, Wolfram, *The Optimal Monetary Unit* (Frankfurt: Campus Verlag, 1981).

Frenkel, Jacob A., and Harry G. Johnson, eds., *The Monetary Approach to the Balance of Payments* (Toronto: University of Toronto Press, 1976).

————, eds., *The Economics of Exchange Rates: Selected Studies* (Reading, Massachusetts: Addison-Wesley, 1978).

Commentary*

ARMANDO P. RIBAS

In analyzing Mr. Bilson's paper I will surely be unable to cast aside the "underdeveloped" bias of my economic training, even though it may perhaps interfere with my understanding the subtleties of the industrial countries' economic problems. I therefore hope that this audience will excuse these shortcomings, but it seems likely that the following general remarks will reflect my background. I note that economists continue to analyze economic behavior as if the concept of the welfare state had never come into being or spread. As a result, the activities of the government and its bureaucracy, extending all the way to the public enterprises engaged in rendering services and producing basic inputs (particularly in the underdeveloped countries) are conveniently ignored in all the models.

Perhaps there is an epistemological justification for skirting this small problem, namely, that economics assumes economic rationality and therefore disregards any behavior that implies economic irrationality. Regrettably, more and more often that which is considered to be political rationality is the counterpart of economic irrationality. Consequently, any attempt to analyze economic problems in terms of economic optimization can lead us to decidedly false conclusions.

For example, in his celebrated article "A Theoretical Framework for Monetary Analysis," Friedman compares the virtues of the quantitative theory with the so-called Keynesian income-expenditure model. To simplify his analysis, Friedman eliminates all equations which include government expenditure. As you know, it was Friedman who postulated the dictum that "money matters" even though, in the article in question, he qualified it by saying that money is all that matters where prices and nominal income are concerned. My own biased view, however, is that what matters is government and that, what is more, it is almost all that matters; and the greater its participation in the economy, the more it matters, as is the case in our countries.

I would now like to refer to a number of individual aspects of Bilson's paper. In the first part, "Institutional and Accounting Features," the author raises the subject of liquidity, relating it to the bankruptcy problem. To distinguish between the two, Bilson states "both domestic and international banking have been concerned with the liquidity problem; that is, the assets of the bank are sufficient to cover the liabilities but immediate reserve assets

---

*The original version of this paper was written in Spanish.

58

are insufficient to cover the demand for them. . . . The problem of bankruptcy, on the other hand, arises when the value of the debt, expressed in terms of the reserve asset, falls below the level required to maintain the commitment to the par value" (page 37).

This is truly an important topic, which we will analyze within the framework of a fixed exchange rate system, a special case of which would be what has been called a preannounced exchange rate system when the depreciation rate is zero (see chart, page 42). My first remark is that what Bilson calls the liquidity problem and the bankruptcy problem are equivalent to what the IMF refers to as disequilibrium and fundamental disequilibrium, respectively. For example, the second case requires an adjustment of the exchange rate or, to use Bilson's terms, the restoration of the balance between the value of the assets and the value of the liabilities in the bank portfolio. If my understanding is correct, Bilson analyzes this problem both for the case of central banks and for that of private banks even though the devaluation solution would be applicable to the former.

Unfortunately, Bilson once again approaches this problem from a strictly monetary point of view, which prevents him from investigating the root causes of monetary problems, such as public spending and the terms of trade, for example. This is a fundamental question which could be explained as follows: in the case of the terms of trade, when relative prices change definitively against a country, we have a fundamental disequilibrium or a bankruptcy situation which cannot be resolved by monetary management. One example of this was the increase in oil prices, which in my opinion has been the principal factor behind the current disequilibrium of the international financial system.

I should like in this connection to refer briefly to a theory I have been supporting for some time. Because of certain restrictions, among which political factors must be included, equilibrium in the economic world is not possible with any system of relative prices. Whenever the financial system tries, and for some time succeeds, in financing a particular structure of relative prices which, in the medium and long term, lead to the increasing impoverishment of one sector in favor of another—or of some countries in favor of others—the obvious result ultimately occurs, namely, debtors cannot pay and creditors cannot collect. This is a bankruptcy situation, or a fundamental disequilibrium, which is currently affecting the world economy as a whole and cannot be solved by any devaluations which may be applied in future.

Accordingly, at one moment or another creditors conclude, because they cannot collect, that credit is excessive. They therefore endeavor to reduce what they call their exposure. The debtors, however, consider there to be a scarcity of credit, since when there is a reduction in the credit which they had been using in the place of revenue, the demand for credit increases. The result is an increase in interest rates which harms debtors and creditors alike because, as noted by Antwerp bankers in the Middle Ages, usury is not a sin, it is bad business.

The second question I wish to raise relates to the impact of public expenditure on the domestic and external equilibrium of the economy, and on domestic interest rates in particular. This brings us to Section 2 of Bilson's paper, where he discusses the monetary approach to the balance of payments. According to this model, the only variable directly under the control of the monetary authorities is the stock of domestic debt. In other words, the monetary authorities can influence the composition of the monetary base but not its total quantity. According to Bilson, the main criticism of the monetary approach is its assumption of complete price flexibility and integrated commodity markets. This assumption implies that there is purchasing power parity of the currency, which historically has been demonstrated not to exist.

The model also assumes the parity condition of domestic and external interest rates, a condition shared by the "asset market approach" model. I shall now try to examine both models at the same time in that the problem of public expenditure I referred to earlier relates primarily to the integration of these two parities.

The only difference between these models, as shown in equations (10) and (16), is that the second incorporates $(p - p^*)$, namely, the possibility of disparity between domestic and external prices. The first problem posed by the theory of purchasing power parity is that this parity is treated homogeneously in both models and there is no differentiation between marketable and nonmarketable goods. The effect on the overall balance of payments, particularly the current and the capital accounts, depends on changes in the relative prices of marketable and nonmarketable goods. In other words, a change in these relative prices has an impact on the balance of payments even if on average they are raised or kept on a par with international prices.

Let us now examine the mechanics of this process, which also has an impact on the relationship between domestic and external interest rates, thereby eliminating the interest rate parity condition from both models. Disregarding for the moment Bilson's observation on the relationship between domestic credit and the reserves target (or the demand for reserves of the monetary authorities), we shall take as valid the assumption made in both models that domestic credit is the only variable under the direct control of the authorities. This principle amounts to saying that the expansion of domestic credit is the determining factor in domestic equilibrium (price stability) and external equilibrium (no change in international monetary reserves).

In accordance with this principle it is the budget deficit, the major component of domestic credit, which is the most important determining factor in this equilibrium. In other words, it is the budget deficit which affects external equilibrium and not the level of expenditure, in that the latter may be compensated for by higher taxes. This is where I disagree most, however, for in my view, overall expenditure, and principally the change in government spending, is the greatest single determining factor of domestic and external disequilibrium.

I would like at this juncture to restate the concept of domestic and external equilibrium. For domestic equilibrium I shall adopt Wicksell's definition, whereby equilibrium occurs when the domestic market interest rate coincides with its natural rate. I would define external equilibrium as the existence of parity between domestic and external interest rates.

Public expenditure is the greatest single determining factor in domestic interest rates. When public spending increases, the domestic interest rate goes up. When the domestic interest rate rises, two things can happen. One is that there is a budget deficit, and therefore domestic credit expands. Unlike the case in the monetary approach with fixed or preannounced exchange rates (see chart, page 42), reserve losses will not occur so long as the domestic interest rate exceeds the international rate, or

$$i > r \ (tp) \tag{1}$$

where

i = nominal domestic rate of interest
r = external rate of interest
tp = exchange rate.

The second possibility is that there is no budget deficit, with the result that domestic credit will not expand. In this case, the difference between the domestic and external interest rates will result in a capital inflow which will finance domestic inflation. Argentina from 1977 to 1981 serves as an example of the first case, while Chile from 1979 to 1982 illustrates the second.

Let us turn now to an examination of what happens to domestic prices. Gradually, the prices of nonmarketable goods (including government services and wages) increase by more than the prices of marketable goods if the latter are subject to external competition. We therefore have the following:

$$p = P_1 + P_2 \tag{2}$$

where

p = general price level
P_1 = prices of marketable goods
P_2 = prices of nonmarketable goods.

Logically, the domestic interest rate will have to be somewhat higher than the average rate of inflation, and therefore well above the rate of prices for marketable goods. The change in relative prices even further disrupts the activities of producers of marketable goods as a consequence of the increase in their costs resulting from price increases for nonmarketable inputs. Many fail, others go into debt abroad in order to take advantage of the difference between domestic and external interest rates, while still others continue to borrow domestically in order to cover operating losses.

As a result of this process, the current account deteriorates in that the change in relative prices makes exporting more difficult and provides an incentive to import. The interest rate differential gives rise to a capital inflow, making it possible still to record a balance of payments surplus and, as a consequence, a net inflow of international reserves. This would mean that the international reserves target is neither a function of domestic credit (monetary approach) nor, as Bilson argues, a factor limiting the expansion of domestic credit. The change in reserves will in each case depend on the difference between the domestic interest rate and the external interest rate. The expression "in each case" is not used lightly. Rather, it has a specific and particular meaning. It means that when the current account increases, the rate differential required to avoid reserve losses also increases. For example, when the current account deficit expands there is a risk of devaluation, as a result of which the difference between domestic and external interest rates will reflect the increased exchange risk.

Demand for Money

Another matter which must be discussed is the very notion of the demand for money. Traditionally, and in Bilson's view, money is considered strictly as M_1, or currency outside banks plus current account deposits. As Bilson states: "Within the traditional monetary approach, the only role for interest rates was to influence the demand for money." This deviates sharply from Keynes's view, wherein the demand for money is considered infinitely elastic to the interest rate after a certain level has been passed.

The problem to which I wish to refer, however, is the concept itself. Regardless of whether the demand for money influences the interest rate or vice versa, we would have the following function:

$$MD = f(r) \tag{3}$$

According to the earlier concept of the demand for money, whenever the interest rate falls the demand for money decreases, after which the opportunity cost for maintaining idle balances increases. In other words, the interest rate and the demand for money are inversely proportional.

When an inflationary process is under way, the opportunity cost of the demand for money is without question the rate of inflation. When the interest rate on time deposits and savings accounts is greater than the rate of inflation, there is a shift away from M_1 to what is known as quasi-money, and if interest is paid on current accounts, the difference between M_1 and quasi-money becomes blurred. We thus come back to the question of what is the demand for money? If money is, as Friedman once observed, anything that acts like money, we would have to include M_2 in its entirety in this definition. This being so, we find that the relationship between the demand for money and the interest rate is reversed. That is, the demand for money becomes a function of the interest rate.

Let us then analyze the implications of these definitions on the demand for international reserves. In the first case, an increase in the domestic interest rate brings about a decline in the demand for money. This drop-off in the demand for money, however, is not transformed into an increase in the demand for international reserves. To the contrary, when M_2 is taken to be money, the decline in the demand for money corresponds to a reduction in the interest rate, which can mean an increase in the demand for international reserves.

Bilson's confusion on this matter is apparent on page 43, where he writes: "To maintain the long-run viability of the fixed rate system, the central bank should sell its domestic debt in order to absorb the reduction in the demand for money." In other words, in order to absorb the reduction in the demand for money, it would be necessary to increase the market interest rate. But it happens that, if we follow the traditional terminology adopted by Bilson, the increase in the interest rate brings about an even greater reduction in the demand for money (M_1). Nevertheless, Bilson describes a process similar to the one I described earlier in connection with the interest rate and reserves. Bilson states: "When interest rates rise, the central bank realizes a loss on its holdings of domestic debt instruments. This loss could reduce confidence in the ability of the central bank to maintain the parity and create a further drain on reserves and a further increase in interest rates" (page 43).

We see here that an interest rate increase is perceived to be a symptom of disequilibrium, and that therefore there is greater pressure on reserves, giving rise to a further increase in interest rates. It may be noted, however, that the dynamics of this process are the same as those I have pointed out, except that Bilson provides no explanation outside the monetary framework of the why and wherefore of the initial pressure on reserves. In the case I referred to, I identified the change in relative prices as the determining factor in the deterioration of the current account and the subsequent pressure on the capital account.

In my view, it is the absence of an exogenous explanation of the behavior of reserves that prompts Bilson to state the following: "In fact, the fixed exchange rate system is inherently unstable whenever the dollar value of the assets backing the monetary base falls short of the dollar value of the base" (page 43). According to this assumption, the stability of the system depends on the level of reserves; presumably, when this level declines, in Bilson's view, a devaluation becomes necessary. I hold the opposite view, namely that reserves are not necessary when the system is stable, or when the exchange rate does not give rise to growing current account deficits, but when, to the contrary, such deficits do arise, no level of reserves can impart stability to the system.

Asset Market Approach

In explaining the asset market approach, Bilson reaches the following conclusion: "...the general point that fixed exchange rate regimes lead to correlated inflation rates independently of the degree of commodity arbitrage will continue to hold. In essence, the fixed exchange rate correlates the monetary policies of the two countries through the interest rate parity condition, and it is the coordinated monetary policies that lead to the coordinated inflation rates" (page 46).

Here, we once again return to the problem created by the condition of parity between domestic and external interest rates. This problem stems from the assumption followed in both models that monetary policy alone has the power to solve or define the balance of payments position. In reality, however, the interest rate structure reflects purchasing power parity.

The differences in inflation rates per se determine different nominal rates of domestic and external interest. When the exchange rate is fixed or the preannounced changes in it do not keep up with the difference between domestic and external inflation rates, the greater the difference in those rates, the greater will be the differential between domestic and external interest rates. As a result, the assumption that there will be no capital flows does not hold; instead the problem actually lies in the fact that such flows are insufficient at all times to bring domestic and external interest rates into line. This is because both rates respond not to different levels of productivity or of return on capital, but to different rates of inflation.

Although Bilson does acknowledge the weakness of the interest rate parity condition, this weakness affects both models equally. Here again we arrive at some confusion with regard to the demand for money, and Bilson states: "The increase in interest rates decreases the demand for money and lowers the local currency value of fixed rate long-term government debt held by the central bank. We consequently have an additional balance of payments deficit and a reduction in the bank's ability to defend the parity" (page 47).

We thus have, according to Bilson and in line with the asset market approach, the increase in the domestic interest rate vis-à-vis the world interest rate causing an increase in the balance of payments deficit. This is the same process described with regard to the monetary approach, and thus calls forth the same remarks made earlier in that regard.

Choice of a Parity

In Section 4, Bilson presents the problem of the choice of a parity in a world of floating exchange rates. By definition, however, this problem is not posed for countries that are part of the floating exchange rate system. Bilson's first proposal is that to avoid losses in the capital value of their assets, central banks should hedge in the markets.

Bilson appears to be more concerned by capital losses on the domestic debt component of the monetary base. From the standpoint of the balance of payments, this has only an indirect impact, that is, the effect of interest rate increases on the demand for money.

Bilson goes on to describe an exchange rate system functioning along the lines of a money market fund. I will not discuss the form of the model itself but do wish to refer specifically to the conclusion he reaches on page 50, where he states: "Then an investor who currently holds dollar-denominated assets could transfer these assets into local currency. Since all of the dollar interest is paid through the appreciation of the local currency, and since the local currency also pays interest, the investor would be unambiguously better off. It is reasonable to suppose that enough investors would be willing to take advantage of this opportunity to drive the local interest rate to zero."

As is obvious from the recent histories of Argentina, Chile, and Uruguay, at no time has there been a situation in which capital inflows matched the differential in domestic and external interest rates. As I will explain below, this is because the difference in question basically corresponds to differences in inflation rates. Furthermore, revaluation of the domestic currency causes increased commercial account and current account deficits as a result of larger debt service payments. Consequently, the exchange risk and even the risk of default on the debt become greater, which increases the interest rate differential required to maintain the level of reserves.

This process is touched upon by Bilson when, on page 51, he writes: "This characteristic of the model should correctly be of concern to exporters, who would find the world price of their goods, calculated as the product of a fixed local currency price and an appreciating exchange rate, rising when high real interest rates are depressing world demand."

In view of the fact that the criterion of achieving interest rate parity is not met for the reasons expressed earlier, it would appear that all the other conclusions derived from the model are fundamentally in error. This does not imply, however, that the criterion is wrong with regard to the advisability of maintaining reserves in a basket of currencies, provided that and so long as the market itself does not equalize their purchasing power through differences in interest rates. However, it is not at all certain that the concept of bankruptcy refers to the value of the central bank assets which constitute its external debt. Likewise, it is by no means certain, except in Bilson's utopia, that the domestic interest rate would be driven to zero, that the money supply is infinitely elastic, or that the rate of inflation will be equal to the negative of the real rate of interest.

Current Account Implications

Here we find another assumption that I believe I have disproven in my earlier remarks. Bilson begins his comments by stating that: "Within a conventional system of fixed exchange rates, we have seen that the real rate of interest on domestic debt is basically determined by the real rate of interest on the reserve currency" (page 54). He goes on to observe that this is of little importance since all the debt of the developing countries is denominated in dollars.

Bilson nevertheless proceeds to establish a golden rule with respect to decision making on the currency in which each country should incur debt. Assuming that the relative weaknesses of different currencies are discounted in the market through the interest rate mechanism, this problem does not arise since the results would be the same for all currencies. Let us assume that this is not the case, however, and follow Bilson's reasoning on page 54. There, he states that oil exporting countries should borrow in pounds sterling, since when the price of oil falls, the value of the pound will also. But what about when the price of oil rises? Does the value of sterling go up as well? What advantage is there for the oil exporting countries to borrow in a dearer currency?

Bilson goes on to say the obverse, namely, that the oil importing countries should borrow in yen or deutsche mark. I fail to see why, since for any country it is best to have the debt in the currency which is devalued or depreciates, provided and so long as this is not offset by the interest rate.

Conclusions

I should like to end my remarks by referring briefly to Bilson's conclusions. The first of these is that both models, the monetary approach and the asset market approach, yield the same results in the case of fixed exchange rates. The problem is that the results are not valid because in no case are the assumptions made with respect to purchasing power parity or interest rate parity borne out.

We of course agree on the greater difficulties represented by floating exchange rates for setting the parity in small countries. Once again, however, Bilson refers to the instability in real interest rates, real exchange rates, and real raw materials prices, without explaining them. In other words, he makes no effort to trace and understand the problem posed in his paper, namely the adjustment process.

Bilson then recommends that small countries endeavor to insulate their economies from the rest of the world (although to my way of thinking, he must mean the industrial countries). But this suggests less reliance on external financing, which in my opinion is ambiguous. External financing is essential for the real investment and development needs of the (small) developing countries, as is the stability of raw materials prices. What must be avoided is the artificial financing that has arisen as a consequence of policies on revaluing domestic currency which created differentials between domestic and external interest rates even when the latter were reaching their maximum levels.

Although I may not have properly understood the model proposed in Section 4, I do not believe that its approach to interest rates and exchange rates really serves to insulate the small countries from events in the rest of the world.

The IMF's Conditionality Re-Examined

E. WALTER ROBICHEK

The subject of the IMF's conditionality is somewhat shopworn, so much so that I should perhaps have given my paper the title "The IMF's Conditionality Re-Re-Examined." But it would seem that there is room for shedding some new light on certain aspects of the IMF's conditionality that are still not fully understood. This paper is organized in four sections: The first section establishes the legal basis for the IMF's conditionality; the second explores the constraints of the margin of flexibility that the IMF has for accepting those adjustment programs that it can support with its resources; the third examines the rationale of the policy instrumentation of such adjustment programs; and the fourth addresses certain dilemmas that the present world economic conditions pose for the IMF's conditionality.

I. LEGAL BASIS FOR THE IMF'S CONDITIONALITY

The principle that access to the IMF's resources in the upper credit tranches under its general purpose facilities, that is, under stand-by and extended arrangements, should be subject to conditions has found increasing acceptance over time, but certain doubts linger on. It is a matter of record that the controversy over the principle of conditionality was not settled at Bretton Woods; that the signals in the early years of the IMF's existence, in fact, pointed to the acceptance of a considerable measure of automaticity of access to its resources; and that these signals proved to be false in the end. There is a wealth of documentation on this subject, including such in-house sources as the IMF's official history[1] and several articles by its former General Counsel, Sir Joseph Gold. A fairly recent exhaustive treatment of

---

[1] J. Keith Horsefield, and others, *The International Monetary Fund 1945–1965: Twenty Years of International Monetary Cooperation* (Washington, 1969).

this subject by an outside source is an excellent article by Sidney Dell.[2] The author concedes, albeit somewhat grudgingly, that the IMF's Executive Board in the end settled the argument definitively in favor of conditionality when it created the stand-by arrangement on February 13, 1952.

It is no secret that the argument was settled under pressure from the U.S. Government, against the solid opposition of the rest of the IMF's membership, for fear that the universal shortage of dollars would cause a run on the IMF's resources unless access to them was made subject to conditions. A strong case can nevertheless be made in favor of the logic of the decision. The original Articles of Agreement foresaw two types of balance of payments deficits: a structural deficit that called for an exchange rate adjustment and a temporary self-correcting deficit that qualified member countries for access to the IMF's resources. What the founding fathers apparently had not foreseen is that the typical balance of payments deficit is neither structural nor self-correcting inasmuch as it is caused by faulty domestic and external policies. The stand-by arrangement provided a solution for this typical intermediate case in that it assured a member country access to the IMF's resources provided the member undertook to follow domestic and external policies designed to correct its balance of payments problem within a reasonable period of time.

Notwithstanding the historical record, and the inherent logic, challenges to the IMF's right to impose conditions for access to its resources are still heard from time to time. What is invariably ignored by these challenges is that the IMF has the statutory authority and obligation to intercede with all its member governments in those aspects of their external and domestic policies that are customarily covered in programs supported by stand-by and extended arrangements, irrespective of their financial relationship with the IMF at the moment.

The IMF's jurisdiction over the exchange rates and exchange practices of member governments was firmly established in the original Articles of Agreement; and its jurisdiction over the gamut of external and domestic policies and policy instruments that have an impact on a country's balance of payments was given explicit recognition in the Second Amendment to the Articles of Agreement. Thus, Article IV, Section 1, states under the heading "General obligations of members":

> Recognizing that the essential purpose of the international monetary system is to provide a framework that facilitates the exchange of goods, services, and capital among countries, and that sustains sound economic growth, and that a principal objective is the continuing development of the orderly underlying conditions that are necessary for financial and economic stability, each member undertakes to

---

[2]Sidney Dell, "On Being Grandmotherly: The Evolution of IMF Conditionality," *Essays in International Finance*, No. 144, International Finance Section, Department of Economics (Princeton, New Jersey: Princeton University Press, October 1981).

collaborate with the Fund and other members to assure orderly exchange arrangements and to promote a stable system of exchange rates. In particular, each member shall:

  (i) endeavor to direct its economic and financial policies toward the objective of fostering orderly economic growth with reasonable price stability, with due regard to its circumstances;

 (ii) seek to promote stability by fostering orderly underlying economic and financial conditions and a monetary system that does not tend to produce erratic disruptions;

(iii) avoid manipulating exchange rates or the international monetary system in order to prevent effective balance of payments adjustment or to gain an unfair competitive advantage over other members; and

 (iv) follow exchange policies compatible with the undertakings under this Section."

Further, Section 3 of the same Article states under the heading "Surveillance over exchange arrangements":

"(*a*) The Fund shall oversee the international monetary system in order to ensure its effective operation, and shall oversee the compliance of each member with its obligations under Section 1 of this Article.

 (*b*) In order to fulfill its functions under (*a*) above, the Fund shall exercise firm surveillance over the exchange rate policies of members, and shall adopt specific principles for the guidance of all members with respect to those policies. Each member shall provide the Fund with the information necessary for such surveillance, and, when requested by the Fund, shall consult with it on the member's exchange rate policies. The principles adopted by the Fund shall be consistent with cooperative arrangements by which members maintain the value of their currencies in relation to the value of the currency or currencies of other members, as well as with other exchange arrangements of a member's choice consistent with the purposes of the Fund and Section 1 of this Article. These principles shall respect the domestic social and political policies of members, and in applying these principles the Fund shall pay due regard to the circumstances of members."

The IMF carries out this surveillance mandate by means of periodic consultations with all its member countries. Those who are inclined to challenge the legitimacy of the IMF's insistence on changes in a member government's external and domestic policies as a condition for granting access to its resources, therefore, should face up to the fact that the institution is mandated to follow essentially the same approach in its relations with all member countries, regardless of whether or not they seek access to its resources; they should also realize that they are on the weakest possible ground when they single out the IMF's advocacy of exchange rate changes and the liberalization of exchange regimes for challenge as undue interference with a country's sovereignty.

2. CONSTRAINTS OF THE IMF'S FLEXIBILITY IN SUPPORTING ADJUSTMENT PROGRAMS

Frequent criticisms of the IMF's approach to adjustment for being insufficiently flexible and too restrictive ignore the limited degree of freedom that the institution has in supporting adjustment programs with its resources. A cardinal rule for any IMF-supported adjustment program is that the contemplated balance of payments deficit can be expected to be fully financed from drawdowns of a country's own international reserves, the IMF resources committed to it, and its access to other sources of balance of payments finance. Countries typically seek to enter into stand-by or extended arrangements with the IMF when their own international reserves are close to exhaustion and when their access to other external sources of finance is severely curtailed. When this is the case, the limits of the flexibility that the IMF has in supporting an adjustment program are essentially set by the amount of its resources which it is prepared to commit to the country concerned.

It is true that a number of IMF-supported programs call for the retention in a country's international reserves of part or even all of the IMF resources committed under stand-by or extended arrangements, or the application of some or all of these resources to the repayment of reserve liabilities of the country's monetary authorities and of its external payments arrears. The division of the resources, which the IMF commits under a stand-by or extended arrangement, between those that the member country can spend and those that it is expected to put into its international reserves or use to repay reserve liabilities (including external payments arrears) is determined either by an explicit balance of payments performance test or by a balance of payments target implicit in the difference between the projected growth of the pertinent monetary variable and the explicit credit ceiling. Thus, this allocation of a country's use of IMF resources is mandatory under a test and notional under a target.

The balance of payments performance test or target is negotiated with the authorities, but in most cases within the constraints dictated by the country's disposable international reserve holdings and its reserve liabilities (including, as appropriate, external payments arrears) repayable within the program period. It is logical that part or even all of the IMF resources committed under stand-by or extended arrangements be earmarked for these purposes, in appropriate cases, considering that a central bank can manage its exchange market efficiently only if it disposes of a minimum of international reserves and that external payments arrears almost always deprive a country of normal trade credits from abroad.

In negotiating adjustment programs the IMF takes full account, wherever this is appropriate, of its role as a catalyst beyond the commitment of its own resources, owing to the influence which it exerts over the flow of funds to deficit countries from other official sources and from private banks. The IMF has been able to bring this influence effectively to bear essentially only on behalf of countries with stand-by or extended arrangements. Thus, relief from government-to-government debt service within the framework of the so-called Paris Club is now invariably conditioned on the prior negotiation of a stand-by or extended arrangement with the debtor country, as is relief from debt service to foreign banks. When it comes to mobilizing new funds for debtor countries, the IMF has exerted its influence over government-to-government aid flows within the framework of country-specific donor groups, customarily chaired by the World Bank, by pointing to the financing gap in a program supported or expected to be supported by a stand-by or extended arrangement, and rarely, when there was neither prospect of such an arrangement nor a clear need for it, by a broad endorsement of the aid recipient government's economic policies. The IMF's experience with inducing private financial institutions to maintain their capital flows to debtor countries is new and is still subject to much experimentation. But it is already abundantly clear that the IMF could not consider going that far in its advocacy of a borrowing country's case until the country has negotiated a stand-by or extended arrangement.

The IMF has been under perennial pressure to allow countries more time for adjustment. But the speed of adjustment, like the magnitude of the adjustment effort, is determined by the amount of emergency balance of payments finance available to a country from its own international reserves, the IMF resources committed to it, and its access to finance from other external sources; as already noted, this often comes down solely to the amount of IMF resources committed under a stand-by or extended arrangement. It is clear that the more drawn out the adjustment process, the greater will be the amount of emergency balance of payments finance needed to carry a country from an unsustainable to a sustainable external payments position; for example, an adjustment will require double the emergency balance of payments finance if spread smoothly over two years rather than one, triple the emergency finance if spread over three years, and so on.

3. POLICY INSTRUMENTATION OF ADJUSTMENT PROGRAMS

The point has been made repeatedly that the IMF tends to place undue reliance on demand management and insufficient reliance on supply-oriented structural adjustment; and, even among the ones who concede that demand management is of relevance there are those who allege that the monetarist approach to the balance of payments is not valid in certain country-specific conditions or at a given stage in the economic cycle. Dogmatic though it may sound, the monetarist model is a universally valid analytical framework, derived as it is from the balance sheet identity. The changes in the net international reserve position cannot but help to fully reflect the difference between changes in money and credit. The dismissal of the validity of this model on theoretical grounds, therefore, can only be explained by an altogether understandable human tendency to resist any form of determinism.

The argument that adjustment programs built on this approach are excessively vulnerable to errors in forecasting cannot be dismissed quite that easily. Programming errors do occur with some frequency because of lack of foresight about external market conditions or domestic production trends, for example, crop prospects. Such errors also occur because programmed policy measures, for example, discretionary government revenue measures, changes in exchange rate management or in the interest rate structure, the removal of exchange restrictions, or the liberalization of foreign trade, do not yield the expected results. But the potential implications of such programming errors for the balance of payments, the bottom line of any Fund-supported adjustment program, should not be exaggerated.

When it comes to the balance of payments outcome, there can be no specification error under a test, and under a target such an error is necessarily confined to the projected behavior of the critical monetary variable. Monetary projections obviously are subject to considerable margins of error, given that they are derived from forecasts of changes in real output, in domestic prices, and in the income velocity of the monetary variable selected, as well as from assumed levels of interest and exchange rates. But, if the programmed credit ceiling is observed, the departures from the implicit balance of payments target will of necessity equal the difference between the projected and the actual change in the pertinent monetary variable; and if the projection is reasonable, it is as likely that the balance of payments outcome will exceed the target as that it might fall short of the target.

The IMF has been experimenting with formulas for automatic adjustment of balance of payments performance tests to protect member countries from unforeseen contingencies and errors in forecasting, particularly shortfalls from projected levels of capital inflows. Such automatic adjustment formulas, of course, cannot be confined to the balance of payments performance test alone; for the sake of maintaining the coherence of a program, they must be carried through to all the interlocking quantitative targets and ceilings. It is worth emphasizing, however, that automatic adjustment formulas are possible only if either a country upon entry into a stand-by or extended arrangement disposes of international reserves or the program calls for the retention of at least part of the committed IMF resources in its international reserves, and only to the extent of any such international reserve availability and retention of IMF resources.

The emphasis placed in IMF-supported adjustment programs on demand management does not in any way detract from the frequently critical importance of building into such programs effective supply-oriented structural adjustment measures. A taxonomy of the latter is virtually endless. There can be no doubt that improvements in education, public health, and the distribution of land holdings will in time have a significant impact on national output. But leaving aside the fact that the IMF was designed to be a specialized doctor and not a general medical practitioner, and that as a consequence it lacks the technical competence to deal with problems in many important fields of socioeconomic policy, the structural improvements such as the ones just referred to have a gestation period that exceeds by many years the permissible time frame of a stand-by or extended arrangement. Another supply-oriented factor with far reaching implications for future output but beyond the IMF's purview is the quality of domestic investment; not only are the requisite technical judgments within the competence of the IMF's sister institution, the World Bank, but investments, too, typically have a gestation period exceeding the time frame of a financial arrangement with the IMF.

What remains of supply-oriented measures for the IMF to address in negotiating adjustment programs is essentially pricing policies, and foremost among them are those for the prices with the most pervasive effects throughout the economy, that is, the exchange rate, interest rate, and wage policies. My colleague, Mr. Loser, has extensively dealt in his paper with this particular subject. I will confine myself to only a few observations of a general character. Adjustment programs supported by stand-by or extended arrangements with the IMF have always focused on these economy-wide prices because of their relevance as supply-oriented instruments, as well as their critical relevance to demand management.

Therefore, it is largely in the eyes of the beholder whether to classify these or any other pricing policies as demand management tools or as instruments of a supply-oriented policy thrust. But it is worth stressing that, given the close linkages between exchange rate, interest rate, and wage policy, it would not be sensible to address one without taking the others into account. It is somewhat astonishing, therefore, that one hears so many argue that wage policy is none of the IMF's business.

The IMF has also been taken to task for recommending the elimination of consumer subsidies, allegedly because of an ideological bias against policies benefiting the underprivileged. These critics go to the extreme of denying that subsidies have balance of payments implications either in the short or the long run. The truth of the matter is that subsidies paid by governments are a charge to the budget and as such have adverse balance of payments effects in the short run, and subsidies paid by producers discourage production and as such have an adverse balance of payments effect that is somewhat more delayed. Given the frequency of criticisms of the IMF along these lines, and their apparent lack of rationality, one is left to wonder whether there really is any general desire to see the IMF be supply oriented in its approach to adjustment.

4. IMPLICATIONS OF THE WORLD ECONOMIC RECESSION FOR THE IMF'S CONDITIONALITY

The IMF was founded to avert worldwide economic depressions. For this purpose, it was mandated to develop rules for orderly exchange rate changes and other exchange practices by its member countries and it was endowed with financial resources to place at their disposal in order to give them an alternative to their adopting policies that would be detrimental to international trade in goods and services. Until recently the IMF's capability for averting a worldwide depression had not come to a test. It is conceivable that it now faces such a test, and this raises the question whether its approach to adjustment is still appropriate.

Let it be admitted that the IMF now faces a certain dilemma. Although it has increasingly adopted a global analytical framework, foremost within the context of its rather elaborate annual world economic outlook exercise, it is not at present well equipped to deal operationally with balance of payments problems except on a country-by-country basis. The unfortunate consequence of the IMF's country-specific operations is that there is a risk that it may become an accomplice to the very beggar-my-neighbor policies that it was created to avert. Its advocacy of a flexible exchange rate management in the countries of South America has the potential for competitive devaluations when market-determined exchange rates overshoot equilibrium levels, as they have a tendency to do.

Perhaps of more relevance to the subject of this paper is the question that is increasingly being raised of whether in the present state of the world economy the IMF should not relax its standards for adjustment programs that it is prepared to support by stand-by or extended arrangements.

It was noted earlier that adjustment programs which the IMF supports by stand-by or extended arrangements frequently call for part, if not all, of the IMF's resources committed under such arrangements to be retained in a country's international reserves or to be used for repaying the reserve liabilities of its monetary authorities. When this is the case, it could be argued that the IMF's pertinent practices should be liberalized in present world economic conditions. There is a certain logic in pleading for less ambitious balance of payments improvements when export earnings are falling and interest payments are rising and for greater agnosticism about fiscal deficits when government revenues are shrinking. But the margin of flexibility for qualifying a country for a stand-by or an extended arrangement that could be gained by allowing a larger proportion of the IMF's resources committed under such an arrangement to be spent rather than saved would be small for the typical country embarking on an adjustment process. The predominant operational problem is that the resources available to countries are so meager, and, with few exceptions, this situation leaves in practice very little room for maneuver.

The margin of flexibility for framing adjustment programs would be more substantially increased by a liberalization of the IMF's quantitative limits on access to its resources. This access is now limited to 150 percent of quota a year, 450 percent of quota for a three-year period—the maximum term of a stand-by or extended arrangement permissible under present policies—and 600 percent of quota for a country's total outstanding indebtedness to the IMF at any given time; all these limits exclude use of the IMF's compensatory financing and buffer stock facilities.[3] However, the IMF's resources are stretched at present and the general quota increase in train is not likely to improve this situation appreciably for any length of time. What the IMF would need to enable it to finance substantially larger balance of payments deficits is either a much greater capitalization or the authority to borrow on financial markets, or both; either of these options is within the discretion of member governments and not in the hands of the IMF's management and staff.

BIBLIOGRAPHY

Dell, Sydney, "On Being Grandmotherly: The Evolution of IMF Conditionality," *Essays in International Finance*, No. 144, International Finance Section, Department of Economics (Princeton, New Jersey: Princeton University Press, October 1981).

Gold, Sir Joseph, *Conditionality*, IMF Pamphlet Series, No. 31 (Washington, 1979).

Guitián, Manuel, *Fund Conditionality: Evolution of Principles and Practices*, IMF Pamphlet Series, No. 38 (Washington, 1981).

Hooke, Augustus W., *The International Monetary Fund: Its Evolution, Organization, and Activities*, IMF Pamphlet Series, No. 37 (Washington, 3rd ed., 1983).

Horsefield, J. Keith, and others, *The International Monetary Fund, 1945–1965: Twenty Years of International Monetary Cooperation* (Washington: International Monetary Fund, 1969).

---

[3]With the coming into effect of the Eighth General Review of Quotas on November 30, 1983, under a decision adopted by the Fund's Executive Board, access to Fund resources became subject to annual limits of 102 or 125 percent of quota, three-year limits of 306 or 375 percent of quota, and cumulative limits of 408 or 500 percent of quota (net of scheduled repurchases).

Commentary*

GUIDO DI TELLA

The paper by E. Walter Robichek could only have been written by someone with his knowledge and experience, which are evident in every part of his presentation. He touches upon very important topics and, especially, introduces a vital one in the last part: the relation between Fund conditionality and the present crisis, though he does not go into detail on the impact present conditions may have on conditionality. I intend to consider the paper section by section and draw some general conclusions at the end.

The first part explains the legal basis for the Fund's conditionality. In my view this is not open to question, as conditionality, legal or not, does in fact exist, and Robichek explains that it is legal. He also quotes the appropriate Fund Article, the latter part of which reads: "These principles shall respect the domestic social and political policies of members, and in applying these principles the Fund shall pay due regard to the circumstances of members." What more could we ask for? Robichek then shows his annoyance at the criticisms leveled at the Fund for "undue interference with a country's sovereignty." I do not consider this reaction justified. The Fund obviously does interfere, and very considerably so, in member countries; it might be acceptable to speak of appropriate or inevitable interference rather than undue interference, and there is no need to speak of sovereignty, but merely of autonomy. There is no doubt whatsoever that Fund interference is inevitable. This does not lead me to feel any particular annoyance, and I would quite simply adopt an attitude of resignation in this respect: such is the world, and what are we going to do about it. And I would say this with a smile and without bitterness. Developing countries are dependent countries, and all the more so if the financial behavior they adopt is reckless, as has been the case in our countries at times. We can win independence from you if, on our own account, we take the appropriate action. I believe there is no reason to take this question of interference so much to heart. We know it exists and we know how to break free from it.

Robichek then considers the constraints on the Fund's flexibility in the implementation of policies. He presents this subject most logically, observing that limits have to be set, that no policy with unlimited flexibility is possible, that there must be cuts, that generalized pressure on the Fund to allow long adjustment periods implies greater costs, and that the Fund must inevitably resist such pressure. Such push and pull between the Fund and its

---

*The original version of this paper was written in Spanish.

members is not, I would say, a love-hate relationship but rather a debtor-creditor one which is somewhat equivalent. Inevitably there is a certain tension, sometimes ending in reconciliation, other times in anger. It cannot be otherwise. However, the limits to flexibility are not determined only by the limits to Fund resources, but also by the internal situation in a country, which imposes a de facto limitation, one which I fear is becoming more significant. There is thus a twofold limit. Sometimes we speak, as if in a dialogue of the deaf, about the limit on the Fund and about the limits on individual countries, when in reality both exist. Latin America may perhaps still be a relatively "safe" area; consequently, it may appear that the limits of adjustment may still not have been met. In Latin America there are not more than one or two communist countries, not more than two or three countries suffering from civil war, and not more than five or six countries that have had to resort to systematic repression of their population to maintain order; only two of the major four countries, namely, Mexico and Brazil, risk major social upheavals while the remaining two, Argentina and Venezuela, do not appear to be on the brink of such problems. I do not mention this either as a reassurance or a threat, but merely to state the way things are. I believe the limit must be handled with the greatest caution. We are speaking of a "safe" area which is verging on becoming unsafe. To bring together what the creditor countries can do or may have to do, and what the debtor countries can do or may have to do, will require a delicate economic and political balancing act. This is the problem that will need to be addressed in the next few years.

In the third part of the paper I have a problem either with the Spanish translation or with the original. The translation is slightly more aggressive. The original speaks of "the monetary approach to the balance of payments" while the translation reads "the monetarist approach to the balance of payments." Further on, where Robichek adds that "the monetarist model is a universally valid analytical framework," I was extremely surprised and went back to the English version, which allayed my fears somewhat. The monetaristic approach implies a whole series of policies which go far beyond the monetary approach to the balance of payments. For my peace of mind, Robichek clarifies that the monetarist approach is a "balance sheet identity." Nothing can be said against mathematical identities, they always have to be accepted. The monetaristic approach, however, is more than a mere identity. The matter was clarified by Robichek when he made it quite clear that for him it was an operational tool rather than a philosophical concept. I trust this is indeed the case.

Where differences may arise is in the area of economic concepts; as can be seen from other views expressed, these are far from being trivial nuances. We do not propose to give a Fund version and say it is white while the opposite version is black, for this is not the case. These nuances, however, are important and in certain economic situations are at the origin of very considerable differences. These generally relate to the automaticity, stability, and speed with which the market adjusts.

Obviously, the Fund's philosophy holds to the belief that markets adjust speedily and well. This implies believing that markets are competitive, that no oligopoly exists to hamper competitive adjustment, that the markets are transparent, that only a single price exists in each of them, that there are no natural disequilibria and those that do exist are temporary aberrations, that the markets are stable, and that no destabilizing trends exist or that these are temporary and of short duration. Furthermore, there is a particular evaluation of the magnitude of the variables required and the manner in which adjustments may be promoted. If a 1 percent increase in unemployment would permit adjustment of the economic situation, no one, not even the most extreme proponents of full employment, would challenge it. If the figure required were 2 percent or 3 percent, in view of what has occurred in the last decade, this would cause only a mild reaction. But if the unemployment rate required to adjust the system would have to increase from 7 to 20 percent, there would be a very different reaction, and some may believe no such policy can be contemplated. I have not the slightest doubt that by using a sufficient dose of monetary medicine the result can be achieved. I do not consider this model inconsistent, but it assumes a perfect world; in reality there is no automaticity, competitiveness, transparency, or stability in the markets, and the impact of the adjustment variables that need to be used is so great and spread over such a long period of time that they become impossible, if not to say utopian. Contrarily, at best, the Fund gets nervous when faced with 20 percent annual inflation, while we get nervous with a monthly inflation rate of 5 percent, even though we recognize the terrible consequences of this. However, we are often faced with highly disagreeable choices. We do not have antithetical models; however, we suffer from different "allergies," and this is the heart of the matter. This can be seen, for example, in the Fund's attitude toward wages, a matter with which it considers rightly that it should concern itself. However, the Fund fails to speak clearly on the question of income distribution, which it never includes as a "target."

Many of the Fund's pronouncements are valid but only over long periods of time. The time frame of the adjustment appears to me essential in some cases. In reality, it is the transition that is the cornerstone of a policy rather than the target, which for one reason or another is never reached.

In the last part of the paper concerning the effects of economic recession or conditionality, Robichek mentions the fall in world exports and the increase in the interest rate as being problems. I feel, however, that one should elaborate on the consequences, which are extremely serious.

These two problems, in conjunction with that of the price of oil, have led to noteworthy indebtedness. If no mention is made of indebtedness, the central aspect of the present situation is being ignored. More than of indebtedness, this is a question of insolvency, and in proportions never before experienced in the financial history of the world. This is going to affect conditionality, will make it harsher, and especially will require that supervision be extended not only to debtors but also to creditors.

It is obvious that Fund surveillance during the past decade was insufficient. Beginning in 1973, the world which began to free itself to some extent from Fund supervision because of the large amount of international liquidity ended up having greater problems than it would have had had it been supervised by the Fund. I would say that in the past few years the Fund was not sufficiently alert in respect to countries that were plunging themselves into debt. At least as regards my country, we are not aware of any attempt by the Fund to tell Dr. Martínez de Hoz that something strange was happening in connection with indebtedness and overvaluation. In earlier times, governments of a different stripe received "reprimands"—of a much stricter kind for far lesser overvaluations.

I believe that the Fund's surveillance function would have been a good thing. It is not that I am being slightly masochistic, since after all I have said about the Fund it might appear that I want it to intervene more. What I do want is for it to intervene more equitably with debtors and creditors alike. The Fund is going through a very, very delicate phase. It is doing an enormous favor to the international financial community and to our countries, but by staving off the problem of insolvency both for the debtor countries and especially for the creditor countries, it may well lead us into even greater difficulties. I am referring to the refinancing that is so very useful at this time and that allows us to "keep going" with short-term rescheduling, for five to seven years and at very high rates in real terms of 5 to 7 percent, which we all know to be rates the majority of countries cannot afford. The adjustment process required by the Fund needs to be extended over a longer period; the indebted countries are doing this through a reduction of the level of their revenue and lenders will have to do this if they wish to recover their loans, at least in the originally agreed period of time and at the originally agreed rate. Few believe this can be done within the system as it is now. We are approaching the "day of reckoning." I do not know whether this is a year away, or two or three, but I believe it is not far off; what is being done now will merely postpone it. I believe the Fund's efforts at postponement may help debtors and creditors to adapt to the change which will need to be faced, but I also believe that it would be infinitely preferable for the "day of reckoning" to be promoted by the creditor countries, by the creditor banks, and by the Fund, who have a sufficient sense of responsibility to understand the problem in its entirety rather than postpone discussion of the problem until after one of the large debtor countries plunges into scandalous default; this would be catastrophic for the international financial system and especially for the country in question, and would generate enormous pressure in other countries to follow the example of the "default" of the pioneer along that distressful path. I do not think there is time to stave off this situation indefinitely. We are beginning to hear proposals for considerable "stretching out" of the debt, not just by several years but by two or three decades. This, however, is not sufficient in itself, and a drastic decrease in real interest rates is also necessary. If these do not return to the levels they were at before 1973, the situation may well become catastrophic. It would be infinitely better for all these matters to be discussed among the creditors, the large international banks, and the Fund, rather than among the debtor countries. It is this task which poses the greatest challenge to the Fund and where it can make its greatest contribution in the future.

Commentary*

MIGUEL A. FABBRI

Calling on his years of experience as Director of the Western Hemisphere Department of the International Monetary Fund and on the methodological and conceptual skills that characterize his work, the noteworthy economist Mr. Robichek has provided us with a meaningful examination of the controversial topic of conditionality.

The author approached this subject from a traditional point of view, as well as from a new perspective reflecting the changes in circumstances from those prevailing in the years following World War II and in the 1950s and 1960s; as a result, he proposes to re-examine the scope and limitations of conditionality, that is to say, the combination of rules under which adjustment programs are planned and carried out.

Under the Bretton Woods agreement, the role of the Fund was to promote world economic equilibrium; this role was undermined following the reform of the international monetary system carried out between late 1972 and early 1976, when in the second amendment to the Articles of Agreement members were given the right to adopt the exchange arrangements of their choice. This option open to members is making it possible for some of them to maintain the level of their revenues by means of periodic competitive exchange devaluations followed up by restrictive exchange, trade, and tax measures.

As A. W. Hooke has observed, in the 1930s such measures achieved the desired results, namely, of maintaining revenues, but did so at the expense of aggravating the difficulties of neighboring countries. These in turn found themselves obligated to neutralize these restrictive practices by taking similar measures, thus producing a worldwide reduction in trade and employment, one of the principal causes of the Great Depression.

I wonder whether the decision to adopt freely selected exchange arrangements might not be one of the factors that unleashed the present crisis.

Mr. de Larosière would surely agree that successful implementation of adjustment programs by the developing countries is particularly dependent on two critical factors: first, continued recovery of the industrial countries, and second, support from commercial financing sources. Given the dominant characteristics of the present situation, it would appear that the prospects for the immediate future are not very bright; on the one hand, there are lingering rigidities and structural disequilibria which will make it

---

*The original version of this paper was written in Spanish.

very difficult to come up with a satisfactory recovery alternative, and, on the other hand, the international banking system is showing an unwillingness to maintain the level of current financing to the developing countries. If the two factors noted above do not positively reinforce one another, it will be extremely difficult, if not impossible, for traditional Fund adjustment programs to restore the domestic and external equilibrium hoped for in each case, despite the financial authorities' strongest inclination and resolve to implement them.

As regards Fund conditionality and the degree of flexibility for the use of its resources, there are two clearly defined views. The first, supported by the industrial countries, argues that the adjustment programs are too mild. The second, espoused by a sizable majority of the developing countries, is that the conditionality established for access to Fund resources is extremely strict, and that the term "austerity program" would be more fitting than "adjustment program." In my opinion, there is great merit in both these views since the greater or lesser intensity of a program depends on the extent of economic deterioration in a country and on the amount of monetary assets available to it.

A high-ranking Fund official has quite rightly observed that it is not really the Fund that imposes adjustment programs; instead, in the final analysis, they are required by the "scarcity" of external resources.

If conditionality is considered to be an instrument for lessening the balance of payments problems of member countries and facilitating the international adjustment process, the corrective measures must necessarily be paralleled by the necessary financing, failing which the process will be rendered more difficult and serious disorders will ensue. There are three sources for adjustment financing:

    (a) the country itself;

    (b) the International Monetary Fund; and

    (c) third parties (commercial banks and suppliers).

If the three sources make adequate flows of resources available, it may be assumed that adjustments will be implemented normally, giving rise to the hope that the pace of growth will recover in the short term; however, this will not be so if the reserves position is critical and if third-party sources of funds dry up. This latter hypothesis is generally the one that is borne out; from the outset, as regards both the amounts and term involved, the program will be highly rigorous and inflexible, raising the possibility of the adjustments skirting dangerously close to the edge of sociopolitical tolerance. Unfortunately, these factors cannot be overlooked even when the Fund plays an institutional role equivalent to that of a medical specialist. Consequently, the amount and term are the variables that determine the intensity of the adjustment. This problem routinely calls into question the Fund's role in the restoration of international economic and financial equilibrium. I therefore believe that alternative solutions are required to avoid what commonly results: the design of highly inflexible programs. One such alternative would be for the Governors of the Fund to arrange for the rapid and complete publication of the Fund's annual assessments of economic policies following routine and special consultations. Full knowledge of these reports can alert the economic, social, and political leaders, the international community, and financial organizations to a potential crisis that a given country might be approaching owing to its authorities' vacillation in implementing corrective measures in a timely manner.

One other consideration pertaining to the flexibility of conditionality is the increase in quotas. The increase approved as part of the Eighth General Review of Quotas last February will make it possible for qualified member countries to increase their requests by almost 50 percent. However, the maladjustment brought about by the reduction of inflation in the developed countries has significantly weakened domestic demand and further slowed down international trade in the developing countries. These phenomena, compounded by the strengthening of the dollar and high interest rates, have caused serious liquidity problems, which can only be solved by sizable infusions of financial resources. Yet another quota increase is therefore necessary, as is an amendment to the Articles of Agreement raising the amount of Fund resources usable by countries with liquidity problems to at least twice the current percentages, and thereby making conditionality more flexible.

It is a fact that commercial banks are pulling out of the Latin American market. Even though the Fund has announced that in the last three cases it has taken steps to permit the joint participation of international banks in adjustment programs, we believe this to be circumstantial and that it will not become the rule, as there are indications that banks are declining to participate jointly in the adjustment program of the Republic of Uruguay—which is not a large country.

It is vitally important to maintain an adequate flow of the financial resources provided by banks, failing which adjustment programs will be less successful because of their tendency to be more severe. It is therefore necessary to consider the following alternatives:

(a) That international banks guarantee in a formal agreement with the Fund that they will participate jointly in adjustment programs, providing financing in an amount not less than that currently extended;

(b) That the Fund Agreement be amended to authorize it to have recourse to the financial market, as Robichek suggests, to cover shortfalls occurring because of the decreased participation of banks and suppliers;

(c) That the General Arrangements to Borrow (GAB) be extended to other users. This measure will make it possible to deal with an economic situation characterized by a general liquidity shortage in Latin America resulting from the world economic crisis. Of course, the GAB expansion must endeavor to ensure that the benefit of using the financial resources generated in this kind of "private club" of the Group of Ten, the wealthiest countries, is actually extended to others.

Consequently, in view of the need for more financing of the longer terms mentioned and of the structural nature of the adjustments generally entailed in such programs, it is essential that the Fund coordinate its activities more closely with other organizations active in development finance, particularly the World Bank.

I believe that these remarks and various views expressed do, to some extent, confirm the truths expressed by Robichek. In brief, the notion of conditionality itself is not debatable. What does merit discussion is its intensity. Its success requires that it undergo another general review so as to adapt it to current circumstances, characterized as they are by crisis, overburdensome external debt, shortage of liquidity, and inflation. It is clearly of the utmost importance that the international monetary system be urgently restructured.

The Role of Economy-Wide Prices in the Adjustment Process

CLAUDIO M. LOSER*

I. INTRODUCTION

In recent years, the experience of many countries with respect to their macroeconomic management has brought the issues of exchange rates, interest rates, and other prices with economy-wide repercussions into the forefront of economic debate. In many instances, particularly in Latin America, exchange rate policies were significantly modified relative to past practices, while wide-ranging financial reforms resulted in substantial changes in interest rate levels and structure. Countries in other areas experienced similar reforms, for example, Israel, Portugal, and Sri Lanka. The modifications were intended to improve the internal balance of the economy and to restore the medium-term viability of the balance of payments. In the event, some countries failed to achieve these objectives, and because the failure was frequently attributed to the pursuit of specific exchange and interest rate policies, many of the previously established policies were reversed.

The issue of adequate pricing—including appropriate exchange rates, interest rates, and wages—has been a focal point of Fund attention, both in consultations and negotiations of arrangements for the use of its resources. Price adjustment policies have been viewed as an integral part of adjustment, and recent experience with Fund-supported programs indicates that they have been generally successfully implemented; however, programs have occasionally failed in their objectives even when major pricing corrections were implemented.

*The views expressed in this paper represent the opinions of the author and not necessarily those of the International Monetary Fund. The author received helpful comments on an earlier draft from many colleagues in the International Monetary Fund—among them Messrs. Robichek, Beza, Gerhard, and Guitián and Ms. Kelly. None of them, however, should be held responsible for any views expressed in this paper.

Section 2 describes the conceptual framework for analyzing the effect of key prices on the macroeconomic equilibrium of countries entering into an external adjustment process, and its possible shortcomings. The analysis, although general, is of particular relevance to those developing countries with at least moderately developed capital markets. Section 3 reviews recent experience with Fund programs, and Section 4 presents a brief discussion of developments with respect to exchange rates in selected Latin American countries in recent years. Finally, Section 5 provides some tentative conclusions.

2. ECONOMIC ADJUSTMENT AND PRICE CORRECTIONS: A SIMPLE CONCEPTUAL FRAMEWORK

It is now well accepted that balance of payments developments—either the emergence of imbalances or their elimination—are directly linked to monetary phenomena. The accounting framework for the monetary approach to the balance of payments is provided by the identity equating changes in the quantity of money (broadly defined) with the sum of changes in domestic credit and net international reserves. But the policy content is determined by the behavioral relation between demand for money and the sources of money creation (domestic and foreign). Financial programming as practiced by the Fund staff is based on these observed behavioral relations and adjustment policies tend to reflect this approach.[1] The monetary approach to the adjustment process is based on the assumption of a stable demand for money and the observation that an excess supply of (demand for) money would be eliminated through changes in nominal income and through changes in net international reserves. From this standpoint, the balance of payments can be seen as a monetary variable, and its imbalances can be corrected through the control of other components of the money supply—namely, domestic credit, either to the private or public sector. More broadly, adjustment must be viewed as the achievement of a viable relationship between aggregate income and aggregate expenditure—reflected in the current account of the balance of payments.[2] In most instances, the size of the current account deficit—and therefore the possible excess of expenditure over income—will be constrained by the availability of financing, namely foreign reserves and foreign credits and grants.[3] Foreign financing will depend on the quality of domestic

---

[1]See Manuel Guitián (1981) for a description of the approach. Also, Frenkel and Johnson (1976), Johnson (1972), and Mundell (1960) and (1971), and the International Monetary Fund (1977).

[2]See Guitián (1973) and Kelly (1982) for a description of the conceptual framework.

[3]See Loser (1977) and Keller (1980) for a description of the impact of foreign debt in overall economic management.

policies being pursued; in particular, if policies are viewed as adequate, the access to foreign financing will be certainly higher than if policies are viewed as inadequate to solve a country's problems.

The use of domestic financial policies—including credit and fiscal measures—helps relax the financing constraint and also narrows the gap between income and expenditure. But these policies have not been the sole mechanism of adjustment. They have been supported almost always by the use of prices that have a generalized impact on the economy. Adjustments in relative prices, including exchange rates, interest rates, and administered prices, have a direct impact on aggregate demand while at the same time they help increase the availability of resources in the economy through an increased level of savings and investment and through a more efficient use of existing resources. If no appropriate measures are taken, price distortions will continue to affect negatively the appropriate functioning of the price mechanism, aggravate internal and external imbalances, and reduce potential income.

The effects of price changes on resource allocation and demand are traditionally the best understood channels of adjustment, but they are not the only ones. The increasing openness of financial markets in many developing countries has brought about an important change in the speed of reaction and magnitude of capital flows; and more frequently than not, these flows have dominated the outcome of the overall balance of payments, at least in the short run. It is important, therefore, that policymakers bear in mind the effect of domestic policies on the capital account. A shift of confidence caused by altering signals may significantly change the availability of foreign financing or induce capital movements that may result in a path that was not expected for the macroeconomic price variables, thereby rendering the policies pursued inappropriate. The implications of capital mobility for economic management will become clearer in the following sections.

Price adjustments affect not only resource allocations and the income-expenditure balance, but the entailing transfer of resources also results in changes in relative factor incomes and in income distribution, having a direct bearing on a particular policy course. It is frequently asserted that the issue of income distribution is overlooked by the Fund.[4] The apparent shortcoming reflects the fact that programs supported by the Fund deal with emerging or already existing balance of payments crises that require immediate and assertive action. For example, the constraints imposed by deteriorating terms of trade or reduced availability of foreign financing often result in an adjustment effort that, of necessity, modifies relative prices between sectors or between factors of production. The consequences of these adjustments may be burdensome from a political or social point of view but frequently

---

[4]Steward and Sengupta (1982).

cannot be avoided because of existing constraints, although some flexibility may exist as to how the costs are distributed. In any event, income distribution effects are not always clear in terms of who benefits from these changes; thus the impact of pricing measures must be carefully appraised. [5]

Role of the Exchange Rate

Exchange rate action probably constitutes the most conspicuous pricing measure in the adjustment process. The widespread effects of exchange rate changes—or their absence—both on the real and monetary sectors of the economy are well known, and it is not the purpose of this paper to review them thoroughly. [6] Nonetheless, it is important to summarize exchange rate issues relevant to the emergence of internal and external imbalances and their correction.

Exchange rate changes have a direct effect on resource allocation from a medium-term point of view; but as indicated previously, in the short term their overwhelming effects are financial. In the framework of an economy that has close economic connections with the rest of the world—both from the point of view of trade and financing—a pegged or controlled exchange rate policy precludes an independent monetary policy—if no restrictions are imposed on exchange transactions; a floating exchange rate, on the other hand, allows for a domestic monetary policy which can diverge significantly from the rest of the world. The foreign exchange intervention policy can be determined by the perception of national authorities about the minimum inflation rate that can be achieved at any time, without major disruptions to economic activity. If the real exchange rate is to be maintained, [7] the inflation rate determines a minimum rate of depreciation, once appropriate account is taken of foreign inflation. In turn, when an exchange rate path is established, the authorities can program the rate of monetary expansion in the economy, consistent with the rate of depreciation and inflation. An expansion in excess of that indicated by the exchange rate policy, and reflected in a rapid increase in domestic credit, will generate balance of payments pressures that will eventually lead to a change in the level of the exchange rate so as to restore equilibrium, immediately or after some time. Otherwise, policymakers will have to have recourse to stringent credit policies or increasingly complex and restrictive exchange and trade controls.

Expansionary policies will be reflected not only in possible changes in the nominal exchange rate, but also in changes in the real exchange rate. As an

---

[5] Salop and Johnson (1980).

[6] See Frenkel and Johnson (1976) and Dornbusch (1980). Also H.G. Johnson (1958).

[7] The real exchange rate is defined as the relative price of tradable to nontradable goods. From a simple empirical point of view, the movement of the real exchange rate would be measured by the behavior of the exchange rate relative to internal price developments adjusted for price developments in major trading partners.

example, budget deficits will have a direct impact on inflation and the exchange rate.[8] In addition, a shift in expenditure to nontradable goods can result in an increase of the relative prices of nontradables, that is, a change in the real exchange rate. Similarly, the increased availability of foreign financing can affect—in conjunction with fiscal policies—the equilibrium level of the exchange rate and the sustainability of the balance of payments outcome. Increased access to foreign financing—because of changes either in domestic or in external conditions—will eventually result in a widening of the current account deficit, either directly through government spending or through a change in relative prices, that is, an appreciation of the domestic currency in real terms. Similarly, reduced access can lead to a real depreciation of the domestic currency. But the access to foreign financing cannot be considered fully exogenous. A widening current account deficit may be perceived as unsustainable by foreign lenders, when expenditure is seen to expand without a corresponding improvement in productive capacity and when accompanied by a deterioration of competitiveness. If policies are not corrected, the deterioration in the external account can result in a reversal of capital flows that will require sharp adjustments, including the use of the exchange rate, in order to reduce the expenditure-income gap.

In general terms, in the short run, capital flows determine the behavior of the foreign exchange markets when capital mobility is significant.[9] Sharp movements in exchange rates can be explained by shifts between currencies, in the context of a portfolio approach. According to this approach, either foreign exchange flows or exchange rate fluctuations can be explained by the expected differential between domestic and foreign rates of return. A change in expected rates of return may overshadow any effects of exchange rates on real economic activity, in particular in circumstances where countries are confronted with an increasing degree of capital mobility in international financial markets. Certainly the effect of foreign exchange flows will be directly related to the particular features of individual countries, that is, the degree of integration with the world financial system and the importance of the private sector in the economy. Consequently, the dominance of developments in the current account or the capital account will vary for each individual country.

The effects of exchange rates on the production and consumption of tradable goods cannot be viewed as distinct from those described above. For example, a production shift toward tradable goods can only be envisaged to be permanent in the context of a set of policies compatible with a more depreciated real exchange rate, namely, those incomes and financial policies that do not passively reflect the effect of the exchange rate on prices.

---

[8]See Rodríguez (1978).

[9]In this connection, Frenkel and Rodríguez (1982) provide a description of exchange rate dynamics and exchange rate "overshooting."

The impact of exchange rates on production will depend on the ability to transfer resources among productive sectors, a possibility that is frequently questioned because of the possible existence of pervasive rigidities, particularly in developing countries. While the argument may be valid from a short-term perspective, if the adjustment policies are pursued over a longer period of time, their impact can be significant.[10] Moreover, even in the short run and with highly specific resources engaged in certain activities, there may be considerable scope for an increase in output, when these resources are used more intensively. A typical case is that of mining and agriculture, where output can be increased rapidly once appropriate prices are provided to producers—for example, through the exchange rate.

Another perspective of the exchange rate in increasing output and improving resource allocation is provided by the possibility of substitution of an exchange rate adjustment for a system of exchange and trade restrictions. Typically exchange and trade restrictions are imposed as a means of controlling the external sector in a period when expansionary policies exert pressures on the balance of payments. These controls can be successful in closing the economy in the short run, although at a high cost in terms of increasingly complex control mechanisms and of higher rates of inflation. More important, the cost is high in terms of generating major distortions that reduce the level of output and eventually render the measures ineffective. In these circumstances, the exchange rate plays a somewhat different role. Even for given financial policies, an adjustment of the exchange rate in conjunction with measures to liberalize exchange and trade transactions will allow for an increase in output, in particular, in the areas of export and import substitutes with low levels of effective protection; in these cases, the exchange rate can help improve resource allocation and reduce inflationary pressures by increasing output and reducing existing demand pressures which may have prevailed previously, even without the need for major financial corrections.

Interest Rate Policies

The discussion on exchange rates is not complete without an equivalent analysis of interest rates. The literature has extensively covered the effect of interest rates on international economic equilibrium.[11] In a world of increasing economic sophistication and growing financial interdependence, interest rate policies have an impact on aggregate demand and affect capital flows to an extent that overtakes any impact on the real sectors of the economy in the short run. In general, the supply of financial resources will be

---

[10]See Section 3 for a description of recent experience with exchange rates in the context of Fund-supported programs. Also see Donovan (1981).

[11]In addition to authors mentioned in earlier sections, see McKinnon (1969) and (1973).

dependent crucially upon the structure of interest rates in the economy. Financial repression—the establishment of ceilings on interest rates and the allocation of financial resources through nonprice means—results in an ineffective allocation of scarce resources and, more important, in a reduced supply of funds channeled through the organized financial markets; this impairs the normal savings-investment process in the economy. Moreover, the persistence of interest rates below those prevailing abroad—when adequate account is taken of the effect of changes in the exchange rate—generates incentives to channel domestic savings abroad, thereby further reducing the availability of capital in the economy.

The exchange and interest rate policies cannot be dissociated. The two policies have to be pursued consistently for an adequate external equilibrium; but in addition they have to be credible, in light of other developments. A slowly depreciating currency can be supplemented by interest rates equivalent to the rate of depreciation plus the interest rate prevailing abroad and may provide for interest rate parity from an accounting point of view.[12] But other financial variables—domestic credit or the budget deficit—may be expanding at rates that generate the expectation that the exchange rate and interest rate policies are inconsistent and that they are, therefore, unsustainable; active intervention by the authorities may help postpone the required adjustment, but eventually the correction will have to take place.

If the authorities want to preserve a given exchange rate or predetermined depreciation path, and pressures emerge in the foreign exchange market, they can make use either of increased restrictions on payments or of tighter financial policies. If the introduction of restrictions is dismissed because of the negative impact of these measures on resource allocation and confidence, the only available option is to allow for increases in interest rates, to reduce capital flight, and to slow down expenditure. In those circumstances, the costs with respect to output and employment may be considerably higher than if the exchange rate is modified. Most of the adjustment will be reflected in reduced demand; any previous loss in competitiveness will not be corrected, and adequate incentives will not be restored for exports or efficient import substituting sectors. In the very short term, some capital inflows may be observed; but if underlying trends indicate the need for corrective actions, tight credit policies will seldom modify expectations about the eventual adjustment of the exchange rate.

The link between exchange rates and interest rates may be affected by the speed of adjustment in the goods and in the capital markets,[13] but eventually the two variables will have to be aligned, taking into account monetary and

---

[12]Interest rate parity is envisaged as taking into account the risk premium that may be required for an individual country.
[13]Frenkel and Rodríguez (1982).

real developments in the economy.[14] Nonetheless, there may be some degree of maneuver to sever the link in the short run. Capital controls can generate a partial break between domestic and external capital markets. The goods market may also be somewhat isolated from the capital market by the existence of dual rates, where a fluctuating rate absorbs the effect of changes in interest rates and other elements that may affect confidence. Nonetheless, these practices can be seen only as stopgap measures that will eventually require modification. Their persistence may result in distortions that may be costlier than those emerging from excessive fluctuations in the rates, if they are allowed to move freely. In sum, interest rate policies in a world of increasing financial interdependence cannot be seen as separate from exchange rate management; they will have to be compatible with other domestic financial policies.

Other Prices

Administered prices have a similarly pervasive impact as that of exchange rates and interest rates. Producer prices for many export products are frequently subject to the control of the authorities and therefore can have a marked impact on macroeconomic equilibrium. The adjustment of prices may be either the necessary reflection of exchange rate adjustments or of international price changes. A break between domestic and external prices could be justified on the basis of welfare considerations, particularly when price changes are viewed as a windfall to be distributed among all inhabitants of a particular country—a typical example is that of increased oil prices during the period 1974–80. In most cases, however, the lack of adjustment of prices is based on other short-term considerations. For example, producer prices frequently remain unrealistically low because of revenue purposes, although the intended effect is offset by an eroding tax base caused by reduced production and contraband. In turn, utility pricing by the public sector often lags behind inflation and results in a marked deterioration of public finances. In some instances, public utility prices have been used as indicators of future inflation; but more often than not, the use of these policies is a faulty mechanism of inflation control. Price adjustments may result in the short term in a quantum increase in the price level, but because they will eventually result in increased public sector savings and reduced excess demand pressures, they are a more effective anti-inflation device. Moreover, frequently administered price changes can constitute an effective form of taxation, with a distributional impact that can be viewed as fair, a case in point is that of gasoline prices.

---

[14] A discussion of the link between interest rate differentials and exchange rate risk is presented in Blejer (June 1982).

Wages

The adjustment of prices, exchange rates, and interest rates will necessarily be reflected in a decline in real wages. If the gap between expenditure and income is to be narrowed to help achieve a sustainable balance of payments, competitiveness should be improved and expenditure reduced. To this end, payments to most domestic factors would have to be reduced in the short term. The implications for wages are clear. Real returns to labor would decline—a counterpart to a more depreciated real exchange rate—unless increases in productivity offset the decline. The declining real wages may lead to social and political pressures that can preclude the achievement of an adequate adjustment process; but a reduction in real factor costs may be inevitable because of a deterioration in the terms of trade or reduced availability of foreign financing. If the available resources to the economy have declined, the costs of adjustment have to be shared by all sectors of the economy, although some flexibility exists with regard to the impact on various groups. In any event, a lack of adequate real wage corrections, in the context of an adjustment process, will most likely result in a marked increase in unemployment, beyond the levels that would have prevailed in the presence of lower real wages.[15]

3. EXPERIENCE WITH FUND PROGRAMS

Recent Evidence

Over the last 25 years, adjustment efforts in many countries have been carried out in the context of economic programs supported by the use of Fund resources in the form of stand-by and extended arrangements. The cooperation between the Fund and member countries has been particularly important because economic adjustment frequently imposes a sharp turnaround in policies. In particular, the pervasive existence of distortions and unrealistic prices has required a widespread use of economy-wide price adjustments in stabilization efforts, either in the context of market or centrally planned economies.[16]

Outsiders have viewed adjustment programs supported by Fund resources as restraining aggregate demand and thereby providing for an improvement in the internal and external balance.[17] While the importance of demand management cannot be sufficiently stressed in the context of adjustment efforts, price adjustments have been central to adjustment—with an impact

---

[15]See Dornbusch (1980) for a discussion of real wages and the process of adjustment. Also Steward and Sengupta (1982) for a critical view of stabilization programs.

[16]See Allen (1982) and Guitián (1981).

[17]See Cline and Weintraub (1981) for a general collection of papers on economic stabilization.

both on supply and demand. Typically, a country entering into a program supported by Fund resources in recent years could have been characterized by the existence of widespread balance of payments problems, high inflation, and low growth, relative to past performance or that of its trading partners. This is shown in Table 1, which is based on the evidence of recent stand-by and extended arrangements.[18,19] While the particular nature of the problems depended on the features of each individual country, in general, a combination of internal and external factors contributed to the difficulties. Adverse exogenous factors occurred in most of the period 1973–81—the period covered by the table. Table 1 also describes the factors associated with economic performance at the time of program inception and shows the importance of exogenous problems, including external and domestic elements beyond the control of the authorities. The effect of deteriorating terms of trade, in part caused by the sharp increase in energy prices, was compounded by a slowdown in world economic activity, creating serious balance of payments difficulties. But expansionary demand pressures, mostly associated with the performance of the public sector, were at the center of imbalances. Moreover, the growing imbalances generated not only pressures on the current account and the overall balance of payments, but also gave rise to market distortions that further aggravated the emerging crises. Frequently, the authorities did not change the exchange rate policy course; instead, they made use of exchange and trade restrictions in order to reduce emerging pressures on reserves and thereby created bottlenecks and shortages. The restrictions affected aggregate supply and reduced output because of the negative effect on competitiveness. Moreover, restrictive practices were introduced in conjunction with other controls on administered prices and interest rates, thereby aggravating the effect of unrealistic exchange rates. The pursuit of these policies sometimes provided a short-term respite but was insufficient to arrest the deteriorating economic performance. Moreover, the expansionary demand pressures frequently resulted in mounting debt problems and capital flight—reflected in increasing problems of accumulation of arrears—further deteriorating the credit-worthiness of the country and reducing the availability of foreign financing. The general pattern was not too different among countries and reflected an inconsistent pursuit of monetary, fiscal, pricing, and exchange rate policies.

---

[18]The experience with Fund-supported programs in the early 1970s is discussed in Reichmann (1978), Reichmann and Stillson (1978), and Johnson and Reichmann (1978).

[19]In general terms, stand-by arrangements have been oriented to correct imbalances in a period of not more than two years and have stressed to a large extent shorter term policies. Programs supported by extended arrangements cover three-year periods and are designed so as to help achieve internal and external balance by the use of financial and structural modifications that improve the structure of the economy and enhance growth prospects. Nonetheless, structural changes are also an integral part of stand-by arrangements.

**Table 1. Characteristics of Economic Problems Prior to Program
in Recent Stand-By and Extended Arrangements[1]**

(Number of cases)

	Stand-By Arrangements		Extended Arrangements
	Approved in 1973–76	Approved in 1977–80	(1975–81)
General characteristics of problems			
Total number of programs	24	50	16
Balance of payments difficulties	24	48	16
Inflation	23	40	13
Economic growth	21	49	13
Public sector performance	22	48	13
Factors associated with economic problems			
Total number of arrangements	24	50	16
Expansionary demand policies	22	44	15
Cost and price distortions	23	50	16
Related to exchange rate	18	31	8
Other prices	20	48	15
Exogenous factors	21	45	11
External debt problems	...	37	14

Sources: Reichmann (1978), Johnson and Reichmann (1978), and Fund staff estimates.
[1]Subtotals do not add to totals for each group owing to concurrence of different problems in individual cases. Problems that emerged prior to the program period may have continued during the program period.

Price Adjustments and Fund Policies

Faced with mounting imbalances in a variety of situations, Fund-supported programs have always stressed realistic pricing policies—particularly the need for a modification of exchange rates and prices. The conceptual reasons justifying the approach have been discussed in previous sections. It may be sufficient to indicate here that the exchange rate and other prices were central in the design of macroeconomic adjustment, as reflected in Table 2, which shows the number of cases where price-related actions were included in programs.

This concern of the Fund about pricing adjustments has been reflected in recent decisions related to the use of general resources and stand-by arrangements[20] and Fund policies in general. In concluding the discussions

---

[20]Decision No. 6056-(79/38), March 2, 1979, *Selected Decisions of the International Monetary Fund and Selected Documents* (1981); also see Gold (1979), Guitián (1981), and A.W. Hooke (1983).

Table 2. Selected Pricing Policy Content of Economic Programs in Recent Stand-By and Extended Arrangements[1]

(Number of cases)

	Stand-By Arrangements		Extended Arrangements (1975–80)
	Approved in 1973–76	Approved in 1977–80	
Total number of programs	24	50	16
Policies with regard to exchange rate	14	25	12
Policies with regard to prices and wages	10	45	9
General wage restraint	...	23	6
Wage guidelines in public sector	...	24	5
Producer prices	...	21	3
Retail prices	...	18	5

Sources: Reichmann (1978), Johnson and Reichmann (1978), and Fund staff estimates.
[1]Subtotals do not add to totals for each category owing to concurrence of different problems in individual cases.

on Guidelines on Conditionality, the Executive Board agreed that: "Performance criteria will normally be confined to (i) macroeconomic variables, and (ii) those necessary to implement specific provisions of the Articles or policies adopted under them. Performance criteria may relate to other variables only in exceptional cases when they are essential for the effectiveness of the member's program because of their macroeconomic impact" (Guideline 9).

Clearly, the Executive Board expected that the achievement of adjustment required not only the use of financial variables, but also the use of macroeconomic price variables, namely, exchange rates and interest rates. Nevertheless, the Fund was not expected to review every pricing policy action: the authorities were to decide the particular price corrections that would result in a given adjustment effort. The Guidelines also indicate that: "The Managing Director will recommend [approval] ... when it is his judgment that the program is consistent with the Fund's provisions and policies and that it will be carried out. A member may be expected to adopt some corrective measures before a stand-by arrangement is approved by the Fund, but only if necessary to enable the member to adopt and carry out a program consistent with the Fund's provisions and policies" (Guideline 7).

Two main ideas can be interpreted to emerge from Guideline 7: (a) The Managing Director and the staff have to be convinced about the likelihood that the program will be carried out—implying the need to have an explicit understanding about specific policies, including price adjustments; and (b) early action is needed to establish a credible program. Price corrections typically introduced at program inception—including exchange rate and interest rate adjustments—are the clearest example of early action. In many recent programs, exchange rate and pricing actions were taken prior to Board approval, and were in general fully implemented; that is, among the policies that countries announced as part of programs, pricing adjustments were among the most consistently pursued.

These observations do not imply that the price adjustment policies have been always successful. Restraints on wages, increases in interest rates, and exchange rate adjustments have been introduced and frequently have had the expected impact. Nonetheless, the lack of adequate supportive financial policies often neutralized the corrective effect of these measures, resulting in a deviation from the original course of action. Many programs were interrupted or canceled and created serious doubt about the feasibility of adjustment through the use of the price mechanism. Moreover, the ensuing inflationary pressures observed in the context of many programs was viewed as the consequence of price adjustments and not of the underlying inflationary pressures that had not been corrected in the first place. Nonetheless, it is true that slippages were present in many instances; and in others, excessive reliance was placed on the adjustment of prices alone, when no assurances existed that the supplementary policies would or could be carried out.

Recent Experience on Exchange Rate Actions

The experience with recent arrangements tends to confirm the importance of pricing actions in adjustment programs. In particular, in a recent study, Donovan has reviewed the real responses associated with exchange rate action in selected upper credit tranche stabilization programs[21] and concluded that exchange rates have been central to external adjustment in the period 1970–76. The paper focuses mostly on the effect of exchange rate adjustments on selected variables. In analyzing programs, the study distinguishes between import restraint programs, in which corrections are mostly related to aggregate demand, and import liberalization programs, in which the action is directed mostly to providing an increase in the availability of resources and increasing supply. Table 3 reproduces data from Donovan's article, showing the impact of exchange rate actions on exports and imports during the first one-year and three-year periods after the measure has taken place. The table clearly shows the positive impact of exchange rates in increasing exports and improving the current account, except in those

---

[21]Donovan (1981). A second article (Donovan (1982)) explores the general impact of adjustment programs on economic performance.

**Table 3. Twelve Stabilization Programs: Annual Average Change
in Real Imports (M) and Exports (X), 1970–76**

(In percent)

	Before Adjustment			After Adjustment		
	X	M	(M–X)	X	M	(M–X)
One-year comparison						
All programs[1]	–1.4	1.1	2.4	9.2	3.5	–5.1
Of which:						
Import liberalization programs[2]	–2.7	–0.9	1.8	15.3	17.3	2.0
Import restraint programs[3]	1.0	1.4	0.4	4.3	1.5	–2.8
Three-year comparison						
All programs[4]	0.3	3.2	2.1	6.5	4.0	–2.5
Of which:						
Import liberalization programs[2]	–8.9	–7.8	1.6	6.3	11.3	4.9
Import restraint programs[3]	...	8.4	3.8	...	2.5	–5.0

Source: Based on Donovan (1981).
[1] Afghanistan, Bangladesh, Bolivia, Burma, Ecuador, Israel, Jamaica, Pakistan, South Africa, Sudan, Yugoslavia, and Zambia.
[2] Bangladesh, Burma, Pakistan, and Sudan.
[3] Bolivia, Ecuador, Israel, Jamaica, South Africa, and Yugoslavia.
[4] Excludes Bangladesh and Pakistan, owing to unavailability of data.

instances when imports increased because of liberalization efforts by the authorities. In general terms, the study concludes that (1) the major reason for undertaking exchange rate action was the emergence of balance of payments pressures, reflected in many cases in increasing levels of restrictions, and a real appreciation of the exchange rate; (2) the depreciation was intended to improve export performance and reduce imports in the cases of expenditure-reducing programs. By contrast, imports were expected to increase when depreciations were accompanied by major liberalization efforts; (3) export performance showed a marked improvement after the depreciations, except in certain cases when supplementary measures failed; (4) imports declined in the import restraint group after the depreciation and increased in the import liberalization group, but in most cases the current account improved after the depreciation; (5) inflation rates increased somewhat in the postdepreciation period, but there was no evidence that the programs were associated with any systematic bias in economic growth. Nonetheless, in the demand restraint group, growth declined sharply, a fact associated with the demand-reducing effect of the adjustment program.

No systematic work comparable to that of Donovan's has been carried out for more recent experience, but the evidence suggests similar behavior. In general terms, exchange rate policy was implemented during the program period expected and covered elimination of multiple rates, restrictions, and depreciations of overvalued currencies; moreover, these policies were introduced at an early stage of the program.

Recent Experience on Interest Rate Policies

In general, interest rate adjustments were carried out as originally envisaged and helped attain the required adjustment, although in some cases, the corrective measures failed to bring about the expected results. In many countries, prior to program inception, interest rates were perceived to be too low—mostly negative in real terms—to provide adequate incentives for savings and investment.[22] Specific action on interest rates was frequently included in and carried out by most programs. Nonetheless, in many cases after interest rates were adjusted, velocity tended to increase. The result may appear to be surprising, but in fact velocity could have been expected to increase because of the impact of constraints on the supply of financial resources. Although the original intentions were to increase nominal rates so as to achieve positive real rates, this was not always the case. Sometimes, the changes were marginal and therefore did not result in a turnaround in financial savings. Only in those instances where the changes were perceived to be significant, or a return of confidence was observed, did resources flow into the financial system, resulting in increased savings and reduced demand pressures.

Adjustment of interest rates became more difficult in recent years, because domestic corrections had to reflect the effect of movements in nominal and real interest rates in the rest of the world, in addition to domestic inflation and exchange rate movements. In particular, the rising interest rates in international capital markets through early 1982 brought about the need for restrictive financial policies in many countries and thereby affected the level of economic activity. The high interest rates further aggravated difficulties in debtor countries because of the need to cover interest payments at a time when the availability of foreign financing was declining, also reflecting tighter financial policies in the major financial centers.

Energy and Other Prices

While the most important pricing measures in the context of adjustment programs referred to exchange rate and interest rate policies, other prices

---

[22]See Galbis (1977) for a review of interest rate policies in Latin America in the period 1967–76.

were also central to the corrective process. In particular, energy pricing policies were part of most programs supported by stand-by and extended arrangements, after the first oil shock of 1973–74. Programs sought adjustments in domestic energy prices that were to reflect to the largest possible extent the equivalent international prices. These policies were pursued both in oil importing and oil exporting countries. The policies were aimed at inducing reduced demand, increased supply of substitutes—in importing countries—and an improved budgetary outcome. The budgetary outcome was particularly important; in most cases, energy production was either under direct control of the public sector or prices were controlled, and price-cost differentials gave rise to major subsidies. Generally, energy-pricing policies were successful in attaining their objectives. In a few instances prices were not fully adjusted, but the subsidies were made explicit in the budgetary process and strict guidelines were established to avoid or reduce existing price distortions.

Producer prices were also subject to major corrections in the context of adjustment programs. In many instances high taxes on export commodities precluded adequate incentives to domestic producers and frequently resulted in declining supplies. In others, the effects of a depreciation or of higher international prices had not been passed on and resulted in new distortions. In general, producer price actions tended to reduce the divergences between external and domestic prices, induced output increases, and helped achieve corrections in the external account with a lesser emphasis on reduced expenditure. Because of their immediate impact, these price adjustments tended to be implemented at an early stage and thereby helped contribute to a substantial initiation of adjustment programs.

4. RECENT EXPERIENCE WITH PREANNOUNCEMENT AND FIXING OF EXCHANGE RATES IN LATIN AMERICA

The recent experience with regard to exchange rate management in several Latin American countries has been of great importance in the understanding of economy-wide prices. At different times over the last five years, several major Latin American countries—Argentina, Chile, and Uruguay in 1979, as the most outstanding examples—announced the pursuit of either fixed exchange rates or exchange rates subject to a preannounced schedule of depreciation against the U.S. dollar. In others, the exchange rate remained fixed after a major adjustment—notably Mexico starting in 1977. Policies were supported in Uruguay by successive first credit tranche stand-by arrangements and in Mexico by an extended arrangement through 1979.

In most cases the fixed rate or predetermined exchange rate path was envisaged as a powerful means of sharply reducing the rate of inflation and providing the countries with a more stable financial environment. The exchange rate regime was predicated on the basis of a set of measures that would result in a consistent inflation outcome; the new exchange rate policies were implemented after periods of high inflation in which exchange rates were allowed to depreciate rapidly. The changes in the exchange rate intervention policy were frequently accompanied by a major revamping of the financial system, through interest rate reforms that were projected to result in rapid increases in domestic financial savings. The exchange rate was conceived as the key price, on the understanding that the budget deficit would be under control and that wages and prices of nontraded goods could rapidly converge to the preannounced path. The convergence was to be aided by appropriate fiscal, monetary, and trade policies. During the expectedly short period of adjustment, financing requirements were to be adequately covered from abroad, mostly through private capital flows, while the liberalization of trade was to achieve a greater degree of efficiency through increased foreign competition. [23]

In the event, countries that experimented with the preannouncement fixed rate scheme abandoned the policy and returned to either floating rates, to policies of frequent unannounced depreciations, or to highly restrictive systems. Argentina abandoned its preannouncement policy in early 1981 and Uruguay in late 1982. Chile abandoned a fixed rate policy in mid-1982. Among countries with a tradition of fixed rates, for example, Mexico maintained a virtually fixed rate for four years but allowed the rate to depreciate slowly in 1980 and finally abandoned the peg in early 1982. In general, the exchange rate policies were abandoned in circumstances when the balance of payments was under considerable strain, reflecting both domestic and external developments. In all cases, the exchange rate had appreciated markedly in effective real terms over the previous years (Table 4), while capital flows, which had been significant, reversed and resulted in marked pressures on international reserves and mounting external debt problems.

In these circumstances, the failure of adjustment programs to achieve both internal and external adjustment was attributed by some critics to the pursuit of the exchange rate policies described and the ensuing real appreciation of the currency. While the real appreciation contributed to the economic difficulties, the failure to achieve the original goals can be traced to a combination of domestic and external developments. In particular, an inadequate coordination of policies and the existence of institutional and market constraints precluded the expected internal adjustment and led to the appreciation of the currency, notwithstanding the marked deceleration of

---

[23] A detailed description of the preannouncement model is discussed by Blejer and Mathieson (1981); this discussion reflects many of their views.

Table 4. Effective Real Exchange Rates in Selected Latin American Countries[1]
(1977–81 = 100)

		Argentina[2]	Chile	Mexico	Uruguay
1977	I	135	93	109	116
	II	140	84	111	115
	III	133	90	107	112
	IV	128	99	104	115
1978	I	133	107	102	116
	II	125	107	102	113
	III	117	108	101	121
	IV	109	108	101	123
1979	I	102	108	98	118
	II	94	103	98	112
	III	86	95	98	105
	IV	87	90	97	94
1980	I	87	89	93	86
	II	83	84	90	85
	III	81	82	87	83
	IV	77	79	85	83
1981	I	78	78	82	83
	II	93	76	79	76
	III	93	75	77	71
	IV	100	78	75	71
1982	I	112	78	90	70
	II	118	80	106	70
	III	120	90	122	64

Sources: *International Financial Statistics, Direction of Trade Statistics*; and Fund staff estimates.

[1] Index of exchange rate against major trading partners adjusted by changes in cost of living index for the same group of countries, weighted by total trade between individual country and trading partner. Increases reflect depreciations of the domestic currency.

[2] Commercial rate, for the periods of split rates—June–December 1981 and July–December 1982.

inflation—a key objective sought in the pursuit of preannouncement policies (Table 4 and Charts 1–4).

The reasons for the rigidity of inflation to decline in line with the rate of depreciation can be explained by the concurrent impact of continued indexing of wages to past inflation in a period of declining inflation, by high increases in the prices of nontradables, and by the slow progress achieved toward trade liberalization. These domestic elements were exacerbated by the pegging of local currencies to the U.S. dollar, which appreciated markedly against other major currencies in the period 1980–82.

This enumeration provides a somewhat mechanistic explanation of the slow decline in inflation. Actually, the reasons for the continued pressures on prices and the balance of payments are to be found to a large extent in the

**Chart 1. Argentina: Rates of Change, Exchange Rate, and U.S.
Inflation Effect Versus Domestic Inflation**

(Percentage change over same quarter of previous year)

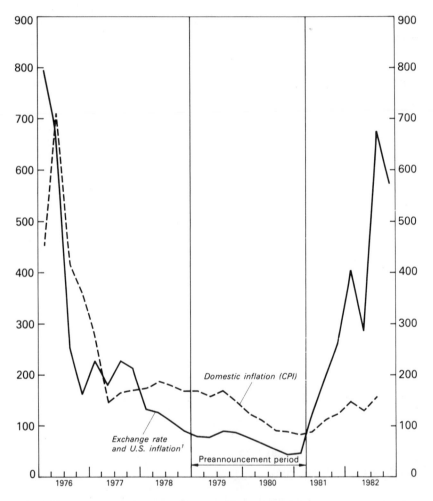

Sources: *International Financial Statistics*; and Fund staff estimates.
[1]Combined effect of percentage change in exchange rate against the U.S. dollar and U.S. CPI.

pursuit of expansionary domestic policies. The continuous increase in the
public sector expenditures—with the clear exception of Chile and, to a lesser
extent, of Uruguay—and the consequent financing requirements rendered
inconsistent the exchange rate and the fiscal policy. Public sector financing
requirements generated pressures on domestic resources and resulted in

Chart 2. Chile: Rates of Change, Exchange Rate, and U.S. Inflation Effect Versus Domestic Inflation

(Percentage change over same quarter of previous year)

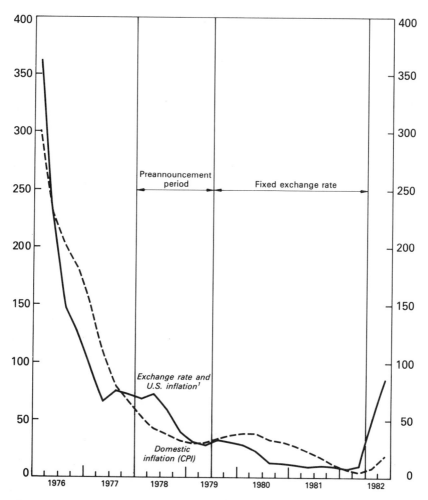

Sources: *International Financial Statistics*; and Fund staff estimates.
[1]Combined effect of percentage change in exchange rate against U.S. dollar and U.S. CPI.

increases in the relative prices of nontraded goods, higher interest rates, and the widening of the current account deficit. While the public sector policies could be identified as a major factor behind the failure of preannouncement policies, overexpansion of private sector expenditure was also an important source of pressures. Concurrently, the loss of competitiveness of export and

Chart 3. Mexico: Rates of Change, Exchange Rate, and U.S. Inflation Effect Versus Domestic Inflation

(Percentage change over same quarter of previous year)

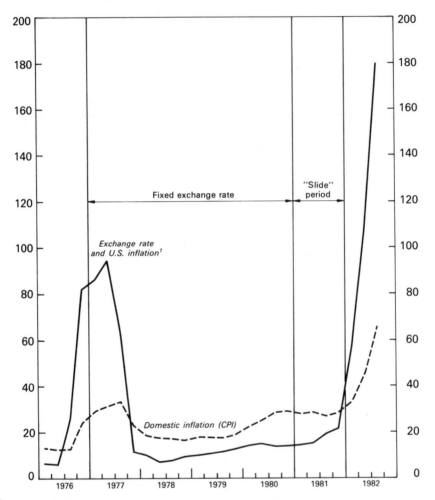

Sources: *International Financial Statistics*; and Fund staff estimates.
[1]Combined effect of percentage change in exchange rate against U.S. dollar and U.S. CPI.

some import substituting sectors resulted in lower levels of activity, affecting the growth prospects of the economy.

   The initially increased access to foreign financing and its eventual reversal also exacerbated emerging imbalances. At the early stages of financial and exchange rate reforms, the financial integration of domestic and international capital markets frequently proceeded at a rapid pace, resulting in sharp

Chart 4. Uruguay: Rates of Change, Exchange Rate, and U.S. Inflation Effect Versus Domestic Inflation

(Percentage change over same quarter of previous year)

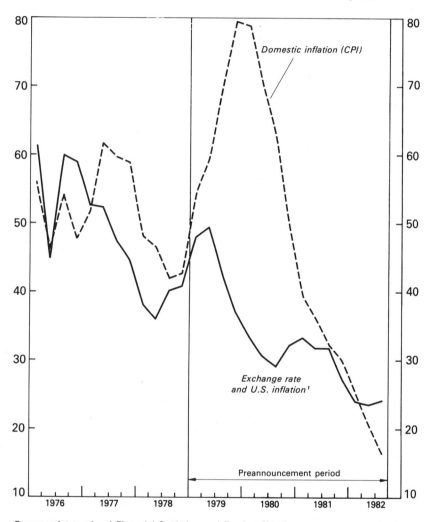

Sources: *International Financial Statistics*; and Fund staff estimates.
[1]Combined effect of percentage change in exchange rate against U.S. dollar and U.S. CPI.

increases in capital flows; but domestic interest rates did not fall in line with the rate of depreciation. To some extent, the slow adjustment in interest rates could have reflected imperfect capital markets; but eventually, the interest rate differential reflected both a perception of exchange rate risk—which was on average different from the announced exchange rate path—and public sector financing needs that continued to induce large capital inflows.[24] The slow pace of trade liberalization was also conducive to the real appreciation observed. The increased capital flows allowed for additional spending, generating pressures on domestic prices but without the required restraint imposed by foreign competition.

Economic performance was further affected by the emergence of exogenous events. Deteriorating terms of trade and higher external interest rates contributed to the widening balance of payments deficits, already weakened by the pursuit of the financial and exchange rate policies described. The ensuing loss of confidence induced more frequent episodes of capital flight and increasing reticence in international capital markets to lend to these countries, further aggravating the problems of employment and balance of payments and eventually resulting in the abandonment of the exchange rate policies pursued.

In summary, the failure of exchange rate preannouncement or pegging mostly reflected a lack of adjustment of other domestic financial policies, compounded by the effect of changing external circumstances. The exchange rate path became the main objective of economic policy, and its pursuit implied high costs and disturbances for economic activity. Eventually, the exchange rate policies had to be abandoned in the midst of growing financial difficulties that reflected to a large extent a loss of confidence in the policies pursued and forced a major correction effort that may not have been required otherwise.

5. CONCLUDING REMARKS

Two main conclusions can be drawn from the previous discussion. First, pricing policies are an essential component of adjustment programs, insofar as they affect both aggregate demand and supply; in their absence, corrective policies may be more detrimental to output and employment. Second, in order to attain adequate adjustment, pricing policies can only be pursued successfully if they are supported by adequate financial policies. These points cannot be considered original, but they summarize in a simple manner the essence of many adjustment programs.

No particular policy can help fully to deflect the consequences of reduced foreign financing or a decline in the terms of trade. Any of these circumstances will require an accommodation of aggregate demand to aggregate supply and will result, in most instances, in a reduction in real disposable incomes, in a slowdown in investment, and in transfers of resources to the external sector. The issue to be addressed is what policy mix

---

[24]Blejer (1982) presents an analysis of interest rate differentials and exchange rate risk in the context of recent Argentine experience.

is the most adequate to achieve a smooth process of adjustment. A combination of demand restraint policies, trade liberalization, and pricing policies—in particular exchange rate policies—provides conditions for the restoration of domestic and external confidence, thereby allowing for less stringent demand adjustments in the context of a Fund-supported program. But the reduction in expenditure is unavoidable, and the costs of adjustment have to be borne among the different sectors of the economy, with only a narrow scope for flexibility.

The existence of political and social pressures makes adjustment more difficult, in particular when sharp corrections are required in real wages. In these instances, exchange rate action will help provide the needed correction if supported by sufficiently strong financial and incomes policies. Otherwise, pricing policies will only provide a short-term respite and in the medium term will possibly result in higher rates of inflation with no balance of payments relief. Moreover, the credibility of both current and future policy actions can be jeopardized, and any new corrective attempt may require a more prolonged period in order to produce the desired change in expectations and the restoration of confidence.

Finally, price targets in themselves should not be made the objective of policies, unless supported by other adequate measures. In different instances, the maintenance of a fixed exchange rate, or the commitment to a given preannouncement path, became in itself the objective, usually in the context of an anti-inflationary policy. Exchange rate policies were maintained even when it became clear that developments in other financial magnitudes did not allow for the achievement of medium-term viability in the context of the external policies pursued. The appropriate policy course required the restraint of public sector deficits and reduced wage pressures, but previous policy slippages, noneconomic constraints, and the dynamics of adjustment made the abandonment of a predetermined exchange rate path unavoidable. In many instances the exchange rate modifications came too late and were too abrupt, therefore worsening emerging balance of payments difficulties. A more flexible approach or an earlier correction both of exchange rate and demand policies would have allowed for a less drastic adjustment. Moreover, it would have precluded the conclusions made by many critics that the failure of controlled exchange rates have rendered useless the use of appropriate pricing policies in the context of adjustment efforts.

BIBLIOGRAPHY

Allen, Mark, "Adjustment in Planned Economies," *Staff Papers*, International Monetary Fund (Washington), Vol. 29 (September 1982), pp. 398–421.

Blejer, Mario I., and Donald J. Mathieson, "The Preannouncement of Exchange
Rate Changes as a Stabilization Instrument," *Staff Papers*, International
Monetary Fund (Washington), Vol. 28 (December 1981), pp. 760–792.

───────, "Interest Rate Differentials and Exchange Risk: Recent Argentine
Experience," *Staff Papers*, International Monetary Fund (Washington), Vol. 29
(June 1982), pp. 270–280.

Cline, William R., and Sidney Weintraub, eds., *Economic Stabilization in
Developing Countries*, The Brookings Institution (Washington, 1981).

Donovan, Donal J., "Real Responses Associated with Exchange Rate Action in
Selected Upper Credit Tranche Stabilization Programs," *Staff Papers*, International Monetary Fund (Washington), Vol. 28 (December 1981), pp. 698–727.

───────, "Macroeconomic Performance and Adjustment Under Fund-Supported
Programs: The Experience of the Seventies," *Staff Papers*, International
Monetary Fund (Washington), Vol. 29 (June 1982), pp. 171–203.

Dornbusch, Rudiger, *Open Economy Macroeconomics* (New York: Basic Books,
1980).

Frenkel, Jacob A., and Harry G. Johnson, eds., *The Monetary Approach to the
Balance of Payments* (London, Allen and Unwin, 1976).

───────, *The Economics of Exchange Rates* (Reading, Massachusetts: Addison-
Wesley, 1978.

───────, and Carlos A. Rodríguez, "Exchange Rate Dynamics and the Overshooting
Hypothesis," *Staff Papers*, International Monetary Fund (Washington), Vol. 29
(March 1982), pp. 1–30.

Galbis, Vicente, "Inflation and Interest Rate Policies in Latin America, 1967–76,"
Staff Papers, International Monetary Fund (Washington), Vol. 26 (June 1979),
pp. 334–366.

Gold, Joseph, *Conditionality*, IMF Pamphlet Series, No. 31 (Washington, 1979).

Guitián, Manuel, "Credit Versus Money as an Instrument of Control," *Staff Papers*,
International Monetary Fund (Washington), Vol. 20 (November 1973),
pp. 785–800; reproduced in International Monetary Fund (1977), pp. 227–42.

───────, *Fund Conditionality: Evolution of Principles and Practices*, IMF
Pamphlet Series, No. 38 (Washington, 1981).

Hooke, Augustus W., *The International Monetary Fund: Its Evolution, Organization, and Activities*, IMF Pamphlet Series No. 37 (Washington, 3rd ed., 1983).

Johnson, G. G., and Thomas M. Reichmann,, "Experience with Stabilization
Programs Supported by Stand-By Arrangements in the Upper Credit Tranches,
1973–75" (Unpublished, February 28, 1978).

Johnson, Harry G., *International Trade and Economic Growth: Studies in Pure
Theory* (London: Allen and Unwin, 1958).

───────, "The Monetary Approach to Balance of Payments Theory," *Journal of
Financial and Quantitative Analysis*, Vol. 7 (March 1972), pp. 1550–71.

International Monetary Fund, *The Monetary Approach to the Balance of Payments:
A Collection of Research Papers by the Staff of the IMF* (Washington, 1977).

───────, *Selected Decisions of the International Monetary Fund and Selected
Documents*, 9th ed. (Washington, 1981).

Keller, Peter M., "Implications of Credit Policies to Output and the Balance of Payments," *Staff Papers*, International Monetary Fund (Washington), Vol. 27 (September 1980), pp. 451–77.

Kelly, Margaret R., "Fiscal Adjustment and Fund-Supported Programs, 1971–80, *Staff Papers*, International Monetary Fund (Washington), Vol. 29 (December 1982), pp. 561–602.

Loser, Claudio M., "External Debt Management and Balance of Payments Policies," *Staff Papers*, International Monetary Fund (Washington), Vol. 24 (March 1977), pp. 168–92.

McKinnon, Ronald I., "Portfolio Balance and International Payments Adjustment" in *Monetary Problems of the International Economy*, ed. by R. Mundell and A. Swoboda (Chicago: University of Chicago Press, 1969), pp. 199–234.

———, *Money and Capital in Economic Development*, The Brookings Institution (Washington, 1973).

Mundell, Robert A., *International Economics* (New York: Macmillan, 1968).

———, *Monetary Theory, Inflation, Interest and Growth in the World Economy* (Pacific Palisades, California: Goodyear, 1971).

Reichmann, Thomas M., "The Fund's Conditional Assistance and the Problems of Adjustment, 1973–75," *Finance and Development*, Vol. 15 (December 1978), pp. 38–41.

———, and Richard T. Stillson, "Experience with Programs of Balance of Payments Adjustment: Stand-By Arrangements in the Higher Tranches, 1963–72," *Staff Papers*, International Monetary Fund (Washington), Vol. 25 (June 1978), pp. 293–309.

Rodríguez, Carlos A., "A Stylized Model of the Devaluation-Inflation Spiral," *Staff Papers*, International Monetary Fund (Washington), Vol. 27 (March 1978), pp. 76–89.

Salop, Joanne, and Omotunde Johnson, "Distributional Aspects of Stabilization Programs in Developing Countries," *Staff Papers*, International Monetary Fund (Washington), Vol. 27 (March 1980), pp. 1–23.

Steward, Frances, and Arjun Sengupta, *International Financial Cooperation* (Boulder, Colorado: Westview Press, 1982).

Commentary*

CARLOS BOLOÑA

Mr. Loser's paper is intriguing and has several strengths, including the coherency and correlation between the theoretical framework and the experiences of Latin American countries. However, it would benefit from a few additions and clarifications.

My first remark refers to a basic and crucial distinction made in Mr. Robichek's paper. The adjustment process and the role of prices in it take on particular special characteristics when the following are involved:

(1) isolated cases of countries;

(2) a worldwide economic depression, affecting a large group of countries.

Loser's article draws several general conclusions for the first case, which implicitly is the one he is dealing with. For the second case it would be necessary to analyze how, in the area of price adjustments, the policies of some countries cancel out or counteract the policies of others (e.g., competitive devaluations). There would also be a need for other instruments, such as joint renegotiations of the external debt and a reordering of the international monetary system, should there be a desire to avoid exaggerated price adjustments and demand management measures (not a viable course in our countries and one with little guarantee of success). Given the current circumstances and prospects for the immediate future, it is the second case which should be analyzed.

A second remark relates to the (clear and explicit) distinction drawn by the Fund between demand management measures and supply-oriented measures. The first of these are generally associated with credit and fiscal measures which narrow the gap between income and expenditure. Some look upon price adjustment policy as if it were supply oriented. This is partially true, as adjustments of prices (exchange rates, interest rates, and real wages) have a short-term effect on aggregate demand and a longer-term effect on aggregate supply.

Third, Loser perceives market forces to be correct, meaning that in one way or another there is competitiveness between markets, stability, and automaticity. But rigidities do exist and must not be discounted.

Fourth, and summarizing Loser's paper to the point of caricature, adequate pricing measures must take the following into account:

(1) *Exchange rate.* The real exchange rate must be maintained; that is, the exchange rate must change in line with the domestic rate of inflation

---

*The original version of this paper was written in Spanish.

adjusted by international inflation. This should be accompanied by measures to liberalize exchange and trade transactions (with low levels of effective protection).

(2) *Interest rate.* The interest rate should be equivalent to the rate of depreciation plus the interest rate prevailing abroad plus a risk premium.

Exchange rate and interest rate policies have to be pursued consistently. It is less efficient to make use of the second rather than the first to bring the balance of payments into equilibrium and reduce expenditure. Financial liberalization measures must be pursued at the same time.

(3) *Other prices.* Controlled or administered prices should be shifted toward the level of external prices adjusted by changes in the exchange rate. Prices for public utilities must be indexed for inflation. This is done with a view to improving the public finances.

(4) *Wages.* Upward adjustment of the above prices will of necessity be reflected in a decline in real wages.

Loser's prescriptions must be clarified in several respects:

(i) To what degree of trade liberalization is he referring? Which is to be preferred, uniform tariffs or tariffs with small variations of 10, 20, or 40 percent? The implications and results differ widely.

(ii) It is necessary to analyze the risk of competitive devaluations, the desire to overcome the exchange lag (depending on the base year considered), and the pressure of expectations (prompted by political factors) generated by an easing of the concept of a real exchange rate.

(iii) Should the real interest rate be zero or positive? In the second case, should it be 2, 10, or 30 percent? The economic implications vary widely in each case. In a situation where external financing is available, a high positive real interest rate may attract international reserves (if other conditions are stable), making it possible to maintain the fixed exchange rate with a moderate rate of inflation. This is the situation prevailing in Chile in recent years.

The temptation to maintain high positive real interest rates raises another problem: a significant proportion of the money supply is generated abroad and the central bank loses the ability to control it.

(iv) I agree with the approach toward other prices, apart from very rare exceptions.

(v) The decline in real wages is deduced by its residual effect. Nothing is said about the liberalization of the labor market, the conditions required for this, or the need to reduce other labor costs.

(vi) Real wages continue to fall and unemployment continues to increase.

(vii) The application of temporary export subsidies on manufactured goods is not a feasible alternative. This would imply a different exchange rate for this type of product, which detracts from the coherency of the recommendations. This policy, followed by some countries in Southeast Asia, has been discarded.

Fifth, the implementation of these measures has not been taken into account:

(i) Gradualism versus sudden (or total) adjustment.

(ii) On page 84, we are told that the programs have been implemented successfully, but then we see that they are not functioning adequately in Argentina, Chile, Uruguay, Peru, etc.

(iii) Something always turns out wrong: exchange rate, budget deficit, programs in which some problem occurs.

Does this mean that the technocrats are unable to implement the measures? Is there some shortcoming on the part of the economic team? Are there exogenous factors which alter the rules of the game completely? Is this wisdom the product of hindsight or foresight?

(iv) The suitability of, or "the right time for," liberalizing when surrounded by protectionist tendencies, for example, or, as in the case of Peru, deregulating when the country is losing reserves.

(v) Is inflation caused by the budget deficit or excessive private sector expansion?

(vi) Exogenous factors always alter and distort these policies.

My sixth remark relates to the evaluation of adjustment programs, in which only imports are analyzed but not the good effects as regards supply. There are already enough cases to make it possible to evaluate such program recommendations in overall terms, studying the effects in the real sector. Which sectors benefit and which are changed (e.g., the manufacturing sector)? What is the size of the financial sector and its relationship with the real sector, and what distortions arise therefrom? And what is the impact on income distribution?

Commentary*

In his paper, Claudio Loser provides an excellent analysis of the main problems arising in the course of implementing stabilization policies in open economies. In accordance with the subject of this seminar, Loser confines his presentation largely to those economies experiencing balance of payments difficulties.

There is much literature exhaustively analyzing the role of various instruments that can be used to achieve external equilibrium. Loser offers an overall analysis of the problem in the very positive spirit required if the objective is to assist in the implementation of rules for action by an institution such as the International Monetary Fund.

Among the numerous instruments customarily used in connection with adjustment programs, Loser distinguishes two main categories:

(1) Aggregate quantitative instruments that directly affect the differential between income and expenditure of the community, such as the size of the budget deficit or the amount of domestic credit.

(2) A group of prices which, because of their significance, may exert a considerable macroeconomic effect on the allocation of resources and thereby on the resultant external equilibrium. Furthermore, the use of such price variables may have a significant effect on the cost of the adjustment process for a given use of the aggregate quantitative variables (AQV).

In Section 2 of the paper, Loser concentrates on analyzing the interaction of the price variables with the traditional AQVs. The price variables he examines are the exchange rate, the interest rate, wages, and a set of "other prices," which includes prices of exports and imports and rates for public services. In all cases Loser shows the strong interdependence between the different price variables and between these and the AQVs. He stresses the inevitable relationship between exchange rate policy and interest rates, and the interdependence of wage policy and exchange rate policy. Similarly, aggregate credit policy cannot be adopted independently of exchange rate policy, nor can the rates of public sector services be arbitrarily set without affecting public sector finances and, as a result, the budget deficit. In this connection, I would like to mention a couple of additional examples which I believe are of some significance, at least as regards the situation of several countries in southern Latin America.

The first is the relation which exists between the so-called real exchange rate (relative price of tradable to nontradable goods) and real wages. In an

---

*The original version of this paper was written in Spanish.

economy that allocates its resources effectively, equilibrium must exist between the two variables and, unless there is proof to the contrary, such a relation should be respected within the framework of any stabilization program. Were this not done, it would necessarily imply rationing both markets. The relation between the two variables depends on the intensity with which factors are used in the trading and nontrading sectors. In the case of Argentina, which I know best and which I have examined empirically, the noncommercial sector is relatively labor intensive. The so-called Stolper-Samuelson ratio indicates that an increase in the relative price of the labor-intensive sector will lead to an increase in the demand for labor, and hence to an increase in real wages. In terms of our variables, this indicates that increases in real wages will be associated with falls in the level of the real exchange rate. In Argentina, the period during which the so-called Exchange Schedule (Tablita cambiaria) was in effect, that is, 1979–80, was marked by a continual deterioration in the real exchange rate and an increase in real wages. It is interesting to see that subsequent administrations have assigned themselves the task of improving both the real exchange rate and real wages, an objective that clearly is unattainable if the earlier results are true. It is also indicative that during the period of efforts to increase the relative price of labor and the real exchange rate, inflation increased to the point that it has averaged 14 percent a month during the last eight months. I find it surprising that the Argentine Minister of Economy should have announced at the time of the last stand-by arrangement with the International Monetary Fund that under their economic policy the real exchange rate would be indexed so as to maintain its present real level (high, in my view) and that wages would be indexed so as to increase them by a minimum of 5 percent in real terms during the first year the arrangement was in effect.

The second example is the relation that exists in the short term between the level of government spending and the real wage level. This is so true that in the case of Argentina many specialists refer to both variables without distinction. This is because surely in Argentina the greater portion of government spending is on goods not traded internationally: education, justice, defense, public services, etc. A reduction in public spending implies a reduction in the relative demand for labor and, as a result, in real wages. In the medium and long term, if the usual arguments on the inefficiency of the public sector are valid, the productivity of the economy and hence, perhaps, wages as well, should increase. However, the short-term effect is practically undeniable and, I believe, creates a very real political constraint when it comes to implementing stabilization programs based on a reduction of the size of the public sector which hold out promise of popularly satisfactory results in the short term.

In Section 3 of the paper, Loser presents data on the origin, contents, and results of stabilization programs recently undertaken with the support of the Fund. This section is mainly based on the recent work of Donal Donovan. Frankly, I find it very difficult to comment on this topic as I have no experience of the problems of these countries nor can I easily obtain the necessary statistical data. I shall, therefore, limit myself to one small suggestion in this regard, all the more so as I have not read Donovan's article (1982). Loser presents tables analyzing recent stand-by arrangements taking into account the problems which led to them, the instruments used, and the results obtained with regard to exports and imports; he also mentions the effect of these stand-by arrangements on the rate of inflation. One of the most discussed aspects of stabilization policies guided by the Fund is whether its adjustment programs are based on a contraction of domestic demand (usually associated with "monetarist" policy) or on the expansion of aggregate demand (obviously a more popular method of adjustment). For example, the recent Fund stand-by arrangement with Argentina, though it was never officially published, was announced by the economic authorities as being an economic recovery program which should lead to an increase in the rate of growth and to the increase in real wages mentioned above. In the spirit of this section, which seeks to determine what has happened with plans already carried out with the agreement of the Fund, it would be of interest to provide a table showing the evolution of supply and aggregate demand both before and after implementation of the program. This would serve to show whether Fund programs are directed toward increasing supply or restricting demand in the economy. Whatever the results may be, however, what is done is done and should not be used as an argument to invalidate any of the conclusions given in the second part of the paper (commented on above), based on theoretical analysis and on common sense.

Section 4 of the paper discusses the recent experience with stabilization efforts in southern Latin America (Argentina, Chile, and Uruguay), the main instrument used being a pre-announced exchange rate. There is a common element in the cases of these countries: at the time these policies were adopted, none of them had external payments problems of significance. The exchange policies adopted were just additional instruments within an overall plan to reduce the inflation rate and liberalize the economy. Prior to the introduction of the Exchange Schedule, all these countries decontrolled their financial markets, though in varying degree. They also permitted capital outflows to differing extents (Uruguay at one extreme, the most liberal, Chile, at the opposite extreme). Similarly, all these countries implemented an opening of the economy to international trade in goods, either before (Chile, through a prior reduction of tariffs) or at the same time (Argentina and Uruguay, through a more timid approach). I do not intend here to go into a detailed analysis of the three stabilization programs, as this would go beyond my duty as commentator, and I believe Loser has produced an excellent synthesis. The author mentions a number of the problems that arose during implementation of the programs, such as the inconsistency between the guidelines of the Exchange Schedule and the development of the budget deficit, or the overvaluation of the currency resulting from the decrease in the devaluation rate and the demand pressure caused by government expenditure. I also agree with Loser that the timing of developments on international markets played an important role in the subsequent failure of the policies adopted; those policies were confronted with deteriorating terms of trade and unprecedentedly high interest rates at the very time all these countries had adopted a strategy of promoting external indebtedness with a view to reducing, or distributing over time, the initial costs of the policy of stabilization and opening of the economy.

I would, however, wish to mention two problems which Loser has not referred to but which are relevant, at least if one is to understand the case of Argentina. One is the political error of implementing simultaneously a tariff policy (to open the economy) and a policy of pre-set exchange rates (to reduce inflation). Both measures penalized heavily the import substitution sector (both the exchange lag and the reduction of tariffs) and, in my view, seriously affected confidence in continuation of the economic strategy. The other problem is that, simultaneously, with the loss of credibility, the maintenance of government guarantees on bank deposits enabled the enterprises affected by the joint impact of tariff reductions and exchange rates to launch "apparently" suicidal policies of seeking to survive by borrowing from the financial system while waiting for the system to change. The resulting high degree of indebtedness further damaged the credibility of the existing system and, contrary to the wishes of each successive minister, the winners were those who bet against. The result was that the exchange strategy and the opening of the economy were abandoned and were replaced by controlled rates of interest in the midst of a resurgence of inflation in order to permit settlement of the debts contracted during the previous stabilization program.

BIBLIOGRAPHY

Donovan, Donal J., "Macroeconomic Performance and Adjustment Under Fund-Supported Programs: The Experience of the Seventies," *Staff Papers*, International Monetary Fund (Washington), Vol. 29 (June, 1982), pp. 171–203.

Fiscal Deficits and Balance of Payments Disequilibrium in IMF Adjustment Programs*

VITO TANZI AND MARIO I. BLEJER

CONCEPT OF FISCAL DEFICIT

One of the most important and lasting contributions of J. M. Keynes's thought to the development of modern economic theory has been the central role he assigned to fiscal policy in stabilizing output. Within the Keynesian framework, the economic result of the fiscal sector, whether a deficit or a surplus, is the most important balancing factor in the economy. The magnitude of the deficit or surplus is the central piece in the determination of the levels of aggregate demand, income, prices, and, eventually, in an open economy, of the balance of payments.

A point that has been considered as fundamental in the theory developed by Keynes is that an economy may converge to an equilibrium that is stable but which may be suboptimal or undesirable since it may involve unemployment or inflationary pressures.[1] In the Keynesian model, fiscal policy is the main instrument that has the power of shifting the economy from one equilibrium position to another. The implicit assumption of this Keynesian view is that the government has the means and the will to regulate the size of its revenues and expenditures and, in such a way, direct the economy toward a desirable level of equilibrium. This view is based on the conception that it is feasible for the fiscal authority to control, at each point in time, the size of the fiscal balance so as to bring it close to what the government wants it to be.

---

*This is a substantially revised version of a paper presented at the seminar on "The Role of the International Monetary Fund in the Adjustment Process," held in Viña del Mar, Chile, in April 1983.

[1]Don Patinkin has characterized this element as the focal point of Keynes's *General Theory of Employment, Interest and Money* (1936) and as one of the central issues on which Keynes differed from his contemporaries. See Patinkin (1982).

Later developments, particularly during the 1950s, made clear that there are dynamic elements, endogenous to the system, which are beyond the control of the authorities and which ultimately affect the outcome of the fiscal sector. For example, due to the built-in flexibility of tax revenue and without specific measures being taken by the authorities, the deficit is likely to increase automatically in recessions and to fall, or even disappear, in booms. In other words, fiscal imbalances are, at least partially, determined by the level of economic activity. Clearly then, while deficits influence and affect economic activity, they are themselves strongly affected by it. This behavior came to be considered desirable as a larger deficit was exactly what was thought to be needed in periods of recession, and a smaller deficit, or a surplus, was needed in periods of high economic activity.

It would be difficult to argue today that, in most countries, the fiscal deficit reflects exactly the level desired by the policymakers. Pressures on governments to increase public expenditure and to provide preferential treatment to some taxpayers, coupled with political constraints on their ability to act, have created many situations in which the fiscal deficit has acquired dynamics of its own.

The difference, over a given period of time,[2] between total expenditure and ordinary revenue is determined by three major factors: (1) the long-run or trend level of taxes and expenditures; (2) the stage of the business, or commodity, cycle; and (3) the (temporary) policies that may have turned, in the short run, the current levels of expenditure and/or revenue away from their trends. As a consequence one could estimate:

(a) the actual fiscal balance, ignoring all the factors that may be influencing it;

(b) the balance that would exist, if, ceteris paribus, the economy were neither in a recession nor in a boom, but was instead moving along its "normal" trend;

(c) the balance that would exist, given the stage of economic activity, if revenue and expenditure had not been affected by short-term policy actions; and

(d) the balance that would exist if the economy were on its trend and no temporary measures had distorted the level of taxes and expenditure.

The second of the definitions given above has often been referred to as the *structural* deficit. This concept has been used almost exclusively in connection with industrial countries where, by and large, the fiscal deficit has been affected by cyclical fluctuations but not by temporary policies. If this deficit is defined in relation to a level of income assumed to reflect potential output, it becomes identical to the full-employment budget surplus

---

[2] As budgets normally cover a year, the most common period of time considered is a year.

(FEBS) that played such a large role in the New Economic Policy pursued in the United States by the Kennedy and Johnson administrations in the 1960s. At present there are doubts as to whether the "normal" trend for the economy is equivalent to its "potential" trend.[3] There are serious doubts as to how to define potential income. For example, what rate of unemployment implies "full employment"? We seem to be far less certain today than we were in the 1960s about how to answer that question.[4] Because of this, the U.S. Council of Economic Advisers has suspended the calculation of potential income. In conclusion, while one may be able to define, in theory, a structural deficit, it is nevertheless very difficult to agree on its measurement.

In developing countries temporary policies have often played a substantive role in artificially raising or, more often, reducing the size of a country's fiscal deficit *for a given year*. Examples of such policies are: (1) the anticipation of future tax payments from some taxpayers;[5] (2) the use of occasional tax amnesties that allow taxpayers who have evaded taxes in past years to "clean their slate" by making a once-for-all payment equal to some fraction of tax due;[6] (3) campaigns to collect tax arrears; (4) the use of temporary taxes or surtaxes;[7] (5) the postponement of payments to suppliers; (6) the postponement of wage payments to public employees; (7) the postponement of inevitable wage increases; and (8) the increased sale of public property, including exploration rights.

When the deficit of a given period is corrected for the effect of economic fluctuations *and* temporary measures, the developing countries' analogue of the structural deficit is obtained. This analytical concept can be called the "core" deficit.[8] Between two countries with identical (actual) fiscal deficits, but with different core deficits, one would expect somewhat different policies for adjustment and, of course, different conditionality in a program with the International Monetary Fund. The proper long-run fiscal policy of a developing country should be oriented toward the core deficit rather than the actual deficit. However, as the core deficit is difficult to measure, economic

---

[3] For example, suppose that the balance of payments result consistent with potential output is not sustainable, can one still assume that the "normal" trend of the economy is its "potential" defined in terms of a natural rate of unemployment?

[4] M. Friedman, for example, has claimed that institutional rigidities and variability of the inflation rate may change the "natural" rate of unemployment. See Friedman (1977).

[5] In this case, the government is essentially borrowing from the taxpayers, but the tax payments so received are not considered as financing.

[6] This technique that has been used, for example, in Argentina, has at times generated, for a given year, revenues equal to as much as 1 percent of gross national product (GNP). Obviously, these are not recurrent revenues even though the country may from time to time provide these "amnesties." In each case, the amnesty is publicized as being the last one ever.

[7] The United States has also experimented with temporary taxes as witnessed by the "surtax" imposed in the late 1960s.

[8] The measurement of the "core" deficit may be even more difficult than that of the structural deficit.

policy is likely to continue to be based largely on the common measure of fiscal deficit.[9]

Although most economic observers have some notion of what a fiscal deficit is, there are so many definitions of it as to warrant a brief discussion. The definition outlined in the International Monetary Fund's *Draft Manual on Government Finance Statistics* (which is related to the actual deficit) arranges the payment and receipt elements for the government's accounts as follows:

Fiscal Deficit = (Revenue + Grants) − (Expenditure on Goods
    and Services + Transfer Payments + Net Lending);

    or, alternatively,

Fiscal Deficit = Borrowing + Net Decrease in
    Cash Holdings − Amortization.

This definition emphasizes cash flows rather than accrual concepts of revenues and expenditures. This is the definition that is more relevant in a discussion of the connection between the fiscal deficit and the balance of payments and is the one that is adopted in this paper. Nevertheless, we must point out that even this definition suffers from various shortcomings of which the following deserve mention.

First, and somewhat related to our discussion of the core deficit, cash flows may at times not fully reflect underlying trends. For example, if a government engages in additional purchases of goods and services but delays making actual payments (thus building up arrears), the cash concept may not reveal in the current year that the level of spending is being changed.[10]

Second, the classification of grants as revenue (rather than as a financing item) raises some questions as these grants are often not permanent sources of revenue but often fluctuate from year to year and may even vanish at the wrong time. Thus, if a government bases its multiyear expenditure commitments on this source of revenue, it may expose itself to the possibility of unpleasant surprises. For our purpose, it would thus seem better to consider grants as a financing item rather than as an ordinary source of revenue.

Third, in a situation where the rate of inflation is significant, it becomes difficult to distinguish in an economic (rather than legal) sense interest payments from amortization changes. As all interest payments are considered an expenditure, and as no allowance is made for the repayment element

---

[9]For a discussion of related issues, see Tanzi (1982).

[10]Thus, while capturing the *monetary* impact of the budget, the cash concept may not capture the income-creating (i.e., the Keynesian) impact. It is for this reason that during the heyday of Keynesian economics (the mid-1960s) the emphasis was on an accrual rather than a cash concept.

implicitly included in the interest payment, the size of the deficit may be distorted, thus potentially leading a country toward wrong policies.[11,12]

In addition to the issue of measuring the deficit, it may also be important to consider the normative questions referring to the desirability of budget deficits. A deficit exists, of course, because the government has been unwilling or unable to raise ordinary revenue to the level of the country's expenditure. It must be recognized that apart from stabilization reasons, there may be allocative reasons which, especially for developing countries, justify the existence of a (core) deficit. Thus, suppose that additional tax revenue would be associated with considerable disincentive effects on the country's productive capacity; and suppose that the additional expenditure associated with the deficit is highly productive so that it will increase the capacity of the economy to grow over future years. In such a situation the deficit may be fully justified. But, even in this case, there must be a close correspondence between the stream of repayments and the stream of income that the deficit has generated. This issue is taken up again in connection with foreign financing. The basic point to be made here is that some (core) deficit may be justified in some developing countries. But the justification will depend on a cost-benefit evaluation of what the country gets from the expenditure associated with the benefit and the price it pays in terms of distortions, inflation, etc.

SOURCES OF DEFICIT FINANCING

The way in which a fiscal deficit is financed determines to a large extent the impact that it will have on the economy. For analytical purposes the financing of the deficit can be distinguished in different ways, all important, but emphasizing different aspects. One could distinguish between domestic and foreign financing, between inflationary and noninflationary financing, and between voluntary and compulsory financing.

Foreign Financing

Up to recent years, the recourse to foreign financing of a fiscal deficit was somewhat limited. In the second half of the 1970s, however, as foreign loans became more readily available and deficits larger, and as this occurred at a time when politically, or technically, tax limits seemed to have been

---

[11] But again this distortion is more important within a Keynesian framework than within a monetarist framework. If the deficit is financed through monetary expansion, the impact on prices and the balance of payments (if not on output) will be the same regardless of whether the expenditure for interest payment is a genuine expenditure or is an amortization.

[12] There is a lengthy discussion in the literature about the appropriate coverage and measurement of the fiscal budget. For some unconventional proposals, see Boskin (1982) and Buiter (1983).

approached or reached in many countries, foreign financing became more and more common. This financing must distinguish between grants[13] and concessionary loans on the one hand, and commercial credit on the other; and between short-run and long-run financing. If a country can finance its fiscal deficit through foreign grants (or through concessionary loans with a long maturity period), then the deficit may not have detrimental implications for the economy.[14] If the additional expenditure is directed mainly toward imported goods, the additional demand can be satisfied by higher imports financed by grants. However, the country must avoid locking itself into types of public expenditures (such as pensions, consumer subsidies, larger bureaucracy) that cannot be reduced without great difficulties should the grants dry up, unless it has a sure commitment from the relevant sources that this revenue will continue at the needed level for the foreseeable future. Unfortunately, there are experiences of developing countries that came to rely on these grants for the types of expenditures described above and that faced serious hardships when these revenue sources dried up.

The second most attractive foreign source of financing of the fiscal deficit is provided by loans with long maturity (say, over ten years). If these loans carry real interest rates low enough to make many potential projects pass a relevant cost-benefit criterion, and if they are, in fact, used toward those projects that rank highest in terms of a cost-benefit (or present value) criterion, then the country will be fully justified in running the deficit and in financing it in this way.[15] The problems arise, and, unfortunately, they are common ones, when (1) the loans carry interest rates high enough to disqualify most projects, (2) the loans are not utilized to finance productive expenditures but are used to support subsidies of various kinds, and (3) when long-run projects are financed with short-term loans.[16]

Fund programs always paid attention to the level and the time profile of a country's total foreign borrowing, and particularly, to the public sector's borrowing, to ensure that the limitations on the fiscal deficit imposed by

---

[13] In this discussion we consider grants as a financing item rather than as revenue. This is in contradiction with the treatment in the *Draft Manual on Government Finance Statistics*.

[14] If the deficit is associated with productive uses of resources, it will bring substantial benefits to the economy.

[15] This, of course, is the same criterion that is used by successful corporations to finance their investments through bond issues.

[16] The stream-of-loan repayment must bear some relation to the stream of additional income (including foreign currency earning) if the country is to avoid difficulties and maintain its creditworthiness. This is necessitated by the imperfection of the international capital market. A country that borrows short and invests long may face difficulties even when all the other criteria (low interest rate on loans, high cost-benefit ratio on projects) are met. Some countries have, in fact, tried to finance investments with long gestation periods with loans of a few months of maturity. Inevitably, they have run into financial difficulties. Short-term foreign credit must be utilized only to allow the government to help finance commercial activities (say, export of crops) that within a short time generate the foreign exchange to repay them.

domestic credit ceilings were not made useless by foreign borrowing. Operationally, this control was achieved by putting ceilings, in a Fund program with a country, on the central government's foreign borrowing with maturities of between one and ten years. This control was not always fully effective as, at times, countries violated its spirit by having public enterprises borrow abroad or by increasing short-run borrowing. Recent programs have thus often attempted to make these controls more effective by extending them to public enterprises and to short-term credit.

Noninflationary Domestic Financing

Shifting attention now to domestic financing, we need to make the basic distinction between domestic financing through inflationary means and domestic financing through noninflationary sources. Of somewhat less importance is the further distinction between voluntary and compulsory financing.

Noninflationary financing is normally associated with the sale of bonds to the public. The extent to which this source of financing is possible in a specific country at any given time depends on two considerations.

The first is the size and sophistication of the country's capital market. As is well known, there is great disparity among developing countries as to the scope and sophistication of their capital markets. In some, the capital market is as developed as that of many industrial countries; in others, the financial structure is still relatively undeveloped, so that, under the best of circumstances, there would be substantial limitations to the sale of bonds to the public.

The second important factor, and one that is emphasized in Fund programs, is the interest rate policy being followed. A country that wishes to finance a substantial share of its fiscal deficit through the domestic sale of bonds cannot, at the same time, pursue a policy of financial repression whereby interest rates are maintained at levels that are below, and sometimes much below, the expected rate of inflation.[17] Financial investors buy bonds when their return is attractive.[18] Whenever their return is low or negative, the possibility of financing the fiscal deficit through this source will be severely limited, regardless of the size and financial sophistication of the country's capital market. In this situation, savers will buy goods, or will try to invest their financial assets abroad, thus reducing the capacity of the government to finance its fiscal deficit, while at the same time aggravating the balance of payments problem (see Tanzi and Blejer (1982)).

---

[17]In reality it may be difficult to determine what the expected rate of inflation is.
[18]Of course there will always be some investors who, because of money illusion or other reasons, may buy some bonds even when their rate of return is negative.

In passing, it may be worthwhile to point out that when the rate of inflation is high and interest payments are taxable, the nominal rate of interest required to sell the bonds will have to adjust for both inflation and taxes. Thus, it may have to be substantially higher than the rate of inflation. This increase will be reduced when tax administration is poor so that many taxpayers will not pay taxes on their interest incomes or when the monetary correction portion of the interest payment is either not considered an income or is specifically exempt.

The connection between the financing of the fiscal deficit and financial policies has been recognized in Fund programs for a long time and this has been part of the reason, although not the only one, why Fund programs have emphasized the need for positive interest rates. One important aspect to recognize here, however, is that when interest rates are positive, and especially when they are significantly positive, and the fiscal deficit is large, the continuation of that deficit in future years will inevitably raise the share of the public debt in the GNP, especially when the rate of growth of the economy is not high. As a consequence, the proportion of total public expenditure that will go to the financing of that debt will also increase. In other words, the fiscal deficit will, in time, feed upon itself through the interest rate component of public expenditure. It is for this reason that Fund programs have often pursued the parallel objective of removal of financial repression *and* reduction of the size of the deficit. Unless these two objectives are pursued jointly, the results are likely to be disappointing over the long run.

Shifting now briefly to the other noninflationary way in which the government can finance its deficit, some compulsory means must be mentioned. Of these, two are worth mention. The first concerns the sale of bonds to social security institutions and to other pension funds. In some countries these institutions are required by law to buy public bonds and, to the extent that these bonds pay interest rates that are negative, this becomes in part an additional source of taxation, so that, in a proper sense, part of this financing should be classified as a tax revenue.[19] Furthermore, if these institutions run deficits that must be financed by the budget, what the government gains on the one hand it will lose on the other. The second compulsory source of financing is the building up of arrears.

Arrears are created when the government purchases goods and services and does not make the payments on time. These arrears can be accumulated with respect to the private sector or the public enterprises. When the arrears are created against the private sector, there need not be any necessary inflationary effect as no monetary creation takes place. In this case it is just

---

[19]Furthermore, in some countries public employees may be subject to moral pressure to buy the bonds.

as if the private sector had bought government bonds at zero interest rate for the period until payment is made. However, there is indirect evidence, at least for some countries, that the providers of the goods or services (especially in connection with capital projects), knowing that they will be paid with delay, have bid up the prices at which they sell those goods or services to the government thus raising the price level as well as the size of the deficit. Therefore, although one may not expect a connection between building up of arrears (in respect of purchases by the public sector) and the rate of inflation, indirectly there is a connection.

If the arrears are accumulated against public enterprises, as is often the case, these public enterprises will run deficits (or higher deficits); and if these deficits are either financed directly by the central bank or indirectly through the budget, they will end up creating inflationary pressures in the country.[20] Thus, even forms of financing that at first glance do not appear inflationary may, in fact, create pressures on prices. Recently, the Fund has been paying particular attention to arrears and various Fund programs have had clauses specifically directed to this issue.

Inflationary Financing

Insofar as the specialized interest of the Fund is in the balance of payments of a country, the fiscal deficit acquires particular importance when it increases the money supply. As will be discussed in detail in the next section, the major connection between the fiscal deficit and the balance of payments comes from the effect that the deficit is likely to have on money creation. A deficit that is not associated with an expansion of the money supply can, of course, still have several effects on the economy, which, depending on the situation, may be desirable or undesirable (Penati (1983)). However, for the majority of developing countries, it is rare when a sizable fiscal deficit does not bring about an expansion in the money supply. It is for this reason that the fiscal deficit plays such a large role in the Fund's adjustment programs.

The connection between financing of the deficit and monetary expansion (normally referred to as inflationary finance) can come in several ways. First, the central bank may buy government bonds directly, in which case monetary expansion is immediate. Second, the government may sell bonds to the public, including the commercial banks, and the central bank may in turn buy the bonds from the public. In this case, the connection between financing of the deficit and monetary expansion is not as immediate and direct as in the previous case, but the end result is the same. Third, the central bank may extend credit to public enterprises at highly concessionary rates. In this case,

---

[20]If these public enterprise deficits are financed directly by the central bank, they will not show in the central government's deficit.

the monetary expansion may not show up as a direct financing of the deficit, so that one may fail to recognize the connection between the fiscal deficit and money creation (see Wattleworth (1983)). However, consideration of the whole public sector and not just of the central government would make this connection more explicit.

In all these cases the net result is an increase in the amount of money, in nominal terms, in circulation. If the economy is growing at a fast pace and the income elasticity of the demand for money is high, its growth will be accompanied by an increase in the demand for money; therefore, part of the monetary expansion will satisfy this additional demand without necessarily leading to price increases or to balance of payments deterioration. However, given the income elasticity, the greater the growth of the money supply compared with the growth of the economy, the more likely are inflationary pressures to arise. The effect of monetary expansion on prices and on the balance of payments will depend on variables such as inflationary expectations, the size of the monetary base, and the elasticity of the liquidity preference schedule. Normally, an increase in inflationary expectation will lower the real stock of money that people wish to hold. A fall in the real stock of money will imply that the financing of a given deficit through monetary expansion becomes more inflationary.

To conclude this section, a brief mention should be made of the fact that monetary expansion can also reduce the share of tax revenue into national income thus raising further the size of the deficit itself. This will occur because of (1) the reliance on the part of developing countries on specific taxes (excises and imports), (2) long lags in the collection of income taxes and some other taxes, and (3) the tendency of exchange rates to become overvalued in periods of inflation, thus affecting revenues from ad valorem import duties. When inflation is high, this factor can become very important (see Tanzi (1978)).

FISCAL DISEQUILIBRIUM AND THE BALANCE OF PAYMENTS

The consequences of fiscal disequilibrium on the external sector of the economy cannot be separated from the overall macroeconomic effects of fiscal policy. However, in order to consider the role of fiscal adjustment in the stabilization process, we will concentrate here mainly on the direct consequences of fiscal disequilibrium and of its financing on the balance of payments.

Although there is no full agreement in the literature about the channels through which fiscal policies and alternative financing strategies affect the balance of payments, it is clear that expansionary fiscal policies, which are not financed in a manner that implies a commensurate reduction in the use of resources by the private sector, would entail pressures on output, prices, and the balance of payments. By how much each of these three variables would be affected by fiscal-induced excess demand depends on the specific conditions of the economy. Prices will be affected more and output will expand less the closer is the economy to its full employment level and the more anticipated is fiscal expansion. With respect to the balance of payments effects, alternative models have stressed different channels of adjustment but, in general, the stronger is the effect of fiscal expansion on output and the less it affects prices, the less will it tend to affect the external position of the country.

The two mainstreams of analysis of the effects of fiscal expansion on the balance of payments are the monetary model of the balance of payments and the more traditional macroeconomic models based on the Keynesian framework. Within the context of our analysis the monetary model would focus on the effects that fiscal deficits and their financing have on the composition of the financial assets portfolio of the private sector and would compare these effects with those on the overall availability of goods and services. The interaction of these two effects would determine the balance of payments outcome. Within the more conventional Keynesian framework, the focus is on the impact of fiscal policy on the savings and investment functions or, more precisely, on the gap between domestic income and expenditures. Although much of the analysis of the effects of fiscal policies within this type of open economy model has been based on the relationships between marginal propensities to consume and to import, more recent models have considered in detail the characteristics of the real sector and the differential impact of fiscal actions under alternative assumptions. Thus, for example, it has been shown that an expansionary fiscal policy has larger negative impact on the balance of payments the more rigid are real wages and the smaller is the portion of government expenditures falling on nontraded goods.

In order to illustrate the functioning of the monetary model, let us consider an expansionary fiscal action, defined as an increase in public sector expenditures, fully financed by taxes. As postulated by the well-known balanced-budget-multiplier hypothesis, such an expansion would lead to increases in aggregate demand throughout the economy which in turn would result in output expansion and inflationary pressures.[21] Unless the economy was operating substantially below its capacity level, and therefore most of the effect of fiscal expansion would eventually result in an equivalent increase in the level of output, the tax financing of government expenditures would tend, in the short run, to reduce the level of disposable income. The monetary approach to the balance of payments stresses the effect of such a

---

[21]It is assumed here that the additional public expenditures do not take the form of transfer payments.

contraction in income on the demand for financial assets of the private sector. Because a reduction in the level of real disposable income reduces the transaction demand for real balances, it may induce substitutions from money to real goods with the consequent expansion in aggregate demand. Clearly, however, the reduction in the disposable income of the private sector tends to reduce consumption and offset the effect on demand associated with portfolio substitutions. The net effect on the balance of payments depends therefore on the relative strength of these two effects. If the monetary effect dominates, it is likely that the contractionary effect on demand caused by tax increases would be partially offset by the results of portfolio substitutions and, as a consequence, private sector demand would contract substantially less than the increase in government spending. In that case, spillover effects on the external sector are likely to arise with a consequent deterioration in the balance of payments.

Financing Aspects of Expansionary Fiscal Policy

Our analysis so far has disregarded the financing aspects of fiscal expansion. However, the financing mechanism of fiscal disequilibrium is of central importance in the determination of its impact on the balance of payments. The alternative ways of financing government expenditures and fiscal deficits were surveyed in the previous section. In terms of their effects on the balance of payments there are two important distinctions. First, we can distinguish between those mechanisms of financing that entail an expansion of liquidity and those which, while raising the stock of government liabilities, do not directly imply an increase in the nominal value of liquid assets in the hands of the public. Second, it is possible to differentiate between the effects of domestically and foreign-financed deficits.

Financing through monetary expansion

The most negative effect on the balance of payments, as measured by the impact on the level of international reserves, is likely to arise from fiscal expansion financed by direct borrowing from the central bank. Since this mechanism implies, in general, an increase in the money supply, it tends to create an excess of liquidity in the hands of the public. Such excess liquidity will tend to increase the demand for domestic and foreign goods, as well as for alternative financial assets, including foreign assets, and will, therefore, tend to put pressure on prices and on the balance of payments.[22] This is the

---

[22]In a fast growing economy some monetary expansion may not be inflationary as additional money is needed to fuel additional transactions.

well-known mechanism of adjustment postulated by the monetary approach to the balance of payments and implies that the excess supply of money created by the monetization of the deficit would only be eliminated as foreign exchange reserves have been depleted enough to restore equilibrium in the money market. In addition, the pressure put by excess liquidity on the level of prices has an additional equilibrating effect by reducing the real value of the outstanding money stock.

In an economy operating under a fixed exchange rate system, it can be said that, the more open is the economy (the higher the share of traded goods in total expenditure), the larger will be the role of the balance of payments adjustment in the equilibrating process, and, therefore, the larger the losses of' reserves and the less the impact of monetized deficits on domestic inflation. Clearly, if the exchange rate is allowed to adjust, the monetization of fiscal deficits will put upward pressure on the exchange rate, reducing the losses of reserves and increasing the inflationary impact. In the limit, with a fully flexible exchange rate, most of the burden of restoring monetary equilibrium would be carried by the changes in the exchange rate operating through changes in the price level. The level of international reserves will clearly be affected much less in this case.

The monetary impact of central bank expansion of domestic credit to finance public sector deficits can be reduced if sterilization measures and other types of contractionary monetary policies are adopted. The expansion of domestic credit to the public sector must be accompanied by an equivalent contraction of credit to the private sector through changes in reserve requirements or through the imposition of other restrictions on the ability of the banking system to expand lending. This will certainly limit the credit available for the private sector and, if interest rates are market determined, it will tend to push up the levels of interest rates and will lead to the well-known "crowding out effect."[23] The stronger is the crowding out effect, the lesser will be the balance of payments impact of central bank financing of public sector deficits. Thus, in financing large deficits through the central bank, the authorities are confronted with the trade-off between compromising the achievement of monetary targets, with the consequent balance of payments and inflationary results, and constraining the financing of the private sector, with the ensuing effects for economic activity and investments.

This type of consideration may help to explain the motivation behind some of the measures included in a typical Fund program. It is common to observe that total credit ceilings are normally accompanied by a subceiling on the amount of credit to the government. Without such a subceiling, the private

---

[23] A more direct form of crowding out is through credit rationing; if crowding out occurs through credit rationing, rather than through interest rate adjustment, capital flight becomes more likely with greater deterioration in the balance of payments.

sector might run the risk of being fully excluded from the credit market and the stabilization program would probably cause a sharp fall in economic activity.

It should be mentioned, in this context, that the external sector's effects of monetary finance are likely to be similar whether the expansion of central bank credit is captured by the central government or whether it takes the form of concessional credit to public enterprises. Some differential impact effect may arise from differences in the expenditure patterns of the various components of the public sector, but the ultimate effect, working through excess liquidity, will have similar balance of payments consequences.

Financing through borrowing from domestic private sector

An alternative to monetary finance of fiscal deficits is domestic borrowing from the bank and nonbank private sector. The appropriate theoretical framework to deal with the effect of debt financing is provided by the portfolio models of balance of payments and exchange rate determination. Portfolio models depart from monetary models in that they assume imperfect substitution between domestic and foreign bonds and, therefore, they are viewed as different assets with different demand functions for each of them. These demands depend, among other variables, on the domestic and foreign interest rates, on the expectations about future exchange rate movements, and on differential tax treatment of domestic and foreign investment income. Within this framework, the sale of bonds in order to finance budget deficits may lead to an excess supply of bonds denominated in domestic currency, especially if the capital market is small and, more important, if interest rates are constrained. In order to restore portfolio equilibrium, the domestic private sector will attempt to move into foreign-currency-denominated assets, which will lead to a balance of payments deterioration, particularly through the capital account. The loss of reserves arising from the diversification toward foreign-currency-denominated assets may also result in expectations of exchange rate devaluation with the consequent additional worsening of the capital account and, also, in a deterioration of the current account.

The increase in the supply of domestic bonds may not lead to excess demand for foreign assets, or to a deterioration in the balance of payments, if the domestic rate of interest is free to adjust enough to restore portfolio equilibrium. But the magnitude of the increase may have to be quite substantial.[24] Such an increase in interest rates is bound to result, again, in crowding out effects by, for example, redirecting bank credit away from the private sector and, as indicated earlier, making the fiscal deficit worse over the longer run unless effective measures aimed at its reduction are taken

---

[24]In reality, there must be some limit to how many bonds can be sold; that is, the demand for bonds will become vertical.

immediately.[25] It is clear, therefore, that debt financing will affect the balance of payments more if financial yields are not allowed to clear the market. Compulsory bond issues (and, to some extent, the building up of arrears with the domestic private sector) are likely to have stronger negative external effects than interest-rate-induced increases in the demand for bonds of the public sector, although the latter will certainly crowd out more private sector spending.

An additional way by which debt financing may have balance of payments effects depends on the question of whether government bonds are net wealth. The extent to which government bonds constitute net private wealth has not been resolved in the literature. It is sometimes argued that the public does not consider these bonds as additions to real wealth since they discount the future tax liabilities implied by an increase in the government debt.[26] If this so-called "Ricardian equivalence" does not hold and, therefore, if government bonds are indeed regarded as net wealth by the private sector, a deficit will be perceived as increasing private sector wealth. When real wealth is an argument in the consumption function, debt-financed deficits will increase consumption and imports and, therefore, the balance of payments will tend to deteriorate. In addition, the asset model postulates another channel of balance of payments worsening. If the composition of the financial portfolio is to remain unchanged, the increase in wealth leads to increases in the demand for foreign-exchange-denominated bonds with the consequent deterioration of the capital account.

Financing through foreign borrowing

The effects of *foreign* finance of budget deficits depend, as in the case of domestic finance deficits, on the magnitude of the increases in liquidity in the hands of the private sector. Direct borrowing from abroad by the treasury or by public enterprises, as well as concessionary loans and foreign grants, will have, if fully monetized, a similar effect as central bank financed budget disequilibrium on aggregate demand. But, of course, to the extent that foreign borrowing allows greater imports, the supply of goods is also increased. This would make foreign financing of the deficit less inflationary than central bank financing. This lower impact on domestic inflation is more marked when foreign borrowing is directly used by the government to purchase traded goods or for direct imports for its own use.

---

[25]The fiscal deficit is also likely to deteriorate in the short run if the fall in economic activity reduces, as it is likely to do, tax revenue.

[26]For a discussion of this issue and further references, see Barro (1974) and Buiter and Tobin (1979). Some recent empirical evidence, however, indicates that most o f the basic implications of the "Ricardian equivalance theorem" is contradicted by the U.S. data. See Feldstein (1982).

The excess liquidity arising from the monetization of foreign transfers generally results in excess demand for goods. It thus puts pressure on the price level and on the balance of payments.[27] Foreign borrowing may, therefore, raise the level of gross foreign exchange reserves, but will tend to deplete net, or owned, reserves. In other words, policies that reduce the domestically financed overall government deficit by inducing foreign capital inflows will, ceteris paribus, have positive effects on the overall balance of payments performance but not necessarily on the current account. An implication of this is that although the domestically financed government deficit is the appropriate macroeconomic fiscal target in considering policies that influence the overall balance of payments position, foreign finance of the fiscal deficit has crucial importance for the *composition* of the balance of payments outcome. Moreover, external financing of fiscal deficits has implications for the longer-term external performance of the country by increasing external indebtedness and, therefore, by raising the burden of future debt service.[28]

It should be pointed out that foreign financing of the fiscal deficit does not always succeed in maintaining the level of gross reserves. In fact, the increase in the service ratio and the anticipation of future devaluations may induce private sector capital outflows which, on balance, may offset the capital inflows generated by the government. Expected devaluations may, of course, lead to further, although probably temporary, deterioration of the current account due to the advancing of imports and postponements of exports.

Fiscal deficits have sometimes been used for stabilization purposes, particularly to smooth the macroeconomic impact of business cycles. In that case, the use of previously accumulated foreign exchange reserves for financing government expenditures may be the most desirable procedure since interest rates will be less affected, and therefore less crowding out effects are likely to arise, and also, the level of the country indebtedness will remain unchanged. However, if expectations, foreign credit ratings, and financial stability are largely affected by the observed level of reserves, the optimality of this type of financing may not be absolute.

---

[27]Clearly, the more open is the economy and the less flexible is the exchange rate, the stronger will be the impact on the balance of payments and the smaller the effect of excess liquidity on the price level.

[28]There is not necessarily a complete connection between official foreign borrowing and fiscal imbalance. In many countries, for example, external borrowing is undertaken by the government or by public enterprises in order to increase gross reserves and strengthen confidence. Moreover, in many cases, governments undertake all commercial foreign borrowing because they have better access to foreign markets and can obtain better terms than the private sector. In those cases, official foreign borrowing is similar to trade and supplier's credit.

FISCAL DEFICITS IN FUND PROGRAMS

The International Monetary Fund has primary responsibility among international organizations for balance of payments adjustment and the proper functioning of the international financial system. Therefore, the main objective of Fund financial programs is to reduce or eliminate disequilibrium in the balance of payments. However, difficulties in the balance of payments of a country are often a symptom rather than the basic cause of economic disequilibrium; as a consequence, Fund financial programs aim at eliminating the basic causes of that disequilibrium. Often the basic cause for the external imbalance of a country has been excessive monetary expansion.[29] It is this monetary expansion that brings about changes in relative prices, thus encouraging imports, discouraging exports, and inducing unfavorable capital movements. Monetary expansion does not occur automatically but is itself promoted by other factors. These factors may find their origin in the private sector of an economy but, more often, they find their origin in the public sector. In recent years large fiscal deficits have been the main cause of excessive monetary expansion in many developing countries.

Because of the heterogeneity of the Fund's membership and the different social and economic systems that Fund members have, the Fund is inherently neutral about the size of the public sector of a country. However, for the reasons indicated above, it is not neutral about the size of the fiscal deficit and especially its financing. A fiscal deficit can be reduced by cutting expenditure or by raising revenue. Fund missions look at both sides of a country's budget and recommend expenditure cuts or revenue increases, depending on the particular situation. If the fiscal deficit is caused mainly by substantial and unsustainable recent expansion in expenditure, Fund missions may recommend that expenditure cuts be made. If, on the other hand, a fall in revenue is the major cause of the fiscal deterioration, or if the tax level of the country is unusually low, the Fund may recommend raising that level. In many cases, Fund missions recommend that the country pursue both channels of adjustment, that is, expenditure cuts and revenue increases.[30] As in recent years, the cause of fiscal deterioration is often the expansion of expenditure, rather than the fall in revenue, countries are advised more often to reduce expenditure than to increase revenue. Fund missions are highly sensitive to possible disincentive effects of tax increases, as well as to the distributional and efficiency effects of cuts in public expenditure. In any

---

[29]Obviously, wrong exchange rate policies or interest rate policies can also bring external imbalances.

[30]With respect to revenue increases, administrative improvements have generally been given preference over increase in rates.

event, final decisions as to how budgetary imbalances are to be reduced lie, as they inevitably must, with the authorities of the member country.

Fund programs generally contain statements of goals or objectives in relation to improvement in (1) the balance of payments, (2) growth performance, and (3) the rate of inflation. At times a reduction of payment arrears and economic diversification have also been specified as a program's objectives. Of course not all of these objectives are specified in each program. Most programs mention balance of payments improvement, and many programs specify growth and the improvement in the fiscal accounts.

When a country agrees to a Fund program, it commits itself to the observance of certain performance clauses. The nonobservance of performance clauses interrupts a member's right to use Fund resources under a program until new understandings are reached with the Fund. Most programs include performance clauses related to (1) domestic bank credit expansion; (2) the use of domestic bank credit by the government; (3) the growth of the external debt; and (4) restrictions on external trade and payments. Some programs also include performance clauses related to the size of the fiscal deficit in nominal terms and understandings about economic policies to be pursued during the period of the program. Such understandings may include particular fiscal actions, such as removal of subsidies or changes in particular taxes.

The fiscal deficit becomes important both in relation to the first of these performance criteria, namely, the domestic bank credit expansion, and when it is directly specified in a performance clause. Normally, the program will specify that not more than a certain amount of the total credit expansion will be channeled toward the fiscal sector. In other words, the program specifies what share of the total credit expansion will go toward the government and what share will go toward the private sector. In general, the country will not have any binding commitments related to the level of tax revenue or the level of government expenditure but to the fiscal deficit financed by credit expansion and the overall fiscal deficit. As monetary data are usually more reliable and more timely than fiscal data (and as monetary expansion is often the basic problem, rather than the deficit itself), the behavior of the fiscal deficit (which may be related to the central government or to a broader concept, such as the public sector) is in many cases monitored through the amount of credit expansion absorbed by the government. This credit expansion is broadly an indication of the monetary expansion for which the public sector is responsible. In some cases a Fund financial program will stipulate, not as a performance clause but as a target, the reduction in the fiscal deficit expressed as a proportion of the gross domestic product (GDP) that is considered desirable to attain. For example, in 1980, out of 26 Fund programs, 18 contemplated a reduction in the fiscal deficit of at least 1 percent of GDP, 12 contemplated a reduction of at least 2 percent of GDP;

and 8 contemplated a reduction of at least 5 percent (Doe (1983)). Behind this reduction in the size of the fiscal deficit there were, as indicated, general agreements about policies aimed at cutting public expenditure or increasing public revenues.

Recent studies have indicated that, by and large, observance of fiscal understandings between the countries and the Fund were accompanied by improvements in the countries' current accounts and overall balance of payments (Kelly (1982)). They have also indicated that the nonobservance of the fiscal agreement was often accompanied by a continuation of the serious external imbalances.

BIBLIOGRAPHY

Barro, Robert J., "Are Government Bonds Net Wealth?," *Journal of Political Economy*, Vol. 82 (November–December 1974), pp. 1095–1117.

Boskin, Michael J., "Federal Government Deficits: Some Myths and Realities," *American Economic Review*, Vol. 72 (May 1982), pp. 296–303.

Buiter, Willem H., "The Proper Measurement of the Public Sector Deficit and Its Implications for Policy Evaluation and Design," *Staff Papers*, International Monetary Fund (Washington), Vol. 30 (June 1983), pp. 306–49.

————, and James Tobin, "Debt Neutrality: A Brief Review of Doctrine and Evidence," in *Social Security Versus Private Saving*, ed. by George M. von Furstenberg, Vol. 1 in the Series on Capital Investment and Saving, sponsored by the American Council of Life Insurance (Cambridge, Mass.: Ballinger, 1979), pp. 39–63.

Doe, Lubin, "Fiscal Policy and Adjustment in the 1980 Fund Financial Programs" (unpublished, International Monetary Fund, June 30, 1983).

Feldstein, Martin, "Government Deficits and Aggregate Demand," *Journal of Monetary Economics*, Vol. 9 (January 1982), pp. 1–20.

Friedman, Milton, "Inflation and Unemployment," *Journal of Political Economy*, Vol. 85 (June 1977), pp. 451–72.

Kelly, Margaret R., "Fiscal Adjustment and Fund-Supported Programs, 1971–80," *Staff Papers*, International Monetary Fund (Washington), Vol. 29 (December 1982), pp. 561–602.

Patinkin, Don, *Anticipation of the General Theory?* (Chicago: University of Chicago Press, 1982).

Penati, Alessandro, "Expansionary Fiscal Policy and the Exchange Rate: A Review," *Staff Papers*, International Monetary Fund (Washington), Vol. 30 (September 1983), pp. 542–69.

Tanzi, Vito, "Inflation, Real Tax Revenue, and the Case for Inflationary Finance: Theory with an Application to Argentina," *Staff Papers*, International Monetary Fund (Washington), Vol. 25 (September 1978), pp. 417–51.

——————, "Fiscal Disequilibrium in Developing Countries," *World Development*, Vol. 10 (December 1982), pp. 1069–1082.

——————, and Mario I. Blejer, "Inflation, Interest Rate Policy, and Currency Substitutions in Developing Economies: A Discussion of Some Major Issues," *World Development*, Vol. 10 (September 1982), pp. 781–89.

Wattleworth, Michael A., "Credit Subsidies in Budgetary Lending" (unpublished, International Monetary Fund, May 26, 1983).

Commentary*

CARLOS AMAT Y LEÓN

The paper presented by Mario Blejer sets forth, in a clear and orderly manner, the conventional theory on strategies for financing fiscal deficits and the effects of such strategies on inflation and on balance of payments equilibrium.

As I am basically in agreement with the technical aspects of this paper, I think it would be best for me to focus my discussion on the experience with the financial adjustment process in Peru, where the public sector deficit was a decisive driving force behind rates of inflation unprecedented in this century. The price escalation (CPI) stemmed from fiscal mismanagement and the price policy of the military government.

It is important to note, however, the present Government's inability to reduce the public sector deficit to levels compatible with the financial stabilization program agreed upon with the International Monetary Fund (IMF). The proposed target is 4.2 percent of gross domestic product (GDP), compared with the results of 8.2 percent in 1981 and 6.6 percent in 1982.

This gap between the desired and actual levels of the public sector deficit has surely been one reason for the distortion of the stabilization programs intended to control inflation and stimulate output and employment.

It is more germane, however, to inquire as follows: Why is it that the rate of inflation has ranged between 60 percent and 70 percent in the last five years? All indications are that inflation will exceed 70 percent in 1983 in spite of the stabilization agreement with the IMF.

Hence, it would be worthwhile to try to explain this phenomenon. This obliges us to recognize existing circumstances for what they are and requires us to add new criteria to our analysis and to conceptualize the functioning of the economic system in a manner other than the traditional one.

In the following tentative explanation, I will present a theoretical framework, which highlights the major lines of the argument. The new analytical components stem from recognition of the following facts:

(1) The production structure is heterogeneous and distorted, in that a small number of producer units—the central government and the large businesses which employ modern technology—account for the bulk of installed capital, output, and value added.

(2) A small proportion of the population controls the production process and the distribution of value added. This control is exercised by workers (16

---

*The original version of this paper was written in Spanish.

to 20 percent of the labor force) and by the owners of the capital, who receive profits and income from it.

(3) This structure of production and of the distribution of value added results in a highly asymmetrical income distribution, where 10 percent of households receive 44 percent of total income. This fact is graphically depicted in the lower panel of the chart.

(4) The producer groups and the population which receives its income from the operations of each have been represented in two segments (A and B) for the sake of simplicity. Group A is the modern sector, which supports the small, high-income group. Group B includes small and medium-scale businesses of the household and cottage industry type, which support the vast, low-income majority.

(5) These two groups are further distinguished by their average and marginal propensities to spend, consume, import, pay taxes, save, invest, etc. In other words, their economic and financial behaviors are at different levels and have different elasticities.

(6) The economic significance of Group A gives it monopoly control over the system, so that it is able to pass on the higher costs entailed by financial stabilization and incomes programs. Therefore, it has a relatively greater ability to defend its market position as regards the use of the real and financial resources available to the system as a whole.

(7) If we examine the manner in which these two groups of economic agents respond to the measures taken by the Government to stabilize the country's finances—in the areas of exchange rates, interest rates, taxes, energy prices, fees for public services, and wages and salaries—it will be noted that the public sector and the monopoly entrepreneur group maintain their positions and even increase their real incomes. This is the case, for example, of certain industrial concerns, such as those in the food industry, which sell mass consumption goods and have inelastic prices.

The graph at the top of the chart shows the different behavior of the two groups in the context of Peru's current inflationary process. On one side, Group A shows systematic increases in the levels of demand, expressed by the upward shift of its demand curve D_{1-4}. In addition, its supply curve S_{1-4} shifts to the left as nominal costs rise.

The axes of the graph are the price level and the gross domestic product. Group B does not set prices; instead, it is subject to the levels determined by Group A. This has two consequences. Its demand successively shifts downward reflecting declining real income. As for supply, as consumption and buying slacken, the productive apparatus which depends on this market enters into recession and the possibility of business failures arises, giving rise to equally systematic leftward shifts of the supply curve, which also shifts upward as production costs rise—the logical outcome of the adjustment program for the system as a whole.

The results of this operating mechanism are
(1) higher inflation;
(2) deeper recession;

Functioning of the Economic System

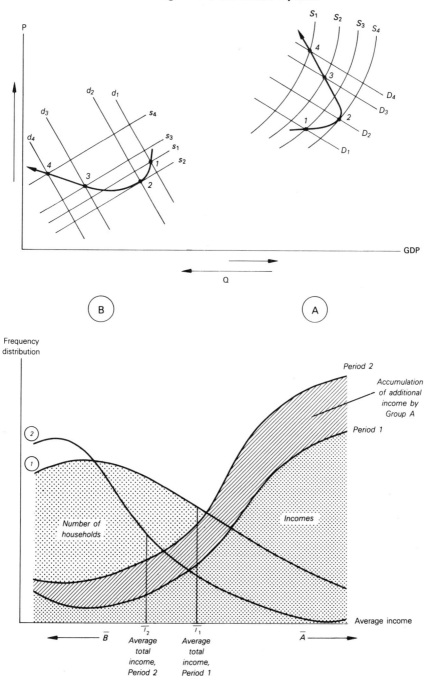

(3) increased polarization in the distribution of income; and

(4) a continuing process of disequilibrium and destabilization.

This process cannot continue indefinitely over time, as the system is subject to constraints. First, there is a constraint on external indebtedness; when the borrowing limit is reached, as in the case of Peru, Group A cannot continue to demand additional resources. Second, there is a limit to the economic and social repression of the population dependent on Group B, which imposes a political constraint; in a democracy, it becomes increasingly difficult to continue such a process of social disequilibrium and inequality.

The strategy for economic stabilization and revitalization will have to be carried out through concerted management on the part of government, the enterprises, and the labor unions functioning in Group A, so as to bring the production process and the distribution of value added into line with a program which specifically takes into account the following.

(1) The capacity to import, established after determining the limits on the country's external indebtedness and on the availability of external resources, projected net exports, and reserve targets;

(2) The level of economic activity for the system as a whole, determined by the capacity to import;

(3) The program for the central government, public enterprises and social security, and the output, productivity and financing targets;

(4) Contracts with monopoly enterprises with respect to the levels of production, financing, and profits;

(5) Contracts with labor unions as regards a schedule of wage increases designed to maintain real incomes.

In short, this is an effort to design and propose a new and consistent economic program under which the agents comprising Group A can have real and financial targets that fit in with the stabilization program, the program is not distorted by a desire on the part of the government in power to reach short-term political objectives, and excess profits on the part of monopoly enterprises can be avoided.

If the sacrifices are shared and visible, Group B will not suffer excessively and the political management of the stabilization program will be feasible, and therefore effective.

Commentary*

SERGIO DE LA CUADRA

The authors provide a conceptual analysis of the relationship between budget deficits and the balance of payments; in so doing, they call upon those theoretical arguments most pertinent to examination of the topic. As a result, little can be added to the paper on a strictly theoretical basis. Also, empirical research on the relationship between budget deficits and the balance of payments is lacking.

Chile's experience in 1979, 1980, and 1981 provides an interesting case study, as it reflects a government budget surplus which turned into a balance of payments crisis.

The obvious conclusion from these years is that the amount spent by the private sector in excess of its income was greater than the total availability of central bank credit and external resources.

We must therefore examine how these central bank credit and external resources were used by the public and private sectors in the Chilean economy.

To do so, I have compiled a few figures for the 1960–81 period on the inflation tax, external credit and central bank credit, and public and private sector participation in these sources of financing.

In view of the instability of exchange policy during the period, expressing all the values in the same currency requires extremely painstaking calculations. As it was not possible to complete such work for this occasion, the figures presented must be considered merely as a very crude approximation of the variables in question. I have therefore provided only averages for the periods 1960–70 and 1971–81.

Period	Variables		
	X_1	X_2	X_3
	(Percent)		
1960–70	12	5.3	60
1971–81	80	20.0	100

X_1 = Inflation tax as a percentage of legislated taxes.

X_2 = External credit plus central bank credit as a percentage of gross domestic product.

X_3 = Private sector share of external credit plus central bank credit.

(The variables are arithmetical averages for the period.)

---

*The original version of this paper was written in Spanish.

The 100 percent figure for private sector participation in external resources plus central bank credit may be explained as the result of averaging years when a public surplus was recorded with years when there were public deficits.

These figures indicate that the imbalance between revenue and expenditure grew sharply in the 1970s and that private participation in this disequilibrium was more significant than public participation.

This raises the question: Is the policy mix required for adjustment independent of the private and public participation in the disequilibrium? If not, how does it change when private participation is equal to or greater than public participation?

The Role of International Reserves and Foreign Debt in the External Adjustment Process

SEBASTIAN EDWARDS*

1. INTRODUCTION

During the 1970s the developing countries underwent serious current account deficits in their balance of payments, which led, inter alia, to major increases in their foreign debt. Whereas in 1970 the public and publicly guaranteed debt of the low-income countries (excluding the People's Republic of China and India) amounted to 16.5 percent of their gross national product (GNP), in 1980 it had risen to 31.5 percent of GNP. On the other hand, the ratio of foreign public and publicly guaranteed debt of the middle-income countries increased from 11.8 percent of GNP in 1970 to 17.4 percent of GNP in 1980.[1] More recently, some developing countries—Mexico, Brazil, Costa Rica, and Argentina, for instance—have faced serious problems in servicing their foreign debt.

The analysis of the determinants of the current account of the balance of payments, and its relation to macroeconomic adjustment, has lately made significant progress. Particular emphasis has been given to the intertemporal nature of the current account, and the distinction has been made between temporary and permanent shocks.[2] It has been postulated, for instance, that whereas the most appropriate policy to face temporary shock is to increase the level of foreign debt (or reduce the level of international reserves), reduction of the level of internal absorption is the optimum policy in response to a permanent shock.[3]

Despite renewed interest in analyzing the macroeconomic adjustment process in an open economy, most of the papers, theoretical as well as empirical, emphasize the use of a particular tool to achieve such adjustment. Thus, for instance, while certain authors have made a detailed analysis of the

---

*I am indebted to Sergio Málaga and Juan Guillermo Espinosa for their valuable comments. (The original version of this paper was written in Spanish.)
[1]See World Bank, *World Development Report*, 1982.
[2]See, for example, Sachs (1981), (1982).
[3]See Sachs (1981), Obstfeld (1982) and Svensson and Razin (1983).

143

use of foreign debt as an instrument for adjustment, others have focused on the use of reserves, and a third group has examined in detail the role of the exchange rate and its relation to the current account.[4] Exceptions to this rule are Eaton and Gersovitz (1980), who have analyzed the joint determination of international reserves and foreign debt; Edwards (1983 a), who has explicitly considered the use of the exchange rate as an adjustment tool in the analysis of demand for international reserves; and Frenkel and Aizenman (1982), who have theoretically examined the joint determination of the optimum degree of float for a currency and the level of reserves the country wishes to maintain.

The purpose of this paper is to analyze in some detail the role of international reserves and external debt in the process of macroeconomic adjustment in developing countries, with particular emphasis on Latin American countries. The discussion explicitly recognizes that both reserves and debt are alternative instruments that countries may use to achieve external balance.[5] In addition, it is recognized that foreign debt plays a twofold role in the economic process. First, in the short run, changes in the external debt make it possible to cope with temporary external disequilibria. Second, foreign debt plays a long-run role connected with financing gross domestic investment. In fact, insofar as the current account deficit—which is equal to external savings—is partly or totally financed by new (net) foreign borrowing, the foreign debt will be playing a major long-term role in the development and economic growth process. It is precisely this twofold role played by foreign debt that requires developing countries to find ways to manage it carefully. In this context it is important, for example, to make the needs for external resources to finance gross investment compatible with the uses of debt for short-term purposes. Appropriate planning of the evolution of external liabilities and assets of the monetary system will prevent imbalances that may turn out very costly in the long run.[6]

In this paper various problems connected with the role of international reserves and foreign debt in the external adjustment process are empirically analyzed. Section 2 contains a general discussion of the subject, emphasizing the fact that most of the economic literature dealing with demand for international reserves has failed to consider explicitly the role played by debt (or exchange rate variations) in the external adjustment process. This section also presents a discussion—and a word of caution—on the use of dynamic optimization models to determine the optimum degree of debt for a country. Section 3, in turn, presents new empirical evidence on the determinants of

---

[4]See, for example, Dornbusch and Fischer (1980) and Rodríguez (1980).

[5]It is further recognized, theoretically, that adjustments in the exchange rate play a similar role. In the empirical analysis the inclusion of such adjustments did not affect the results, hence they are not presented in this paper.

[6]See Loser (1977).

demand for international reserves in the developing countries, using data for 1975–80. This section also presents results obtained when reserves and debt are considered to be alternative instruments for achieving external equilibrium. The main conclusions reached in this section are that: (a) the demand for reserves in the developing countries has been a stable function in the past few years, although from a legal standpoint the international monetary system has been characterized by a dirty float;[7] (b) demand for reserves in the developing countries displays diseconomies of scale showing that, as a result of economic growth, such countries' need for international liquidity will grow more than proportionately in the next few years; (c) reserves and foreign debt are substitutes, in the sense that both have been used by these countries as alternative ways to finance their external adjustment processes.

Section 4 of the paper examines a critical issue for macroeconomic management of reserves and foreign debt. The section discusses in what way the levels of debt and reserves, among other variables, affect the level of country risk perceived by the international financial community. The importance of this discussion lies in the fact that should a relation exist between these variables and the probability of default perceived by the international financial community, countries may manage these variables in such a way that the degree of risk of default perceived is kept at relatively low levels. This in turn will lead to more favorable terms for obtaining foreign funds and continuing maintenance of such loans. The results presented in this section, based on data from over 700 public and publicly guaranteed loans granted in the period 1976–80 in the Eurocurrency market, show that the higher the debt/output ratio the higher the perceived probability of default. It was further found that a higher international liquidity ratio will result in a lower perceived country risk.

In Section 5 an empirical analysis on the relation between the dynamic adjustment of international reserves and monetary market equilibrium is presented. This analysis shows that international reserve movements over time arise essentially from two factors: (a) discrepancies between desired reserves and reserves actually maintained; and (b) imbalances in the monetary market. These results—which basically correspond to the analysis presented in the monetary approach to the balance of payments—point out that situations of excess supply of money will tend to result in international reserves dropping below desired levels. The above findings, in the light of results obtained from analysis of country risk determinants, have obvious implications in terms of economic policy. Insofar as a country wishes to

---

[7]Of course while the currencies of industrial countries have tended to float (dirtily), developing countries have adhered to the most diverse exchange arrangements. See the introduction in any recent issue of the International Monetary Fund publication *International Financial Statistics* (*IFS*) for a list of such agreements.

maintain an acceptable (conservative) degree of perceived country risk, it must be particularly careful in the way it handles its monetary policy.

Section 6 of the paper contains some considerations on the case of the Latin American countries, with emphasis on the importance of designing a coherent exchange rate policy to deal with macroeconomic adjustment problems. Finally, some concluding remarks are offered in Section 7.

2. INTERNATIONAL RESERVES AND FOREIGN DEBT IN THE MACROECONOMIC ADJUSTMENT PROCESS

There is an extensive literature, empirical as well as theoretical, on the role of international reserves in the external adjustment process, which has been reviewed, among others, by Clower and Lipsey (1968), Gruebel (1971), Williamson (1973), and Bird (1978). Generally speaking, most of the studies on the subject assume that countries maintain reserves both for financing international transactions and for facing unforeseen international payment difficulties. Hipple (1974), for instance, groups studies on international reserves under two headings: one focusing on the transaction motive for maintaining reserves; the other emphasizing the role of international payment variability as a motive for demanding reserves. Most recent studies, however, have recognized the importance of both these motives in the demand for reserves.[8]

Empirical studies recently conducted by Frenkel (1978, 1980) and Heller and Khan (1978) have shown that, even after the change in the monetary system's rules of the game in 1973, the demand for international reserves in the various groups of countries remains stable. Frenkel (1980), for instance, found that in 1972 a structural change took place in the demand function for reserves in the case of developing countries. This finding—also confirmed by Heller and Khan (1978)—shows that the developing countries altered their behavior with respect to the desired amount of international liquidity even before the Bretton Woods system was officially given up in 1973.[9] For practical and economic policy purposes, however, the relevant point about these results is that they show that even during the present international monetary arrangements, various countries' demand for international liquidity has remained stable. This fact may be explained in several ways. For example, at present the international monetary system is based on a dirty float (managed parities) by the industrial countries and diverse systems— pegging to a currency, pegging to a basket, crawling peg, and so on—used

---

[8]See, for example, Brown (1964), Machlup (1966), Clark (1970 b), Kelly (1970), Flanders (1971), Frenkel (1974), (1978), and (1980), Heller and Khan (1978), Saidi (1981), Frenkel and Jovanovic (1980), von Furstenberg (1982), and Edwards (1983 b) and (1984).

[9]In the event that these countries anticipated the breakdown of the Bretton Woods agreement, this result should not prove surprising.

by the developing countries.[10] In the event that the float is dirty, countries will wish to maintain a positive level of international reserves in order to intervene in the exchange market.

Most of the studies on international reserves are based on some concept of optimality for determining the desired level of liquidity for a particular country. Heller (1966), in his pioneer work, equated the marginal benefit to the marginal cost of maintaining reserves to derive his equation on optimum quantity of reserves. Subsequent papers, explicitly based on optimality concepts, include those of Olivera (1969), Hipple (1974), Claasen (1976), Hamada and Veda (1977), and Frenkel and Jovanovic (1981). Such studies assume that maintaining reserves allows countries to survive external crises without having to incur the costs of adjusting internal absorption. This positive effect of maintaining reserves should therefore be compared with the corresponding costs, in order to determine the optimum amount of reserves. Thus, for example, in Clark's (1970 a) well-known dynamic analysis, the costs of maintaining reserves are given by the marginal productivity of capital (representing the alternative cost of reserves) and by the cost of adjusting the quantity actually maintained to the quantity desired. Conversely, benefits are related to the ability to maintain a more stable real-income flow over time. In this way Clark (1970 a) derives a model that, for a given probability that a country runs out of reserves, simultaneously determines the optimum level of reserves and the optimum speed of adjustment between desired reserves and reserves actually maintained.

In a recent paper Frenkel and Jovanovic (1980) develop a stochastic model to determine optimum reserve levels, combining issues on the demand for money for precautionary and for transaction motives. In this study Frenkel and Jovanovic (1980) find that the optimum level of reserves will depend on the variability of international payments, the alternative cost of maintaining reserves, and a variable measuring the country's scale.

One problem affecting most of the empirical studies on demand for reserves is that they fail to consider explicitly that changes in international reserves are only one of the possible policy tools that can be used to face external imbalances. In fact, countries undergoing payments difficulties have at least four alternatives for solving such problems: (1) they may alter the level of reserves maintained; (2) they may resort to policies aimed at expenditure switching; that is, they may devalue (Makin (1976)) or they may implement commercial policies; (3) they may borrow abroad; or (4) they may adjust their level of internal absorption. Theoretically, by means of some optimizing criterion, countries may decide simultaneously what proportion of the adjustment is to be obtained through each of the above instruments.

---

[10]See, for instance, various issues of the *World Economic Outlook: A Survey by the Staff of the International Monetary Fund.*

This decision will be influenced by such considerations as the costs associated with the use of each of these instruments and the nature of the external disequilibria (i.e., temporary or permanent shocks). While some authors have recognized, at a theoretical level, the simultaneous nature of decisions to maintain international reserves and adjust the exchange rate (Edwards (1983 a)), very few have explicitly considered the simultaneous decision to use reserves and foreign debt as alternative instruments for external adjustment. (One major exception is the work done recently by Eaton and Gersovitz (1980), (1981 a), and (1981 b).) Moreover, as far as I know, no author has considered the simultaneous decision to use reserves, debt, and exchange rate adjustment to correct external imbalances.

In a recent paper Eaton and Gersovitz (1980) consider the case of an economy where the decision regarding the level of reserves and debt to be maintained forms part of an overall portfolio problem. In their empirical study these authors find that foreign debt is a substitute for reserves, in the sense that changes in debt level are used (partly) to facilitate external adjustment, "smoothing" the level of internal absorption through periods of significant variations in exports revenue.

From the standpoint of economic policy, however, one major issue that Eaton and Gersovitz (1980) fail to consider is that while international reserves essentially fill a short-run role only—to facilitate smoother external adjustments—foreign debt plays both long-run and short-run roles. In the first place, as mentioned earlier, debt accumulation and disaccumulation help to reduce the costs associated with the external adjustment process. This is a short-run role. Second, foreign debt accumulation in each period will be linked to external savings (if international reserves remain unchanged, the new net debt will be equal to external savings), and hence will play a fundamental part in financing gross domestic investment. This is therefore an essentially long-run role. It is precisely this twofold role of foreign debt that makes it necessary for countries to design financial management programs that will make the short-run variations in reserves compatible with the needs for medium- and long-term external financing. Loser (1977) has stressed the need for financial management suited to foreign debt.

A Note on Optimum Foreign Debt, External Savings, and Economic Growth

The fact that debt accumulation is generally associated with higher foreign savings, and hence presumably with higher economic growth, has led some policymakers to feel that the optimum level of debt is relatively high. The argument usually runs along the following lines: "As more debt involves more capital accumulation, it is advisable to borrow while debt cost is less than the marginal productivity of capital." Moreover, in the economic literature some authors (e.g., Blanchard (1981)), have used dynamic optimization models to postulate that for a country such as Brazil the optimum debt level is approximately equal to 1.6 times GNP. Nevertheless, insofar as in practice debt/output ratios are substantially below 1, it is worth wondering what is wrong with the above argument.[11]

It appears obvious that there are at least three reasons for qualifying the notion that the optimum foreign debt level should be relatively high. First, it is possible that higher external savings are replacing domestic savings (Mikesell and Zinser (1973)). Depending on whether such substitution is total or partial, total saving will increase or remain constant.[12] In other words, in this case it is possible that the higher foreign debt is being used (partly) to finance higher consumption. This seems to have been the case in Chile in 1980–81, where, in spite of significant increases in the level of foreign debt, total savings remained constant, and even declined (see Edwards (1982 a)).

Second, a higher foreign debt will result in higher cost of foreign credit, even to the point of the country concerned being excluded from the international credit market, with all the consequential costs associated with such a measure. (See Section 4, below.) This prospect will of course lead to optimum debt levels significantly below those calculated using methods such as Blanchard's (1981).

Lastly, to the extent that the economy produces tradable and nontradable goods, the allocation of the new investment financed with higher foreign debt is a major consideration, because in the future the foreign debt will have to be repaid through current account surplus.

3. DEMAND FOR INTERNATIONAL RESERVES IN DEVELOPING COUNTRIES: EMPIRICAL RESULTS 1975–80

This section presents the results obtained from the empirical analysis of the determinants of the demand for international reserves for a selected group of developing countries during 1975–80. As discussed in the preceding section, the empirical analyses of Frenkel (1978, 1980), Heller and Khan (1978), and others, have shown that even after the international monetary system legally became a floating rate system in 1973, the various groups of countries have had stable demand for international reserves. The above authors further pointed out that a statistical difference is observed in behavior in regard to reserves before and after the collapse of the Bretton Woods system.

The results presented in this section will therefore be useful for projecting

---

[11] For debt/output ratios, see *World Debt Tables* of the World Bank.

[12] There is empirical evidence that external savings partly replace domestic savings.

future international liquidity needs of developing countries, assuming that the international financial system will retain its present form.

Generally speaking, the relevant literature has assumed that countries demand international liquidity both to finance international transactions and to face unforeseen international payments. Such studies have assumed that the demand for reserves is a stable function of a small number of variables that usually include the size of the country, the degree of variability of its international transactions, the degree of openness to the rest of the world, and the alternative cost of maintaining reserves.

Regarding the size of the country, most authors have assumed that the larger the country (in an economic sense), the larger its international transactions and the higher its needs for international reserves. In empirical studies, the size of a country is usually measured by its domestic product or its level of imports.

With respect to the variability of international transactions, it is assumed that the more variable such transactions are, the higher will be the desired amount of reserves. For empirical purposes various measures of international payment variability have been used: while some authors have used the export variability coefficient (Kenen and Yudin (1965), Iyoha (1976)), others have used some measurement of variation in the level of reserves as such (Heller and Khan (1978), Frenkel (1974), Saidi (1981), Edwards (1983 b)).

Most of the empirical studies have assumed that the more open the economy is to the rest of the world, the more vulnerable it is to exogenous shocks affecting its international liquidity position. Therefore, according to such authors, a greater degree of openness will entail greater demand for international reserves. The degree of openness is usually measured by the average propensity to import in each country. It should be borne in mind, however, that some authors (Heller (1966), Kelly (1970), Clark (1970 b)) have assumed that the relation between the degree of openness and the desired amount of reserves is negative.

Lastly, to the extent that by maintaining resources in the form of reserves countries are incurring a cost, the theoretical analyses have assumed that the alternative cost of maintaining reserves, measured by the domestic interest rate, negatively affects the desired level of reserves. Empirical studies, however, have repeatedly failed to find significant coefficients for this variable.[13] Among the reasons given to explain these results, the following stand out: (a) the variables used as proxies of the opportunity cost of maintaining reserves have been inadequate (Williamson (1973) and Bird (1978)); (b) since a high percentage of reserves are maintained in the form of interest-earning assets, the alternative cost is (approximately) zero, and the nonsignificant coefficient obtained in the empirical studies is to be expected.

---

[13] For a discussion of the subject, see Williamson (1973, p. 696) and Bird (1978, pp. 88–89).

In this paper two approaches have been followed to estimate the function of demand for international reserves in developing countries. First, following the traditional literature on the subject, demand equations have been estimated using a single-equation method. It has been assumed that the desired amount of international reserves depends on a variable measuring the scale of the country (GNP, y), a variable measuring the degree of openness (the average propensity to import, m), and a variable measuring the degree of export income variability (standard deviation of export series corrected by the trend, s). It was further assumed that the adequate specification of this demand for reserves is double logarithmic:

$$\log R = a_0 + a_1 \log y + a_2 \log m + a_3 \log s + u \qquad (1)$$

where, based on the above discussion, it is expected that $a_1 > 0$; $a_2 > 0$; and $a_3 > 0$. On the other hand, u is a random error with the usual characteristics.

The second approach takes into account the fact that international reserves are only one of the possible mechanisms used to face external imbalances. Specifically, it was assumed that in addition to changes in reserves, variations in the level of indebtedness could be used to relieve these disequilibria. Thus, the debt was also included as an additional explanatory variable when the demand for reserves was being estimated. The estimate was accordingly made using simultaneous estimation methods. Following the discussion in Section 2, it was assumed that the quantities demanded of both assets are determined simultaneously and may be expressed as follows:[14]

$$R^d = f(y,m,s,D) \qquad (2)$$
$$D^d = g(y,m,s,r,I) \qquad (3)$$

where R = international reserves and D = level of debt. On the other hand, I is the average propensity to invest and is included in equation (3) to account for the fact that in the long run foreign debt is used (partially) to finance the gross domestic investment of the country concerned. In this paper, the external debt demand function is not estimated, since to the extent that some countries have limited access to external credit, this function cannot be estimated using semi-conventional econometric methods. In this case we are dealing with a situation of markets in disequilibrium, which means it will be necessary to use econometric methods for disequilibrium situations, such as

---

[14]There are some nontrivial problems about estimating equations (2) and (3). In the first place, in the event that some countries face quantitative restrictions regarding the amount of foreign debt they may incur, we will face the problem of estimating markets in a state of disequilibrium. See Eaton and Gersovitz (1980). This problem is not explicitly approached here. Preliminary results, however, including this problem in the estimation process, show that there are no major changes in respect of the conclusions presented here.

those proposed by Goldfeld and Quandt (1976).[15] Consequently, in this paper, analysis will focus on estimating equation (2) using an instrumental variables method.

One difficulty in estimating equation (2) is that, as discussed in Section 2, in theory at least, countries may also use exchange adjustments to balance their external position. This means that in a general equilibrium setting it should be possible to estimate equation (2) simultaneously with an equation describing the determinants of such exchange rate adjustments.[16] This procedure was tried in the present context with negative success; hence the results obtained are not included in this paper.

Demand for Reserves in Developing Countries: 1975–80

Equation (1) was estimated using data for 19 developing countries for the period 1975–80. Cross-sectional data for each year were used for the estimation. (See Table 4, for a list of the countries included.) Table 1 contains the results obtained, where figures in parentheses are t statistics and MSE is the mean quadratic error of the regression.

These results are interesting in several ways. To begin with, the adjustments—as measured by both R^2 and MSE—are highly satisfactory, especially since we are dealing with cross-sectional data. Second, all coefficients have the expected sign and show remarkable stability over time. Furthermore, the result of an F test for stability was 1.584. Third, the fact that the coefficient of log y exceeds the unit value in all cases shows that there are diseconomies of scale in the holding of international reserves by developing countries. That is, economic growth in these countries (increases in y) will result in more than proportional increases in the desired amount of reserves. It is most interesting to find that this result, which had been obtained earlier by the author using data for the Bretton Woods period (Edwards (1983 a)), is still valid for the recent period.

Another interesting point about the results presented in Table 1 is that for every year the coefficient of log m—the average propensity to import—is positive and significant, showing that the more open the economy, the higher is the desired level of reserves. This result has some major implications in economic policy. To the extent that the trend toward greater openness (higher value of m) observed in developing countries in the recent past continues in the future, such countries will face growing needs for international liquidity.

As to the coefficient of log s, although it is positive in all cases, as

---

[15]See also Eaton and Gersovitz (1980). Preliminary results using maximum likelihood methods for markets in disequilibirum show that the conclusions presented here are not substantially affected.

[16]In particular, logit analysis may be used to determine the likelihood that a given country may devalue its currency to facilitate external adjustment.

Table 1. Estimation of Demand for International Reserves, 1975–80

$$\log Rn = a_0 + a_1 \log y_n + a_2 \log m_n + a_3 \log s_n + m_n$$
$$(OLS^1 = 1975{-}80)$$

	Const.	$\log Y_n$	$\log m_n$	$\log s_n$	R^2	MSE
1975	−2.678 (−1.766)	1.342 (6.452)	1.482 (2.842)	0.873 (1.923)	0.751	0.688
1976	−1.679 (−1.353)	1.142 (6.745)	0.752 (1.892)	0.782 (2.075)	0.779	0.486
1977	−2.106 (−1.692)	1.128 (7.082)	0.711 (1.941)	0.455 (1.058)	0.803	0.404
1978	−2.249 (−2.093)	1.117 (8.502)	0.767 (2.437)	0.230 (0.672)	0.855	0.286
1979	−2.603 (−1.932)	1.175 (7.210)	0.812 (2.011)	0.402 (1.047)	0.819	0.409
1980	−2.668 (−1.887)	1.140 (7.372)	0.890 (2.314)	0.236 (0.589)	0.793	0.481

Note: t-statistics are shown in parentheses.
[1] Ordinary least squares.

expected, it is only significant at conventional levels in 1975 and 1976. This contrasts with the results obtained earlier by the author (Edwards (1983 a) and (1984)) using data for 1964–72, where the coefficient of international payment variability proved significant in most of the cases.

Simultaneous Estimation of Demand for Reserves

As mentioned earlier, in addition to estimating equation (1), a log-linear version of equation (2) was simultaneously estimated taking into account the fact that the desired quantities of debt and reserves are simultaneously determined for the various countries. The results obtained are given in Table 2.

These results are quite interesting. In the first place, the negative coefficient of $\log D$ in all years supports the hypothetical substitutability of reserves and debt. The foregoing means, as in the case of Eaton and Gersovitz (1980), that reserves and debt are used as alternative mechanisms to deal with external adjustments. However, it should be noted that the degree of significance of these coefficients is not very high: 5 percent in 1975 and 1978 and 10 percent in the remaining years. Second, the results obtained for the coefficients of $\log y$, $\log m$, and $\log s$ in estimating the demand for reserves confirmed the conclusions arising from the single-equation analysis presented in Table 1, although $\log m$ is now negative in 1976. In particular,

Table 2. Demand for International Reserves
*(Regressions with combined cross-sectional and
time series data; Fuller-Batesse method)*

	1976	1977	1978	1979	1980
Constant	0.273	−1.025	−1.116	−1.027	−0.882
	(0.141)	(−0.753)	(−0.920)	(−0.636)	(−0.482)
Income	1.108	1.376	1.421	1.501	1.652
	(4.227)	(5.489)	(6.299)	(5.062)	(4.745)
Average propensity	−0.048	0.362	0.526	0.470	0.672
to import	(−0.775)	(0.967)	(1.659)	(1.159)	(1.972)
Export variability	0.840	0.532	0.423	0.589	0.473
	(1.578)	(1.204)	(1.139)	(1.316)	(1.468)
Debt	−0.581	−0.442	−0.497	−0.586	−0.796
	(−2.351)	(−1.572)	(−1.946)	(−1.658)	(−1.794)
R^2	0.663	0.805	0.860	0.811	0.790
MSE	0.610	0.404	0.281	0.437	0.504

Note: *t*-statistics are shown in parentheses.

for every year the coefficient of log y is greater than 1, again pointing to the presence of diseconomies of scale.

4. INTERNATIONAL RESERVES, FOREIGN DEBT, AND COUNTRY RISK

This section contains an empirical analysis of the relation between foreign debt, international reserves, and country risk. In the event that sovereign debtors may repudiate their debt without giving up (total) control over the assets financed with it, the international financial community will tend to charge interest rates proportionate to the likelihood of a given country failing to pay its debts. This probability of default is known as country risk.[17]

The assessment that banks and financial institutions make of the likelihood of default will be reflected in the terms under which loans are granted by them to the various countries. In an extreme case, should the probability be deemed very high, the country in question will be totally excluded from the credit market.[18] On the other hand, countries participating in the credit market will tend to pay higher interest rates (and/or to be granted shorter terms), as the likelihood that they may fail to pay is perceived to be higher. In the Eurocurrency market the various assessments of default probability will be reflected in varying degrees of spread above the London interbank offered rate (LIBOR) charged to the different countries.

[17]See, for instance, Buiter (1980), Eaton and Gersovitz (1980), (1981 a), (1981 b), Sachs and Cohen (1982), McDonald (1982), and Edwards (1983 b).
[18]Eaton and Gersovitz (1981 a), (1981 b), and Sachs and Cohen (1982).

In this section data on 727 public and publicly guaranteed loans granted to 19 developing countries between 1976 and 1980 are used to make an empirical analysis of the determinants of country risk. From an economic policy standpoint, the most interesting issue in this analysis is determining how appropriate management of foreign debt, international reserves, and other economic variables will allow a country's probability of default, as perceived by its creditors, to remain at comparatively low levels, thus aiding a continuous flow of foreign funds toward the country in question.

The Model

The results presented in this section are based on Feder and Just's (1977) model on country risk and probability of default. This model assumes monopolistic competition in the international financial market and that banks maximize expected profits. In this context, the interest rate applied to country n will be given by:[19]

$$r_n = \left[\eta_n / (\eta_n - 1)\right] (1/\theta) \left[P_n (x_n) / (1 - P_n(x_n)\right] \bar{h}_n \qquad (4)$$

where r_n is the spread over the LIBOR applied to country n; η_n is the elasticity of demand for foreign credit with respect to the interest rate; θ is equal to $(1 - (1 + r^*)^{-N})/r^*$, where r^* is the average cost of capital of banks and N is the average loan duration; P_n is the probability of default of n, which is assumed to depend upon a vector x of economic variables relevant to that country; and where h is the proportion of the loan that the bank expects to lose in case of default.

Assuming that the default probability $P_n (x_n)$ has a logistic distribution function, we may write:

$$P_n (x_n) = \left\{\exp (\beta_o + x_n \beta_n) / \left[1 + \exp (\beta_o + x_n \beta_n)\right]\right\} \qquad (5)$$

where x_n is the vector of probability determinants, and the β, the associated coefficient.

By combining equations (4) and (5), using the properties of the logistic distribution function, and making some simplifications, Feder and Just (1977) write the following estimable equation with combined cross-sectional and time-series data:

$$\log r_{nt} = \beta_o^* + \sum_{h=1}^{k} \beta_h x_n - \log \theta_t + u_n + v_t + w_{nt} \qquad (6)$$

where u_n, v_t and w_{nt} are stochastic errors; $\beta_o^* = \mu + \log h$, and μ is the expected value of $\log [\eta_n/1 - \eta_n]$.

---

[19]See Feder and Just (1977), p. 227.

The Data

In order to estimate equation (6) the determinants of the probability of default P_n must be established. Furthermore, in this paper the constant is estimated as $\gamma_o = \log \beta_o{}^* - \log \theta$.

In the present study a series of variables were included in vector x_n:

(a) The ratio of public and publicly guaranteed debt to domestic product. It is assumed that this variable, which has been used previously in country risk studies by Frank and Cline (1971), Feder and Just (1977), and Sachs (1981), among others, will have a positive coefficient showing that the higher the debt ratio, the greater the perceived default probability. Data on this variable were taken from the *World Debt Tables* of the World Bank.

(b) Ratio of public and publicly guaranteed debt service to exports. This variable measures the cash flow problems that a country may face in paying its foreign obligations. The coefficient of this variable is also expected to be positive, showing that the greater the proportion of export earnings that must be devoted to serve the debt, the higher the probability of default. Data for this variable were also taken from the *World Debt Tables*.

(c) Ratio of international reserves to output. This variable measures the level of international liquidity maintained by a country at a given time. It is assumed that the greater the value of this variable, the lower the probability of default assigned to this particular country by the international community. The data for computing these ratios were taken from the IMF publication *International Financial Statistics*.

(d) Loan duration. This variable measures the average term of the loans granted in year t to the country in question. Generally speaking, it may be assumed that international banks will use loan duration as an alternative (or additional) way to discriminate among countries with varying degrees of default probability. In this connection, it may be supposed that banks use spread and loan duration simultaneously as cover against that probability. Hence, a negative coefficient would be expected for this variable in the regression analysis. The variable was constructed as a weighted average of the duration of individual loans obtained by each country. The basic data were taken from the World Bank publication *Borrowing in International Capital Markets*.

(e) Average loan amount. This variable, based on information contained in *Borrowing in International Capital Markets*, measures the role of country size (from a financial standpoint) in determining the perceived probability of default.

(f) Ratio of gross domestic investment to output. This variable measures the future ability of the country to pay.[20] A greater propensity to invest points

---

[20]See Sachs (1981), Sachs and Cohen (1982), Edwards (1983 b).

to higher future growth of the country's output, hence lower probability of default. The coefficient of this variable is therefore expected to be negative in the regression analysis. Data on this variable were taken from *World Development Report*.

(g) Ratio of current account to output. This variable, also obtained from the *World Development Report*, measures the requirement of foreign resources to finance gross investment. Its sign in the regression should be negative, showing that greater deficit (lower surplus) increases the probability of default. In regressions where the propensity to invest and the current account ratio are simultaneously included, the coefficient of the latter is interpreted as follows: the greater the current account deficit, with a given propensity to invest, the larger the fraction of capital accumulation financed with external savings. It is then intuitively clear that the larger the fraction of gross investment financed with external savings, the higher the probability of default.

Other variables were also considered in the regression analysis as possible default probability determinants, such as output growth rate, export variability, and size of the public sector in the economy. Their inclusion, however, did not affect the results to any significant degree.

The dependent variable r was constructed for each country and each year as the (weighted) average spread over the LIBOR. The basic data on spread applied to individual loans were taken from *Borrowing in International Capital Markets*. (See Table 4, for a list of the countries included.)

The Results

If it is assumed that errors u_n, v_t, and w_{nt} in equation (6) have the following properties:

$$
\begin{aligned}
E\ (u_n v_t) &= E\ (u_n w_{nt}) = E\ (v_t w_{nt}) = 0 \\
E\ (u_n) &= E\ (v_t) = E\ (w_{nt}) = 0 \\
E\ (u_n u_m) &= 0 \quad \text{si } n \neq m \\
&= \sigma^2 \quad \text{si } n = m \\
E\ (v_t v_s) &= 0 \quad \text{si } s \neq t \\
&= \tau^2 \quad \text{si } s = t \\
E\ (w_{nt} w_{ms}) &= \Omega^2 \quad \text{si } n = m \text{ y } t = s \\
&= 0 \quad \text{other cases}
\end{aligned}
$$

Equation (6) may be estimated following the procedure suggested by Fuller and Batesse (1974) for estimating pooled cross-sectional and time series data.

The results obtained from estimating equation (6) with the Fuller and Batesse (1974) procedure are presented in Table 3.

In the first place, the results obtained show that the international financial community takes into account the behavior of a number of economic variables in order to determine the rate of interest to be charged to any one country. As expected, the coefficient of the external debt/output ratio is positive, which indicates that a higher volume of debt is reflected in a higher interest rate. While debt, reserves, and current account ratios are significant at 5 percent, the debt service ratio is significant at 10 percent.

What is surprising to a certain extent is the high value (in absolute terms) and high level of significance of the international reserves-to-output ratio. This result suggests that with prudent management of international reserves it is possible to keep the country risk premium relatively low. What is surprising, nonetheless, is that the coefficient of the international reserves ratio should differ significantly from the debt/output coefficient. This would mean that if foreign debt is used exclusively to finance accumulation of reserves, a country may in fact bring about a reduction in the default probability assigned to it by the international financial community. This is not easy to understand, since it is well known that reserves are a highly volatile international asset liable to decrease rapidly. A recent instance of a country where a policy of debt with equivalent accumulation of international reserves was followed on purpose was Chile during the period of so-called "neutral monetary policy" (1979–82). The recent results of the Chilean case (1981–83), however, have shown that in spite of that policy the international financial community began in early 1982 to perceive a significant increase in Chile's probability of default.

Table 3. Country Risk Determinants, 1976–80
(Regressions with combined cross-sectional and time series data; Fuller-Batesse method)

Variable	Coefficient	Asymptotic value of t statistic
Constant	0.329	1.422
Debt/output	0.622	2.512
Debt service/output	0.426	1.688
Reserves/output	−1.155	−2.164
Debt duration	−0.012	−0.648
Debt volume	−0.001	−1.340
Investment/output	−0.681	−0.681
Current account/output	0.435	1.966
σ^2	0.022	
τ^2	0.054	
Ω^2	0.019	

Nevertheless, the results presented in this section should produce some doubts on the international banks' ability to discern countries of different risk levels. The fact that some of the most important variables are not significant, or have an incorrect sign, lead one to believe that the origin of the current external indebtedness crisis lies to no small extent in the inability of banks to actually identify the pertinent economic variables. However, the results presented here will be useful for developing countries, as they clearly show what variables banks have taken into account to determine individual country risks. Of particular importance is the finding that if international reserves are suitably managed, the level of perceived probability can be kept at a reasonable level.

Probability of Default

The results presented in Table 3 together with assumptions on possible values of β_o may be used to obtain information on the evolution of the probability of default perceived in each year by the international financial community. By way of illustration, Table 4 presents the probabilities of default for each country between 1976 and 1980, obtained by assuming that $\beta_o = \gamma_o - 1.75$.

As may be observed in Table 4, the perceived probabilities of default, computed in this fashion, differ considerably every year from one country to another and fluctuate somewhat within each country over time. Nevertheless, it may be noted that even in 1980, the international financial community had not grasped the magnitude of the problems countries such as Mexico, Argentina, and Brazil were approaching. In fact, on the basis of Table 4, the perceived probability of default by these countries tended to decrease between 1977 and 1980.

Analysis of Residuals

The preceding sections discussed the economic determinants of default risk perceived by international banks. It is clear, however, that in addition to economic variables there are political considerations that will affect the probability of default perceived for any country. Generally speaking, it will be expected that countries with more political stability will be assigned lower probabilities of default.[21]

While our discussion in preceding sections has not explicitly considered political stability factors, it is possible that they are reflected by the residuals of the regression analysis. In particular, a hypothesis worth pursuing is: The

---

[21] For a discussion of the political risk connected with the spread of interest rates, see Aliber (1980), Dooley and Isard (1980).

Table 4. Estimated Probabilities of Nonperformance, 1976–80
(In percent)

Country	1976	1977	1978	1979	1980
Greece	8.3	7.9	7.9	7.4	7.6
Portugal	10.7	9.8	9.1	9.3	9.6
Spain	8.7	9.0	8.5	8.2	8.5
Yugoslavia	8.1	8.1	7.9	7.0	7.3
Argentina	7.8	8.1	8.1	6.8	5.4
Brazil	8.8	8.9	8.6	7.5	8.1
Colombia	10.1	9.6	8.7	7.9	9.5
Ecuador	7.3	7.5	7.3	7.5	7.5
Mexico	8.9	8.8	9.1	8.1	7.6
Panama	10.4	12.3	12.9	12.1	13.1
Uruguay	9.6	10.5	8.8	8.1	9.5
Venezuela	5.6	6.1	5.7	6.4	6.7
Indonesia	9.7	9.5	9.0	8.2	7.8
Korea	9.9	9.3	8.3	7.7	7.6
Malaysia	8.2	8.0	7.5	7.2	7.0
Philippines	7.5	7.8	7.4	7.4	7.8
Thailand	7.9	7.9	7.7	8.0	8.1
Ivory Coast	10.2	10.1	9.8	9.0	9.0
Morocco	8.9	9.0	9.1	9.2	10.0

most politically unstable countries will show positive (average) residuals in the regression analysis, whereas more stable countries will show negative residuals. If we define average residuals as

$$RES_n = \sum_{t=1}^{5} \left[r_{nt} - \Sigma \beta_h^{GLS} \chi_{nt} \right]/5 \qquad (7)$$

where r_{nt} is the observed spread and $\Sigma \beta_h^{GLS} \chi_{nt}$ is the estimated spread using the GLS (general-least-squares) method of Fuller and Batesse (1974). A positive value of *RES* says that, on average, the spread corresponding to that country exceeds the model prediction. This would be an indication that such a country would be politically unstable in relation to the sample.

Table 5 contains the results obtained from calculation of such average residuals. As may be observed, the results offer some comparatively surprising points. For instance, it is interesting that Spain should have the lowest residual, which, according to our hypothesis, would class it as one of the most politically stable countries in the sample. Conversely, countries with "strong" governments, such as Korea, turn up quite high on our "instability" scale. Undoubtedly, then, although the results presented in Table 5 are not lacking in interest, the analysis of the relation between perceived probability of default and political instability requires much more

Table 5. Average Residuals by Country

Country	Average Residual	Country	Average Residual
Greece	−0.113	Uruguay	0.076
Portugal	0.039	Venezuela	0.059
Spain	−0.202	Indonesia	0.078
Yugoslavia	0.253	Korea	−0.127
Argentina	0.185	Malaysia	−0.248
Brazil	0.111	Philippines	0.120
Colombia	−0.078	Thailand	−0.061
Ecuador	0.117	Ivory Coast	0.225
Mexico	−0.379	Morocco	0.087
Panama	−0.142		

work. The use of residuals obtained from regressions like equation (6) appears to be an interesting avenue along which to conduct this line of research.

5. NOTE ON THE DYNAMIC ADJUSTMENT OF INTERNATIONAL RESERVES AND MONETARY POLICY[22]

A number of studies have analyzed the dynamic adjustment process of demand for international reserves.[23] In general, these papers show that the movement of the logarithm of international reserves over time responds to the discrepancy between desired reserves (log R^*) and reserves actually maintained. In this context, the following partial adjustment equation has been considered:

$$\log R_t - \log R_{t-1} = \alpha \left[\log R_t^* - \log R_{t-1}\right] \qquad (8)$$

Notwithstanding, in an economy with a fixed exchange rate the dynamic behavior of international reserves will *not* respond only to the discrepancy between desired and actual reserves, but also to the situation in the monetary sector of the economy. In particular, the movement of international reserves will be affected by excess demand for (or supply of) money: with a given domestic credit, excess demand for money will result in an increase in actual international reserves. The reason for this is, as indicated by the essential

---

[22]This section is partly based on Edwards (1983 a).

[23]See Clark (1970 b), Iyoha (1976), Bilson and Frenkel (1979), Heller and Kahn (1978), Edwards (1982 b), (1983 a), and (1984).

message of the monetary approach to the balance of payments (Frenkel and Johnson (1976)), that in an economy with fixed exchange rates the quantity of money—both nominal and real—is determined by demand conditions.

In the event that the movement of international reserves is actually affected by imbalance in the monetary market, the partial adjustment equation (8) should be modified to take this into account. Furthermore, exclusion of monetary influence in the empirical formulation might result in biased coefficients in the estimation of demand for reserves. One way to include monetary considerations in the dynamic analysis of demand for reserves, and to integrate the analysis with the monetary approach to the balance of payments, is to use the following equation:

$$
\begin{aligned}
\log R_t - \log R_{t-1} = \alpha \left[\log R_t^* - \log R_{t-1} \right] \\
+ \lambda \left\{ \log M_t^* - \log M_{t-1} \right\}
\end{aligned}
\tag{9}
$$

Equation (9) indicates that the movements of (real) international reserves over time respond to two factors: discrepancies between desired and actual reserves and excess demand for money. While parameter λ captures the speed of adjustment between desired and actual reserves, parameter α gives the proportion of excess demands for money resolved, on average, by accumulation of reserves.

Equation (9) may be estimated in different ways. One, for example, is to postulate the structural forms of $\log R^*$ and $\log M^*$, insert the resulting expressions in equation (9), and estimate a reduced form, using ordinary least squares (OLS), for reserves actually maintained. One difficulty about this procedure, however, is that in the event that both demand for reserves and demand for money depend upon common variables (income level, for instance), it will not be possible to distinguish the individual coefficients of each function. An alternative procedure used in this section is to estimate equation (9) in two stages. In the first stage a partial adjustment equation is estimated for the demand for money:

$$
\log M_t - \log M_{t-1} = \zeta (\log M_t^* - \log M_{t-1})
\tag{10}
$$

In the estimation of equation (10) both M and M^* are expressed in real terms, and it is assumed that long-run demand for money is characterized by a Cagan function.

$$
\log M_t = b_o + b_1 \log y_t - b_2 \pi_t^e
\tag{11}
$$

Therefore the equation to be estimated is:

$$
\log M_t = \zeta b_o + \zeta b_1 \log y_t - \zeta b_2 \pi_t^e + (1 - \zeta) \log M_{t-1}
\tag{12}
$$

From the estimation of equation (12), the coefficients of long-run demand for money are obtained. Then it is possible to estimate the desired quantity of money at any time, $\log \hat{M}^*$. Having obtained these values and assuming that long-term demand for international reserves may be expressed as follows:

$$\log R_t = a_1 + a_2 \log y_t + a_3 \log m_t + a_4 \log s_t + v \quad (13)$$

the following equation may be obtained for dynamic analysis of adjustment of international reserves:

$$\log R_t = \alpha\, a_1 + \alpha\, a_2 \log y_t + \alpha\, a_3 \log m_t + \alpha\, a_4 \log s_t$$
$$+ (1 - \alpha) \log R_{t-1} + \lambda \left\{ \log \hat{M}_t^* - \log M_{t-1} \right\} \quad (14)$$

where $\log \hat{M}_t^*$ is the estimated value of the desired quantity of money, using the coefficients obtained in the first stage of our process. All the equations contained in this section assume that both the quantity of reserves and the quantity of money are expressed in real terms. This assumption was retained for the empirical estimation of the model.

Empirical Results

Equation (14) was estimated using combined cross-sectional and time-series data for 23 developing countries during 1965 and 1972. The countries considered, as well as the period of time used, respond to the need to base the analysis on cases of fixed parity. For that reason the period following the collapse of the Bretton Woods system was excluded from the analysis. In addition, the sample countries maintained a fixed exchange rate throughout the period, which simplified the use of variables expressed in a common currency (U.S. dollars).

In the first stage—estimation of demand for money—all variables were expressed in U.S. dollars and expected inflation was replaced by actual inflation. A well-known difficulty about dynamic analyses using pooled time-series and cross-sectional data is that in the event that the error contains a country-specific element the use of OLS will result in biased coefficients. For this reason, equation (14) was estimated using dummy country variables. In the second stage of the estimation process the coefficients obtained in the first stage were used to construct the excess demand for money ($\log \hat{M}^*_{nt} - \log M_{nt-1}$) variable to be used for estimating equation (14). Estimation of this equation using the OLS method with dummy country variables yielded the following result:

$$\log R_{nt} = \alpha\, a_{1n} + 0.795 \log y_{nt} + 0.061 \log m_{nt} + 0.026 \log s_{nt}$$
$$(4.675) \qquad\qquad (0.345) \qquad\qquad (0.333)$$
$$+ 0.736 \log R_{nt-1} + 0.299 \left\{ \log M_{nt}^* - \log M_{nt-1} \right\} \quad (15)$$
$$(9.873) \qquad\qquad (1.816) \quad R^2 = 0.984$$

As can be seen, all the coefficients have the expected signs. Furthermore, the coefficients of the variables of scale and lagged reserves are 5 percent significant, whereas the coefficient of excess demand for money is 10 percent significant. These results show that for these countries during this period, the movements of international reserves responded with nearly the same speed to monetary imbalances and to discrepancies between actual and desired reserves. On average, a unit imbalance between desired and actual reserves is corrected in 26.4 percent in the first year through changes in the amount of reserves. On the other hand, a unit imbalance between desired and actual quantity of money will be corrected in 30 percent in that year by accumulation or disaccumulation of international reserves.

The interesting point about these results is that they explicitly integrate the monetary sector imbalance with the analysis of demand for international reserves. They show that even if a country is obviously deficient in reserves (i.e., when actual reserves are very much lower than desired reserves), it can disaccumulate reserves if the monetary policy leads to an excess supply of money. From the standpoint of external management policy, these results emphasize the need to maintain compatible monetary and external policies. Although the results were obtained for countries with a fixed rate of exchange, the main lesson—the need to maintain coherent policies—extends to any kind of exchange rate arrangement.

6. SOME CONSIDERATIONS ON THE LATIN AMERICAN CASE

In the past few years the Latin American countries have significantly increased their foreign debt. In some cases public and publicly guaranteed debt has exceeded 40 percent of gross domestic product. Table 6 presents information connected with the level of public debt in Latin American countries in 1980. Column 1 contains the level of public and publicly guaranteed debt (D) on December 31, 1980, in millions of U.S. dollars. Column 2 in turn presents the level of public and publicly guaranteed debt obtained from private creditors, also in millions of U.S. dollars (DAP).

Columns 4 to 6 contain some interesting debt ratios. While column 4 gives the ratio of public and publicly guaranteed debt to gross domestic product (D/y), column 5 contains the ratio of total service for this debt to product (ST/y), and column 6 contains the ratio of total debt service to exports (ST/x). The first quartile (Q_1), the median (M), and the third quartile (Q_3) are shown at the bottom of the table. Column 7 presents the percentage of public and publicly guaranteed debt subject to variable interest rate (LIBOR plus a specified spread, for example). Lastly, column 7 contains information for selected countries on private non–publicly guaranteed debt.

Table 6. External Debt of Latin American Countries, 1980

Country	(1) D	(2) DAP	(3) DPSG	(4) D/y	(5) St/y	(6) St/x	(7) T/V
	(In millions of U.S. dollars)			(In percent)			
Argentina	10,285	8,373	6,593	15.4	3.0	17.7	57.7
Bolivia	2,124	994	n.a.	36.4	4.7	25.9	32.1
Brazil	38,260	31,844	16,605	16.6	3.5	34.5	67.6
Colombia	4,294	1,848	525	13.2	1.7	10.0	33.9
Costa Rica	1,585	911	n.a.	34.3	4.3	16.4	48.1
Chile	4,885	3,317	4,693	18.0	5.2	22.9	51.8
Dominican Republic	1,186	476	253	18.3	2.4	12.2	43.4
Ecuador	2,671	2,017	n.a.	24.5	3.7	13.9	62.7
El Salvador	509	11	n.a.	15.3	1.2	3.7	3.6
Guatemala	541	1	n.a.	6.9	0.8	3.5	0.2
Haiti	249	9	n.a.	17.8	0.9	4.1	3.0
Honduras	892	186	191	36.9	3.9	9.9	19.4
Mexico	33,490	28,998	n.a.	20.6	4.9	32.1	70.6
Nicaragua	1,496	586	n.a.	71.9	3.8	14.9	3.9
Panama	2,276	1,721	n.a.	71.3	14.5	14.0	54.0
Paraguay	667	271	151	15.5	2.1	12.9	9.3
Peru	6,204	3,046	n.a.	33.7	8.1	25.2	25.2
Uruguay	1,041	719	211	10.7	1.9	23.2	23.2
Venezuela	10,867	10,444	n.a.	17.9	4.9	13.2	77.9
Q_1	—	—	—	15.4	1.9	12.2	—
M	—	—	—	18.0	3.7	14.0	—
Q_3	—	—	—	34.3	4.9	22.9	—

Source: World Bank, *World Debt Tables.*
n.a. indicates data not available.

The information given in Table 6 is useful to analyze the degree of (relative) difficulty in which some countries of the region already found themselves in 1980. It is interesting, in the first place, to consider the countries whose debt-to-GDP ratio (D/y) and debt service-to-export ratio are in the top part of the distribution of these two variables. In particular, the following countries have their debt ratio in the top 25 percent: Costa Rica (34.3 percent), Bolivia (36.4 percent), Honduras (36.9 percent), Panama (71.3 percent), and Nicaragua (71.9 percent). In addition, in the following countries the debt service-to-export ratio is in the top 25 percent of the distribution: Chile (22.9 percent), Bolivia (25.9 percent), Peru (31.9 percent), Mexico (32.1 percent), and Brazil (34.5 percent). As may be observed, most of the countries that are facing serious difficulties today in the matter of external payments are found in one of these two groups. Table 7 provides information on the indebtedness of these countries in 1981.

Table 7. External Debt of Latin American Countries, 1981

Country	(1) D	(2) DAP	(3) DPSG	(4) D/y	(5) St/y	(6) St/x	(7) T/V
	(In millions of U.S. dollars)			*(In percent)*			
Argentina	10,506	10,930	12,166	n.a.	n.a.	18.2	59.4
Bolivia	2,422	1,174	n.a.	31.9	3.7	26.9	35.2
Brazil	43,999	44,794	19,792	16.0	3.1	31.9	68.2
Colombia	5,076	3,168	902	14.0	2.0	8.4	40.1
Costa Rica	1,854	1,103	n.a.	14.1	7.2	8.5	45.2
Chile	4,423	3,229	8,138	14.1	5.3	27.2	48.7
Dominican Republic	1,261	471	232	n.a.	n.a.	n.a.	40.5
Ecuador	3,392	2,621	n.a.	26.9	4.3	17.9	62.7
El Salvador	664	355	n.a.	19.3	1.3	n.a.	2.5
Guatemala	684	302	n.a.	8.0	0.6	3.3	1.2
Haiti	295	71	n.a.	18.7	1.3	5.4	1.9
Honduras	1,223	414	172	47.1	4.4	12.7	22.8
Mexico	42,642	38,711	n.a.	18.5	3.7	28.2	75.0
Nicaragua	1,975	772	n.a.	77.4	7.2	n.a.	2.7
Panama	2,377	1,817	n.a.	64.5	13.4	11.5	52.3
Paraguay	707	455	133	13.8	1.4	n.a.	7.5
Peru	5,974	3,956	n.a.	28.6	9.1	44.9	25.8
Uruguay	1,312	1,084	326	12.2	1.6	n.a.	33.5
Venezuela	11,352	11,168	n.a.	163.9	4.5	12.5	81.3

Source: World Bank, *World Debt Tables.*
n.a. indicates data not available.

The increased foreign debt of the countries of the region has been due to a number of reasons. On the one hand, starting in the mid-1970s the Eurocurrency markets made significant amounts of resources available to developing nations. That is, with the boom in the international private capital markets (and with the recycling of petrodollars), the supply of external funds available to developing countries grew significantly. On the other hand, the financial reforms implemented in some Latin American countries (particularly in the Southern Cone) toward the late 1970s resulted in major increases in demand for external funds in those countries.

One extremely important fact that is not properly reflected in Tables 6 and 7 is that a significant volume of the new debt was channeled to the private sector of the debtor countries. Thus, for instance, the private foreign debt of Costa Rica totaled about $1,200 million in 1980, whereas public foreign debt amounted to $1,585 million. In Chile, the private sector foreign debt was approximately $10,000 million in 1981, while public and publicly guaranteed debt amounted to only $5,400 million.[24] In Mexico, the private sector foreign debt amounts to about $35,000 million at the present time (1983).

The growing significance of private external debt in the recent past requires further analysis. Among major issues connected with this topic, the following at least should be mentioned.

(a) Effective regulation and supervision of domestic intermediation activity with respect to the new external resources. In general, as mentioned before, the new foreign debt has gone side by side with a process of liberalization of the domestic-financing sector. Once the financial "repression" ends, new banks and financial institutions emerge in the domestic market, intermediating internal and external resources. However, as shown very clearly by recent experience in Chile and Argentina, the lack of experience of such institutions may result in disastrous management of such resources, which in both the cases mentioned ended in large losses that were eventually absorbed—totally or partially—by the respective governments (i.e., the taxpayers). This points to a need for designing extremely efficient policies for regulating the financial and banking sector. Only in this way will it be possible to prevent new flows of external resources from being misused.

(b) Determination of an "optimum" foreign debt policy. To the extent that increases in foreign debt, as shown in Section 4 above, result in growing cost of debt, it is advisable to restrict the volume of a country's debt. This argument in favor of intervening in the external loan market emerges from direct application of the idea of an "optimum tariff." In fact, while debt cost grows with a larger volume of debt, the country concerned will benefit from imposing a tax on debt equal to $1/e$, where e is the elasticity of the external funds supply curve in respect of the interest rate. It should be noted, however, that the relevant supply curve should take account of perceptions of the risk of default as felt by both creditor and debtor.

A salient feature of the behavior of the Latin American countries is that in spite of considerable increase in foreign debt no equivalent increase has been observed in total savings. While in some cases total savings have remained practically constant (Argentina and Brazil), in others, total savings have dropped significantly as percentage of the product (Chile, Peru, Uruguay). The exceptions to this rule are mainly Colombia and Venezuela.[25] This suggests, as we find in the relevant literature, that a not negligible portion of the new foreign debt has been used in the region to finance consumption.

Under present circumstances, when a significant number of Latin American countries have difficulty in paying their foreign debt, it seems obvious that new efforts must be made in the management of international reserves. In particular, in the event that access to foreign credit is

---

[24]See Edwards (1982 a).
[25]See discussion in Bacha and Díaz Alejandro (1982).

(temporarily) reduced in the next few years, the need for reserves to face external payment difficulties will increase. This fact arises from the results of the empirical analysis contained in Section 4 above and shows that if the use of one of the adjustment instruments utilized to date (debt) is limited, a need to make more intensive use of other available instruments will arise.

In this connection, for the next few years economic discussion in the region should focus on the design of an appropriate exchange rate policy. Recent exchange rate crises in a number of countries of the region (Argentina, Chile, Mexico) show that this precisely has been an area where economic management has been deficient. First of all, it is essential to include in the analysis the fact that these countries are situated in a world of (semi-) floating exchange rates. This means that pegging the exchange rate to a given currency (the dollar, for instance) automatically means floating with respect to the other currencies of industrial countries. As the recent (1981–82) experience in Chile has shown, this may turn out to be disastrous when the value of the currency to which the domestic currency has been pegged varies widely in the short term. The foregoing discussion, then, indicates that under present institutional arrangements prevailing in the international monetary system, the exchange policy becomes even more complex. An area of applied research that the economic policymakers of the region would do well to examine in detail is the determination of "currency baskets" suitable for guiding the country's exchange rate policy.

The second major issue is the determination of exchange rate rules. To date many countries of the area, at varying periods, have followed exchange rules tending to keep a fixed real exchange rate. Such rules known as purchasing power parity (PPP) may, however, prove detrimental to the operation of the economy, in that they set up rigid links between the exchange rate, domestic prices, and international prices. As the real exchange rate is a key relative price, it is important that the exchange rate policy abstain from inhibiting its equilibrium changes.[26]

Lastly, in relation to exchange rate policy, it is also important to define the optimum degree of float or pegging. Generally speaking, from a theoretical standpoint, the optimum degree of exchange rate flexibility will depend on variables such as the degree of openness of the economy and the nature of the shocks affecting it. Frenkel and Aizenman (1982) have stated that the optimum exchange rate will tend to be more rigid as the variance of real shocks affecting the supply of goods and services is greater.

7. FINAL COMMENTS

This paper has analyzed various aspects of the external adjustment process in developing countries. Emphasis has been laid in particular on the role that

[26]See in this respect Dornbusch (1982) and Frenkel (1983).

international reserves and foreign debt play in such adjustment process. The empirical analysis based on data for 19 selected developing countries during the period 1975–80 shows that these countries have made use of reserves and debt as substitutes in the adjustment process.

The empirical analysis also reveals that management of both these variables—level of reserves and level of debt—affect the perception of the international financial community regarding the risk involved in lending to a given country. Higher reserves reduce the perceived country risk, while higher foreign debt increases it. This greater perceived risk will in general bring about different effects among the smaller countries. First, it will take the form of higher cost of any foreign loan they may obtain, and/or a shorter loan term. Second, if the increased risk perceived is high enough it may result in exclusion of the country in question from the foreign loan market. This suggests that in the event that developing countries wish to keep up a stable flow of external funds, they should show care in managing their reserve and debt levels in order not to raise the level of perceived risk above a conservative figure.

In this paper, also, the dynamic analysis of demand for international reserves was integrated with the analysis of equilibrium conditions in the monetary sector of the economy. The analysis performed for 23 selected developing countries with a fixed exchange rate during the period immediately prior to the collapse of the Bretton Woods system points out that the amount of reserves maintained by a country will move over time for two reasons: first, the movement will tend to be related to discrepancies between the quantity of reserves actually kept by a country and the quantity of reserves desired in the long term. Second, the movement of reserves over time will also respond to excess demand in the monetary market. This result, which is consonant with the fundamental propositions of the modern approach to the balance of payments in a monetary economy, shows that international reserve management by the economic authorities should take particular account of monetary issues.

Finally, Section 6 of this paper contains some reflections about the Latin American case. In this connection, it is stated here that in the event that a number of countries of the region face difficulties to service their foreign debt, they will face restrictions for using (new) debt as an active instrument for facilitating the adjustment process in the next few years. This suggests that these countries will face even greater needs for international reserves in the next few years. This section also points out the need to outline effective exchange rate policies that will allow these countries to face situations of external imbalance with the lowest possible cost.

BIBLIOGRAPHY

Aliber, Robert Z., "The Interest Parity Theorem: A Reinterpretation," *Journal of Political Economy*, Vol. 88 (April 1980), pp. 370–84.

Bacha, Edmar Lisboa, and Carlos F. Díaz Alejandro, "*International Financial Intermediation: A Long and Tropical View*" (Princeton, New Jersey: Princeton University Press, May 1982).

Bilson, John F.0., and Jacob A. Frenkel, "Dynamic Adjustment and the Demand for International Reserves," NBER Working Paper, No. 407 (Cambridge, Massachusetts: National Bureau of Economic Research, November 1979).

Bird, Graham, *The International Monetary System and the Less Developed Countries* (London: Macmillan, 1978).

Blanchard, Oliver Jean, "Debt and the Current Account Deficit in Brazil," Harvard Institute of Economic Research Discussion Paper Series, No. 882 (Cambridge, Massachusetts: Harvard University Press, November 1981).

Brown, Wier M., *The External Liquidity of an Advanced Country*, Princeton Studies in International Finance, No. 14 (Princeton, New Jersey: Princeton University Press, 1964).

Buiter, Willem "Implications for the Adjustment Process of International Asset Risks: Exchange Controls, Intervention and Policy Risk, and Sovereign Risk," NBER Working Paper, No. 516 (Cambridge, Massachusetts: National Bureau of Economic Research, July 1980).

Claasen, Emil-Maria, "The Optimizing Approach to the Demand for International Reserves: A Survey," in *Recent Issues in International Monetary Economics*, ed. by Emil-Maria Claasen and Pascal Salin (Amsterdam: North-Holland, 1976), pp. 73–116.

Clark, Peter B. (1970 a), "Optimum International Reserves and the Speed of Adjustment," *Journal of Political Economy*, Vol. 78 (March–April 1970), pp. 356–76.

———, (1970 b), "Demand for International Reserves: A Cross-Country Analysis," *Canadian Journal of Economics*, Vol. 3 (November 1970), pp. 577–94.

Clower, Robert, and Richard Lipsey, "The Present State of International Liquidity Theory," *American Economic Review*, Vol. 58 (May 1968), pp. 586–95.

Crockett, Andrew D., "Control Over International Reserves," *Staff Papers*, International Monetary Fund (Washington), Vol. 25 (March 1978), pp. 1–24.

Dooley, Michael P., and Peter Isard, "Capital Controls, Political Risk and Deviations from Interest Rate Parity," *Journal of Political Economy*, Vol. 88 (April 1980), pp. 370–84.

Dornbusch, Rudiger, "PPP Exchange-Rate Rules and Macroeconomic Stability," *Journal of Political Economy*, Vol. 90 (February 1982), pp. 158–65.

———, and Stanley Fischer, "Exchange Rates and the Current Account," *American Economic Review*, Vol. 70 (December 1980), pp. 960–71.

Eaton, Jonathan, and Mark Gersovitz, "LDC Participation in International Financial Markets: Debt and Reserves," *Journal of Development Economics*, Vol. 7 (March 1980), pp. 3–21.

———(1981 a), "Debt with Potential Repudiation: Theoretical and Empirical Analysis," *Review of Economic Studies*, Vol. 48 (April 1981), pp. 289–309.

———(1981 b), *Poor-Country Borrowing in Private Financial Markets and the Repudiation Issue*, Princeton Studies in International Finance, No. 47 (Princeton, New Jersey: Princeton University Press, June 1981).

Edwards, Sebastian (1982 a), "Deuda externa, ahorro domestico y crecimiento económico en Chile: Una perspectiva de largo plazo, 1982–1990," *Estudios Internacionales*, Vol. 15 (July–September 1982), pp. 260–275.

———(1982 b), "Ajuste cambiario y reservas internacionales: Un analasis empírico," *Cuadernos de Economia*, Vol. 19 (August 1982), pp. 193–202.

———(1983 a), "The Demand for International Reserves and Monetary Equilibrium: Some Evidence from Developing Countries," UCLA Working Paper No. 293 (March 1983).

———(1983 b), "The Demand for International Reserves and Exchange Rate Adjustments. The Case of LDCs, 1964–1972," *Economica*, Vol. 50 (August 1983), pp. 269–89.

———(1983 c), "LDC's Foreign Borrowing and Default Risk: An Empirical Investigation," NBER Working Paper, No. 1172 (Cambridge, Massachusetts: National Bureau of Economic Research, July 1983).

———, "La demanda por liquidez internacional de los países en desarrollo: Un análisis dinámico," *El Trimestre Económico*, Vol. 51(1), No. 21 (January–March, 1984), pp. 131–46.

Feder, Gershon, and Richard E. Just, "An Analysis of Credit Terms in the Eurodollar Market," *European Economic Review*, Vol. 9 (May 1977), pp. 221–43.

Fisher, Franklin M., "Tests of Equality Between Sets of Coefficients in Two Linear Regressions: An Expository Note," *Econometrica*, Vol. 38 (March 1970), pp. 361–66.

Flanders, M. June, *The Demand for International Reserves*, Princeton Studies in International Finance, No. 27 (Princeton, New Jersey: Princeton University Press, 1971).

Frank, Charles R., and William R. Cline, "Measurement of Debt Servicing Capacity: An Application of Discriminant Analysis," *Journal of International Economics*, Vol. 1 (August 1971), pp. 327–44.

Frenkel, Jacob A., "The Demand for International Reserves by Developed and Less Developed Countries," *Economica*, Vol. 41 (February 1974), pp. 14–24.

———, "International Reserves: Pegged Exchange Rates and Managed Float," in *Public Policies in Open Economies*, ed. by Karl Brunner and Allan H. Meltzer (Amsterdam; New York: North-Holland, 1978), pp. 111–140.

———, "The Demand for International Reserves Under Pegged and Flexible Exchange Rate Regimes and Aspects of the Economics of Managed Float," in *The Function of Floating Exchange Rates: Theory, Guidance and Policy Implications*, ed. by David Bigman and Teizo Taya (Cambridge, Massachusetts: Ballinger 1980), pp. 169–95.

———, "International Liquidity and Monetary Control," NBER Working Paper, No. 1118 (Cambridge, Massachusetts: National Bureau of Economic Research, May 1983).

———, and J. Aizenman, "Aspects of the Optimal Management of Exchange Rates," *Journal of International Economics*, Vol. 12 (November 1982), pp. 231–56.

————, and Harry G. Johnson, eds., *The Monetary Approach to the Balance of Payments* (Toronto: University of Toronto Press, 1976).

————, and Boyan Jovanovic, "On Transactions and Precautionary Demand for Money," *Quarterly Journal of Economics*, Vol. 95 (August 1980), pp. 25–43.

————, "Optimal International Reserves: A Stochastic Framework," *Economic Journal*, Vol. 91 (June 1981), pp. 507–14.

Fuller, Wayne A., and George E. Batesse, "Estimation of Linear Models with Crossed-Error Structure," *Journal of Econometrics*, Vol. 2 (May 1974), pp. 67–78.

Goldfeld, Stephen M., and Richard E. Quandt, eds., *Studies in New Linear Estimation* (Cambridge, Massachusetts: Ballinger, 1976).

Gruebel, Herbert G., "The Demand for International Reserves: A Critical Review of the Literature," *Journal of Economic Literature*, Vol. 9 (December 1971), pp. 1148–66.

Hamada, Koichi, and Kazuo Veda, "Random Walks and the Theory of Optimal International Reserves, *Economics Journal*, Vol. 87 (December 1977), pp. 722–42.

Harberger, Arnold C., and Sebastian Edwards, "Lessons of Experience Under Fixed Exchange Rates," in *The Theory and Experience of Economic Development*, ed. by Mark Gersovitz, and others (London; Boston: Allen and Unwin, 1982), pp. 183–93.

Heller, H. Robert, "Optimal International Reserves," *Economic Journal*, Vol. 76 (June 1966), pp. 296–311.

————, and Mohsin S. Khan, "The Demand for International Reserves Under Fixed and Floating Exchange Rates," *Staff Papers*, International Monetary Fund (Washington), Vol. 25 (December 1978), pp. 623–49.

Hipple, F. Steb, *The Disturbance Approach to the Demand for International Reserves*, Princeton Studies in International Finance, No. 35 (Princeton, New Jersey: Princeton University Press, May 1974).

Iyoha, Milton A., "Demand for International Reserves in Less Developed Countries: A Distributed Lag Specification," *Review of Economics and Statistics*, Vol. 58 (August 1976), pp. 351–55.

Kelly, Michael G., "The Demand for International Reserves," *American Economic Review*, Vol. 60 (September 1970), pp. 655–67.

Kenen, Peter B., and Elinor B. Yudin, "The Demand for International Reserves," *Review of Economics and Statistics*, Vol. 47 (August 1965), pp. 242–50.

Loser, Claudio M., "External Debt Management and Balance of Payments Policies," *Staff Papers*, International Monetary Fund (Washington), Vol. 24 (March 1977), pp. 168–92.

McDonald, Donogh C., "Debt Capacity and Developing Country Borrowing: A Survey of the Literature," *Staff Papers*, International Monetary Fund (Washington), Vol. 29 (December 1982), pp. 603–46.

Machlup, Fritz, *The Need for Monetary Reserves*, reprinted in *International Finance* (Princeton, New Jersey: 1966).

Makin, John H., "Exchange Rate Flexibility and the Demand for International Reserves," *Weltwirtschaftliches Archiv* (Kiel), Vol. 110 (1976), pp. 229–43.

Mikesell, Raymond F., and James E. Zinser, "The Nature of the Savings Function in Developing Countries: A Survey of the Theoretical and Empirical Literature," *Journal of Economic Literature*, Vol. 11 (March 1973), pp. 1–26.

Nerlove, Marc, "Further Evidence on the Estimation of Dynamic Economic Relations from a Time Series of Cross Sections," *Econometrica*, Vol. 39 (March 1971), pp. 359–82.

Obstfeld, Maurice, "Aggregate Spending and the Terms of Trade: Is There a Laursen-Metzler Effect?" *Quarterly Journal of Economics*, Vol. 97 (May 1982), pp. 251–70.

Olivera, Julio H.G., "A Note on the Optimal Rate of Growth of International Reserves," *Journal of Political Economy*, Vol. 77 (March–April 1969), pp. 245–48.

Ripley, Duncan, and Esther C. Suss, "An Approach to the Estimation of Inequality in Reserve Distribution," *Staff Papers*, International Monetary Fund (Washington), Vol. 21 (November 1974), pp. 789–99.

Rodríguez, Carlos Alfredo, "The Role of Trade Flows in Exchange Rate Determination: A Rational Expectations Approach," *Journal of Political Economy*, Vol. 88 (December 1980), pp. 1148–58.

Sachs, Jeffrey, "The Current Account and Macroeconomic Adjustment in the 1970s," *Brookings Papers on Economic Activity: 1* (1981), The Brookings Institution (Washington), pp. 201–82.

———, "LDC Debt in the 1980s: Risk and Reforms," in *Crises in the Economic and Financial Structure*, ed. by Paul Wachtel (Lexington, Massachusetts: Lexington Books, 1982), pp. 197–243.

———, and Daniel Cohen, "LDC Borrowing with Default Risk," NBER Working Paper, No. 925 (Cambridge, Massachusetts: National Bureau of Economic Research, July 1982).

Saidi, Nasser, "The Square-Root Law, Uncertainty and International Reserves Under Alternative Regimes: Canadian Experience, 1950–1976," *Journal of Monetary Economics*, Vol. 7 (May 1981), pp. 271–90.

Svensson, Lars E.O., and Assaf Razin, "The Terms of Trade and the Current Account: The Harberger-Laursen-Metzler Effect," *Journal of Political Economy*, Vol. 91 (February 1983), pp. 97–125.

von Furstenberg, George M., "New Estimates of the Demand for Non-Gold Reserves Under Floating Exchange Rates," *Journal of International Money and Finance*, Vol. 1 (April 1982), pp. 81–95.

Whalen, Edward L., "A Rationalization of the Precautionary Demand for Cash," *Quarterly Journal of Economics*, Vol. 80 (May 1966), pp. 314–24.

Williamson, John, "International Liquidity: A Survey," *Economic Journal*, Vol. 83 (September 1973), pp. 685–746.

Zellner, Arnold, "An Efficient Method of Estimating Seemingly Unrelated Regressions and Tests and Aggregation Bias," *Journal of the American Statistical Association*, Vol. 57 (June 1962), pp. 348–68.

Commentary*

JUAN GUILLERMO ESPINOSA

I would first like to extend my thanks, not formally, but very sincerely to the organizers, and particularly the International Monetary Fund, for having afforded us the opportunity to have such frank and systematic discussions of our common concerns about the regional and international economic and financial situation.

The emphatic statements already made on the subject by most participants preclude the need to refer here to the importance and timeliness of including Mr. Edwards's topic as a separate item on the agenda.

We are only too well acquainted with the crisis of payments and new financial resources that is facing the major economies of the region. It has resulted in considerable changes in economic policy, with significant effects on our countries' national products, revenues, employment, and external economic relations.

In trying to comment on Sebastián Edwards's paper, I am faced with the quandary of deciding between taking an "academic" or a "pragmatic" approach. An academic approach is, to be sure, more detached from the urgencies of the moment; it is almost "atemporal." However, the depths of the current crises in our economies and the magnitude of the consequences referred to in other papers have prompted me to take the most realistic and current approach possible.

Furthermore, various participants have referred to the urgency of finding concerted, planned ways of resolving the difficulties before us, and I do not believe that an abstract approach would contribute to this cause.

The paper presented by Edwards is valuable, I think, primarily in that it is an interesting and concise synthesis of recent writings and studies on the topic by Anglo-American scholars. The paper would merit close examination merely for its copious bibliography and numerous references concerning both methodology and the ideas put forward by a wide range of scholars in the field.

Furthermore, it has the great merit of refreshing our memories concerning a number of the major assumptions or hypotheses of prevailing theory. What is more, it reminds us of some of the principal operational concepts or precepts implicit in the normal functioning of international finance and the management of the external debt.

---

*The original version of this paper was written in Spanish.

The facts, however, appear to run ahead of our theories. The crises would appear to be telling us that most of the explanatory factors or variables considered valid for periods of "relative normalcy" are overtaken by circumstances to the point of being rendered virtually irrelevant during periods of economic and financial crisis. That is, it seems we need one theory for periods of "relative normalcy" and another for periods of "crisis," when the financial system is no longer reliable, when we have run out of alternative savings instruments, when expectations begin to change suddenly, and so on.

Speaking constructively, I believe that the major critique that could be made of the paper relates more to what is not said or considered in it than to any errors which may have slipped into the text before us.

In his paper, Edwards is faced with the task of revising many of the concepts used in the first part of his study, which are based on the use of traditional background information and notions of indebtedness, when toward the end of his paper, he measures them against the actual situation in Latin America, which presents a host of new scenarios, with new problems that do not necessarily respond to the "conventional wisdom" we have accumulated over the last two decades. This is perfectly understandable as regards the constraints frequently imposed on us by figures; many of us have tried to verify or contrast various hypotheses in light of the real world— a process which proves to be virtually impossible when based on questionable data, especially in this field.

In other words, the current situation, or the reality we see, prompts us to reconsider various methods and concepts which now seem to be out of touch. I do not say this in order to enter into some abstract discussion of reality, but instead to assess certain key concepts and methods in a practical way in light of the situation we face, which has been very well described by the Fund itself.

One such concept is our notion of public debt and private debt. Recent experience and the experience of many countries in the 1930s suggests that in reality there tends to be no difference between public and private indebtedness. When problems are encountered, it is the economy as a whole which has foreign exchange or does not, which has international reserves or does not, which has a positive trade balance or a current account deficit or does not. The key problem would thus appear to be that almost always, almost inexorably, pressures are exerted to have the private debt paid off, directly or indirectly, by the public sector or the country. In practice, in almost all cases, that which had been the exclusive responsibility of the private sector is slowly but surely becoming a public responsibility which must be assumed by the national economy. Although this is mentioned in the paper, it is not incorporated into the estimates. I believe that due consideration of this matter could lead to changes in both the analysis and the results.

In this regard, though, the author reminds us early in his paper that everything is still set up for our traditional approaches to the public debt even though, in the last five years, the growth of debt originating in and for the use of the private sector has far exceeded the amount of public borrowing in several countries of the region. Consequently, our results continue to confirm the findings of economic writers of the 1960s and 1970s but are not very helpful in the present situation.

What is more, the problem goes much beyond an institutional or legal definition and points to a question which is basic and central to the entire model, namely, that in our economies everything has been set up so as not to impede the growth of the private sector, which we now find overindebted, falling short of expectations, without working capital, and with prospects for an indefinite period of adjustment and contraction.

The old approach assumed, and perhaps still largely assumes, that private sector borrowing without (or even with) a government guarantee was the form of external savings that would be most likely to be invested productively, and that, in the absence of government interference in the making of payments, private sector loans would pose the smallest debt service problems.

In other words, it was expected, or rather assumed, that excess indebtedness was unlikely, which brings us to my next point.

Our traditional belief that external indebtedness plays a long-term role in the financing of gross investment in the region would appear to be one of the assumptions which is the least borne out and the most refuted by recent evidence from various countries of the region, at least from those in southern Latin America. The author himself reminds us that, in recent experience in Latin America, the pronounced increase in external indebtedness has clearly not produced an equivalent increase in total savings. Perhaps what is most impressive is that not only has there not been increased investment, but investment has actually decreased, and that a sizable proportion of new external borrowing has been used to finance consumption.

As a number of authors have indicated, the large-scale recycling of funds over the past five years was a considerable financial success, but it was deceptive. It was not a recycling of savings into investment, but in part a shift from one form of savings into another or from savings into consumption. The old, most orthodox Keynesian theory holds that when the propensity to save is greater than the tendency to invest, a depression is created; this could explain much of the phenomenon we are now witnessing.

Financial recycling from one bank to another for any purpose other than investment is not sufficient—or its effects are not yet clear. From a banker's perspective it may represent a success, but from the standpoint of the economic well-being of the rest of the world, it may constitute a step backward. What I am trying to say, among other things, is that in this financial recycling we have lost sight of the basic criterion for granting resources that was learned during the peak time of international cooperation, the objective of which was to maximize complementary national efforts and not just the income created by each dollar of aid.

Another way of illustrating the same problem is the pace at which credit expanded, from a low proportion of gross domestic product (GDP) in 1974–75 in various economies to levels of 80 to 90 percent of GDP in 1980–81.

Similarly, the "old wisdom" that private banks properly supervise and evaluate the use to which their loans are put appears in some cases not to coincide with the current situation in the major Latin American economies. This observation must of course be attenuated or qualified for at least two reasons: first, a multitude of banks (some estimate about 1,600) are involved in this process, and second, it is a problem of shared responsibility which must urgently be remedied. In other words, if this function has not been carried out by the banks, large or small, with or without their own analysts, or by the Fund (which arrives on the scene only when so requested by the deficit countries and when problems already exist), or by the central banks, which in the majority of the cases have instead tended to see increasing revenues from external credit as a sign of approval and confidence, we are faced with a rather paradoxical, virtually self-destructive situation.

To this must be added the concrete and widely recognized fact that each of these agents inclined (for various reasons, some of them rather creditable) not to provide adequate background information on the figures involved, which makes for an unreliable and lagging data base. This problem of the quality, timeliness, and adequate dissemination of information has not yet been mentioned, and I believe it is at the heart of the problems we are discussing today.

At present it is possible to consider only semitheoretically the alternative roles played by adjustments in domestic activity, the exchange rate, reserves, and external indebtedness in the macroeconomic adjustment process of the countries of the region, after examining the most recent figures on indebtedness and interest rates, among others. At times of economic crisis and declining international liquidity, these roles are no longer the usual ones or cease to have the same significance, as in the case of indebtedness, the mentioned cases of exchange rates, and other variables mentioned. This appears to be equally true of the banking practices we know, which are relevant to periods of normalcy; although it has been recommended to banks on innumerable occasions that they not follow the practice of first lending intensely and then abruptly curtailing their lending, in real life this practice is rather frequent, even when it can be disastrous for all.

Turning to another subject—estimates of country risk—I must stress the author's forthrightness in portraying the results obtained from estimates, despite how disheartening this must have been. These results, like those of other studies, verge on suggesting that the type of analysis or the factors considered are irrelevant and that one or more dummy variables could just as well have explained much of the dependent variable, that is, the probability that a given country will not meet its commitments (probability of default). In other words, the analytical process at present, when it considers only or preponderantly credits to the public sector or government-guaranteed credits, overlooks all of the important and potentially difficult present situation. Therefore, the type of analysis presented still requires further study and more direct observation of reality with a view to learning from experience or from actual practice for forward projections. The quality and timeliness of data are again important here, as this is an effort to estimate risk in advance rather than after the fact. The results obtained from analysis as it now stands are in some cases impressive. To mention but a few of them, the coefficients of the debt service ratio and of the average volume of loans, and the coefficient of the ratio of current account to product have been found not to be significant in estimating country risk. On the other hand, the author stresses his surprise at learning the importance, in absolute terms and in terms of significance, of the ratio between international reserves and national product. This suggests that, by keeping the reserves-to-product ratio high, somehow, a country might sustain the impression among international creditors that it is very unlikely to default.

Finally, I was quite interested in the author's analysis of the residuals factors involved in estimates of the probability of default or the probability that a given country will not meet its commitments. As the author points out, it is clear that in addition to economic variables, considerations of a political nature will affect the community's perception of such a probability. In other words, politically more stable countries would be expected to have a lower default probability. Recent results appear to suggest that further study is still required of both the analytical framework and factors involved. Otherwise, current analytical methods lead us to conclude that there are several hard-to-interpret situations with respect to political stability and support from the international financial system.

Other matters not considered in the paper, but which cannot be examined here in greater detail because I have already spoken so long, include the effects of capital inflows and outflows on key prices in the economy and on the relative prices of tradables and nontradables. Also not considered are the effects of this large-scale financial recycling on aggregate supply and demand, and on the changes in their makeup; that is, the structural shifts which to varying degrees and with different nuances have caused decreases in the importance of the industrial sector and a more than proportional expansion of the financial, commercial, and services sectors of various economies of the region.

Yet another question, which is actually a more general problem that must be reconsidered in our analytical methodologies and is therefore not specific to the work being commented on here, is the concept of short-term indebtedness. Until 1981, or thereabouts, short-term financing was used primarily for purposes of trade. In the past two years, however, short-term financing, which in Latin America has reached an approximate total of about $90 billion, has been increasingly used for interbank support. This changes the basic character of the lending from commercial to financial.

Finally, in these last, more general remarks, no mention has been made of some important limitations derived from a model oriented toward export promotion. On the one hand, the most recent studies of Latin American economies indicate that the export sector of each economy makes a rather small contribution to overall employment. Today, with the stagnation and sizable adjustments experienced in the region in the last two years, unemployment has grown extraordinarily. We must therefore recall that development is fundamentally a question of human progress, and a man with no job can make no progress. On the other hand, while our exports may significantly increase in the near future owing to the new trade agreements between countries of the south, the related export proceeds do not ease the external debt service burden in that the debt is to a great degree, if not completely, made up of credits from the industrial economies whose currency of exchange is the U.S. dollar or another hard currency.

Commentary*

SERGIO MÁLAGA

The study just presented to us by Sebastian Edwards is, first of all, a fine survey of the recent literature on the subject of adjustment of disequilibria in the external sector of the economies of developing countries. This topic is eminently timely in light of recent events familiar to all of us, including the severe contraction of loanable funds available to Latin America, a disproportionate external debt in that part of the world, and the inability of most of its economies to service their external debts.

Second, Edwards takes an especially close look at the role of international reserves and external debt in this adjustment process and in the determination of the risk of default. He uses his own estimates, first individually and then simultaneously, of the demand functions for both reserves and debt, with data from 19 developing countries, to get an empirical handle on a number of hypotheses, some deriving strictly from economic logic and others being less simple to deduce. Thus, he concludes from his research that: (a) the income elasticity of the demand for reserves is greater than unity while that of the demand for debt is not significantly different from unity—hence, the need of the developing countries for international liquidity and debt in the next few years will grow at rates which are, respectively, greater than and equal to those by which their incomes grow; (b) reserves, external debt, and the exchange rate are substitutes whose combined role in the process of financing external adjustment has yet to be adequately examined; (c) the greater the ratio of debt to product and the lower the ratio of reserves to product, the greater the perceived likelihood of default—hence, rational management of their levels can keep the cost of external borrowing lower than it would otherwise be; (d) the greater the openness of the economies, as measured by the average propensity to import, the greater the required level of reserves; (e) both the demand for reserves and the demand for debt are apparently insensitive to the cost of obtaining either; (f) the greater the variability of export income, the greater the demand for reserves and debt, although for most years the coefficients found are significant only in the case of the demand for debt; (g) the greater the ratio of external debt to product and the lower the ratio of reserves to product, the higher the interest rate charged by international banks as a premium for the higher level of country risk; and, finally, (h) the greater the risk perceived by banks, the higher the interest rates and the shorter the maturities on their loans.

---

*The original version of this paper was written in Spanish.

At this stage of the analysis, one wonders whether the demand functions for reserves and debt, estimated on the basis of the observed levels of these variables, can explain the levels desired by the authorities concerned. The discrepancy between observed and desired levels may be due to the fact that, on the one hand, the monetary authorities are following a fixed exchange rate policy or keeping exchange rates within politically established or publicly announced bands and, on the other hand, the fiscal authorities are facing a massive withdrawal of international bank lending.

The first and most common of these cases is resolved by Edwards in Section 5 of his study, where he introduces coefficients of partial adjustment between the desired and observed levels of reserves and of the money supply. In this way it is established that, given fixed exchange rates, international reserves fluctuate in response to partial adjustments in the discrepancies between the actual and desired levels of reserves and money. Introduction of the demand for money into the analysis is, of course, strictly in accord with the assumptions of the monetary approach to the balance of payments; excessive domestic credit, and the resulting excess money supply, will lead to faster inflation if the exchange rate is flexible and to a loss of reserves if the exchange rate is fixed. The money demand function used has as its explanatory variables the expected inflation rate—which is not necessarily equal to the expected cost of holding money balances—and the level of income.

Edwards uses this dynamic analysis to estimate new coefficients for the explanatory variables of the demand for reserves in his first version—the level of income, the mean propensity to import, and the standard deviation of the export series—as well as coefficients for the new explanatory variables—reserves held in the preceding period and the difference between money balances desired in the period and those held in the previous period. While all the coefficients turn out to have the expected sign, only those associated with the income and reserves variables for the previous year are significant at the customary level of 5 percent; the coefficient of the excess demand for money variable is significant only at 10 percent. Curiously, however, the income elasticity of the demand for reserves now achieves a value of about 3.

I believe this dynamic analysis can be exceptionally useful in explaining and ascertaining the demand for reserves, but it is clear that much more work remains to be done. Perhaps the results achieved can be improved (a) if the expected cost, or simply the present cost, of holding money balances, instead of the period's inflation rate, is used as an explanatory variable in estimating the demand for money. Most developing countries, especially those in Latin America, repeatedly experience prolonged periods of high inflation. In these circumstances, banks normally pay high interest rates on current accounts as a partial offset to the loss of purchasing power. My suggestion is even more valid if we use the broader definition of money. In my opinion, the inflation rate may well significantly overstate the cost of holding money balances; (b) if the opportunity cost of reserves and cost of external credit are used in estimating the demand for reserves and the demand for debt, respectively. As Edwards properly points out, earlier empirical studies have failed to find significant coefficients for proxy variables of the cost of holding reserves, such as the domestic interest rate or the difference between that rate and the rate paid on reserves deposited abroad. It is hard for me to believe, however, that the marginal social cost or the marginal social benefit of holding reserves is approximately zero. This assessment may be biased by the international liquidity crisis now being experienced by our economies, but that is not the only such crisis we have experienced and it will not be the last, at least for individual countries. Evidence of a high cost or benefit is provided by the drastic devaluations of domestic currencies which the monetary authorities, very much against their will, often have to accept—as in the recent case of Chile—as well as by the nationalization of banks in Mexico and the deferrals of external debt payment in Venezuela and Peru. This is undoubtedly a case of nonfinancial benefits and costs relating to the domestic and foreign prestige of governments and reflected in the confidence or lack of confidence in their economic management. It would therefore be difficult to incorporate this cost variable in empirical analyses. I would venture to suggest as proxy variables an index of general economic performance, including rates of product growth, employment, inflation, etc., or simply an index of the government's popularity, which will be useful only to the extent that political costs and benefits are more influential than economic ones; (c) if we explore, for both demand functions, the degree of explanatory power of the variable "fluctuation of import value," which in the Latin American case is undoubtedly far less important than the variable "fluctuation of export value" used by Edwards. They could be used jointly if, as appears to be the case, they are not closely correlated.

In Section 6, Edwards gives us interesting data on the external official and officially guaranteed debt of the Latin American countries. Although his data are for 1980, they clearly show the extremely high debt levels already then registered by most of the countries which now have serious external imbalances; their ratios of debt to product and debt service to exports exceeded the third quartiles of the respective distributions, namely 34.3 percent and 22.9 percent. The picture would certainly be even more troublesome if complete data on the private debt were included. Therefore, independent of the efforts the economic authorities must continue to make to hold down the social cost of the adjustment process, it would be well worth their while to follow the interesting recommendations made by Edwards in his study.

(a) Highly effective policies must be developed for regulating the financial and banking system in order to prevent the effects of misallocation of credit from being transferred to the rest of the population.

(b) To the extent that the cost of the debt rises as indebtedness increases, a policy must be developed to optimize private sector borrowing abroad. The need is for an optimum charge, to be applied to public borrowing transactions as well, in the form of an annual percentage rate which ideally makes the marginal social cost of new borrowing equal to the marginal cost to the borrower. Such charges already exist in many countries, although not for the above reasons, in the form of a withholding tax. Governments unfortunately tend to eliminate them or substantially reduce their rate—with the difference sometimes being absorbed by international banks—when they face balance of payments difficulties and are trying to stimulate borrowing as a means of restoring the balance. Moreover, the charge generally does not apply to official or officially guaranteed borrowing, thus adding to the disequilibria between public enterprises, which becomes more profitable, and private enterprises. The proceeds from this charge could partially finance the insurance system for deposits in banks and financial institutions, which, in keeping with the above recommendation, should be revised to introduce variable premiums directly linked to the percentages of bad portfolio investment and credit concentration. The problem with such a charge is, of course, that of estimating the elasticity of the supply of lendable funds, which, moreover, is highly volatile. Nor am I sure that it does not involve externalities imposed by the indebtedness of other economies in the same region. The massive retreat of international banks from Latin America is perhaps evidence of this. The subject is certainly worthy of attention, with a view to the prompt regulation of external credit at optimum levels.

(c) It is necessary to develop an appropriate exchange policy, one which recognizes that pegging the currency to the dollar does not necessarily lead to maintenance of parity with other currencies and that the real exchange rate is also a variable. This tool, Edwards maintains, must be used in conjunction with the others—debt and reserves—in the process of restoring equilibrium to the balance of payments. This is necessary if appropriate levels of international liquidity and external debt are to be maintained.

In conclusion, I believe that Edwards's study is excellent, because I am sure that it will motivate further research on this important subject, which is certainly necessary considering its significance at a time like the present, when most of our economies must go through a severe and painful process of adjusting their external sectors.

The Role of Commercial Banks in the Adjustment Process

Jack D. Guenther

Adjustment can mean many different things, but in this paper it refers to the process of adapting a country's balance of payments to whatever unfavorable shock has upset the equilibrium.

The fundamental role of commercial banks is to accept the world's savings from those who can be induced to save and to channel those savings to creditworthy borrowers with good investment opportunities. When banks do this well, their intermediation can be a powerful force for economic growth in the world.

Banks have a special role when adjustment is taking place. While the main task continues to be to channel savings to creditworthy borrowers, the specific purpose of the lending in this case is to tide the borrower over a difficult period while he adjusts to a new situation. The test of creditworthiness in this situation is whether the borrower, in fact, uses the time well to carry out the required adjustment. In the ideal case, lenders can make an invaluable contribution to easing the adjustment process of their clients. The required adjustment can be less abrupt, the growth of world production can be sustained, and the pain in terms of lost output and unemployment can be held to a minimum.

What is it that we are now adjusting to? One year ago, most of us would have answered, the "second oil shock." In fact, if you were young and lived in an industrial country you might have thought that the only thing the world ever had to adjust to was an oil price increase. But "old-timers" from Latin America are aware that unfavorable shocks, such as declining commodity prices, were a problem long before 1973 and often the adjustment called for in the exporting country was even larger than the adjustment that occurred after the oil price increase.

Until about one year ago, I also thought that the world's main current adjustment problem was to adapt to higher energy prices. I think you will agree, however, that the situation has become more complex than this. In fact, early in 1983 newspapers suddenly decided that the most frightening prospect facing the world was a sharp decline in energy prices. Some of the stories suggested that the world financial system could withstand a drop in oil prices to $25 a barrel, but if prices fell below that, oil exporting countries such as Mexico, Venezuela, Indonesia, and Nigeria would be unable to service their debts and this could lead to the bankruptcy of some of the world's largest banks. The imminent threat of a world financial collapse was presented in almost exactly the same language as two years earlier, when oil prices rose, causing problems for Brazil, Korea, and the Philippines. That many journalists—and some U.S. congressmen—do not believe that the world's economies or the world's financial system are capable of adjusting to fluctuations in commodity prices and other similar shocks is discouraging; we have always had such fluctuations, changes, and uncertainties in the world; we have them now, and we will continue to have them.

In my view, the world's economies and the international financial system are not as fragile as is thought, and, given time, both have proved to be capable of adapting to large changes. Unfortunately, very few people in developed countries realize this and only a few have any in-depth knowledge of developing countries. This lack of understanding may, in fact, itself be the biggest threat now facing the world economy: ill-conceived regulations to limit the flow of capital in the world could lead to a decade of depressed economic activity.

Imperceptibly during the past year, the world's basic problem has switched: it is no longer adjustment to higher energy prices but adjustments to high real interest rates and to a dramatic slowing down of inflation and economic activity. The world, for the moment at least, has stopped growing. Exports of developing countries which grew by 20 percent a year from 1973 to 1980 remained almost flat from 1980 to 1982. This slowdown in activity is what we are now adjusting to, and the required adjustment affects everyone irrespective of boundaries.

But this is getting ahead of my story. To put our present problems in perspective, it is useful to discuss the adjustment process since the first oil shock in 1973.

Section 1 looks at the growth in external debt of the non-oil developing countries since 1973. There is a popular notion that these countries did not adjust adequately to the oil price increases of the past decade, but rather simply borrowed large amounts of money to finance their deficits, and consequently will not be able to service the resulting debt. The section considers, therefore, not only the debt but also interest payments on the debt and the growth of export earnings, which provide the means of servicing the debt. The section ends with a judgment as to the further growth of debt that these countries can safely manage over the next few years.

This is followed in Section 2 with a discussion of balance of payments trends in non-oil developing countries over the past decade. External debt is an outgrowth of the balance of payments, since debt is incurred to cover a deficit on current operations. Any effort to control the growth must, therefore, start by strengthening or adjusting the balance of payments; a reduction in borrowing without an accompanying adjustment of the balance of payments will simply result in payments arrears. Section 2 ends with an estimate of the amount of adjustment that developing countries are currently making in their balance of payments, an estimate of the financing required for the remaining deficit, and, in particular, how much of that financing can be expected from commercial banks.

Section 3 focuses directly on the claims of commercial banks on developing countries and looks especially at the current idea that commercial banks are dangerously overexposed in lending to developing countries.

1. EXTERNAL DEBT OF NON-OIL DEVELOPING COUNTRIES 1973–82, AND A LOOK AT THE FUTURE

The external debt of the non-oil developing countries (including over $100 billion of short-term debt) has now exceeded $600 billion.

Almost everyone agrees that this debt is large, and until recently, was growing too fast. Here, the consensus ends. Opinions differ widely on how the debt became so large, how serious the debt problem now is, and what attitude should be adopted toward growth of debt during the next few years.

Although the size of the debt is worrisome, particularly under present world conditions, most of the recent press reporting on the debt problem is unnecessarily alarmist, and this distorted presentation of the problem has itself become a danger.

The growth of developing country debt in the post-1973 period can only be properly understood if it is placed in the perspective of world developments during the period. From end-1973 to end-1980, the long-term external debt of the non-oil developing countries increased from $97 billion to $375 billion, which represents a compound annual rate of growth of 21.3 percent (Chart 1). It must be remembered, however, that these seven years were a period of unusually high world inflation and also high economic growth. As can be seen in the chart, the exports of goods and services of the non-oil developing countries, which provide the foreign currency earnings to service the debt, also rose rapidly, from $109 billion in 1973 to $404 billion in 1980, or at a compound annual rate of 20.6 percent. In fact, after stagnating momentarily during the 1975 recession, the export earnings of these countries actually grew slightly faster than their debt up to 1980. Furthermore, most other relevant economic variables, such as the gross national product (GNP) and total international reserves of gold and foreign exchange, also rose rapidly, approximately tripling in the seven years.

Chart 1.   Non-Oil Developing Countries:
External Debt and Exports

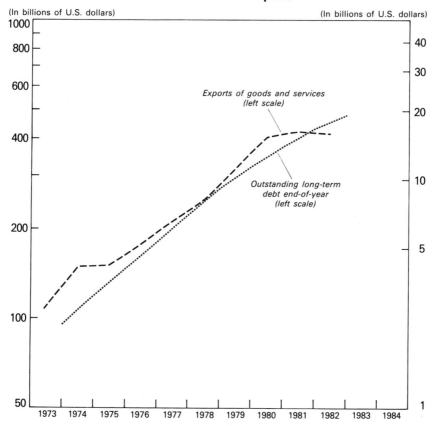

Source: Table 4.

In retrospect, it is my view that while the foreign debt of the developing countries grew too fast from 1973 to 1980, the idea that it was completely out of control or rising out of all proportion to the countries' capacity to service the debt is not borne out by these figures. On the contrary, I will argue that the international capital flows during the 1970s played an indispensable and reasonable role in the health and growth of the world economy in the period. One must remember that a by-product of the 1973 oil price increase was the concentration of a sizable amount of savings in a few oil-rich countries which had quite limited investment opportunities. The international banking system channeled these savings to those parts of the world that were short in savings but had good investment opportunities. This meant mainly developing countries, such as Brazil, with its hydroelectric potential and raw material wealth, Korea, with its disciplined labor force in manufacturing, or Mexico, with its oil reserves to develop. There is no doubt that much of the economic growth achieved by these developing countries and by the world as a whole in the latter part of the 1970s was a direct result of these capital flows.

The success of the recycling effort after 1973 depended on getting the funds to those countries where genuine investment opportunities existed and where the economic policies being pursued assured that the funds would be well used. These countries should then have been able to increase output rapidly, expanding both their own economies and the markets for other producers and, at the same time, generating through their investments the exports needed to service the debts. And this is exactly what happened. Contrary to the pessimistic predictions in 1974, the economic growth of the oil importing developing countries in the latter part of the decade was faster than in any comparable period and also faster than in the industrial countries. The best performance was in precisely those countries that received heavy infusions of capital, for example, Brazil, Mexico, Korea.

The most rapid growth in the developing countries in the late 1970s was in the export sector. This was essential to the adjustment process. It provided foreign exchange to pay for higher-cost energy imports and to service the debts incurred to carry out the required investments. But I will leave the fuller discussion of the balance of payments adjustment to Section 2.

Following these relatively favorable trends in the late 1970s, developments in the world economy in 1981–82 brought an abrupt change. The problem was not that debt began to increase more rapidly—in fact, the rate of increase recorded in long-term external debt seems to have declined slightly in 1981–82 to an annual rate of about 14 percent for the two years—but that the growth in exports of goods and services suddenly slowed down (Chart 1).

There is no doubt that the major single factor in the debt crisis which has spread through much of the developing world is the poor performance of exports in 1981–82. After growing by 20 percent a year for eight years, export earnings in 1982 were not much above the level of 1980. Exports in 1982 were, therefore, almost 40 percent lower than they would have been if the previous growth rates had continued. This, not energy prices, is what the world is now adjusting to. As would be expected, the abrupt halt in export growth is affecting principally those rapidly growing developing countries whose economic success in the 1970s was mainly dependent on exports, who integrated themselves closely into the world economy, and whose development strategy was based on external borrowing being paid for with export earnings. (Mexico, for example, expanded merchandise exports from $2 billion in 1973 to $20 billion in 1981, faster than almost any other country in the group, and it was the sudden downturn of the volume and price of oil shipments in mid-1981 that forced an immediate reassessment of the growth in debt.)

In addition to the unexpected stagnation of exports, the second development in the early 1980s which forced countries to re-evaluate their recourse to foreign borrowing was the sharp increase in interest rates. Average interest rates on the long-term foreign debt of the developing countries had been below 5 percent in 1973, but by 1980, they had risen to about 8 percent, and on the basis of preliminary estimates, they had risen to almost 9 percent by 1982. Because of this shift to higher rates, the growth in interest payments was far faster than growth of debt itself after 1979 (Chart 2). Average interest rates throughout the decade would be even higher, of course, except for the considerable amount of concessionary credit available to the low-income developing countries, but the portion of this type of financing in total debt has declined in the past decade. Nevertheless, for countries receiving large amounts of concessional financing, mainly the low-income countries of Africa and Asia, interest rates do not appear to have increased much over the past decade and real interest rates probably even declined as inflation accelerated.

The rise in nominal and real interest rates has had a particularly adverse effect on countries in Latin America, which borrow most of their funds at commercial rates. Consequently the possibility that real interest rates in the 1980s will remain higher than in the early 1970s cannot be ignored in planning a future debt strategy for these countries. The burden of an $80 million debt takes on a completely different significance when interest rates rise from a nominal 6 percent (real 2 percent) as in the mid-1970s to 16 percent (real 7 percent) as in the early 1980s. A difference of 10 percentage points in the interest rate on a $80 billion debt adds $8 billion to the current account deficit. It is not surprising, therefore, that the most severe payments crisis of 1981–82 occurred in those highly indebted Latin American countries that borrow on commercial terms; that the domestic policies in some of these countries during 1982 were often inadequate, because approaching elections or other political factors did little to alleviate the crisis.

To complete this introduction of the growth of debt, one must say something about the problem of short-term debt, that is to say, debt with an original maturity of less than one year. Even though data on short-term debt are tenuous, most estimates suggest that the short-term debt of non-oil developing countries was around $100 billion at the beginning of 1983.[1]

Traditionally, about the only source of short-term debt used by developing countries was trade-related. Imports would be paid for with a delay, or exports with an advance, of a few days or months. This not only provided balance of payments support to countries, but frequently also was a source of

---

[1]The numbers shown in the charts refer only to long-term debt; this is because the statistics on long-term debt of developing countries are relatively good, owing to the cooperation between these countries and the World Bank and the International Monetary Fund (IMF) over the past three decades.

Chart 2. Non-Oil Developing Countries:
External Debt, Exports, and Interest Payments

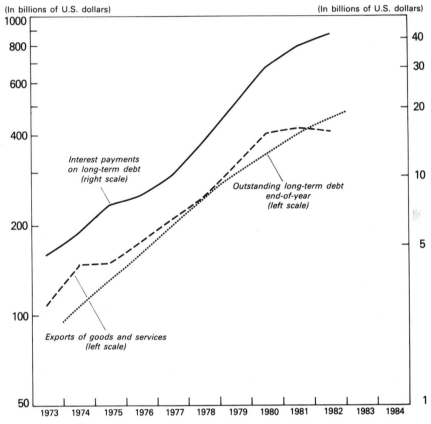

Source: Table 4.

working capital to exporters and importers. Most debt-registration systems established for developing countries, including that of the World Bank, did not attempt to track these constantly changing "debts," many of which existed for only a few days. Almost everything imported or exported by a country gets financed for a few days, at least while the payment is being processed. Current records on the amount of this debt are not only difficult to maintain but are also out of date by the time they become available. Moreover, in normal times one expects a certain stability in the amount of trade credit outstanding, although it must be admitted that some of the rescheduling difficulties in Latin America in the 1950s and 1960s were brought on by an overextension of this type of short-term foreign indebtedness.

During the past few years, a new type of short-term foreign debt has begun to emerge that is totally unrelated to trade and that often involves foreign agencies of commercial banks of the developing countries which have established themselves in New York, London, Paris, and other foreign money centers. These agencies behave like other banks in those centers, funding themselves by taking deposits or placements, often at maturities of 30, 60, or 90 days, or even overnight funds. The banks might channel two thirds or three fourths of their funds back to the country or head office and place the remainder in the developed countries or in other developing countries. The New York agencies of Brazilian banks, for example, might be lending in France, Mexico, and Chile, as well as to borrowers in the United States and Brazil. When the "home" country of the head office of one of these banks has balance of payments problems, the agency may experience a loss of short-term deposits, which adds to the total crisis. Most attempts by countries to measure their debt now seem to record the remittances which the agencies make to the home country. Some important series on lending, however, such as the BIS (Bank for International Settlements) quarterly series on bank lending, fail to capture these claims as part of the total claims on the country. I have brought up this short-term non-trade-related debt for two reasons. First, this type of debt appears to have risen rapidly with the proliferation of developing country banks around the world, and particularly during the past two years when countries were experiencing difficulties in raising funds in other ways. Second, this debt is by nature very volatile because it is funded with short-term deposits, which can be withdrawn suddenly at any sign of problem in the borrowing country, thereby adding to the sense of financial crisis.

To summarize, I think the growth in debt of developing countries until 1980 was not so irrational as is sometimes suggested. The debt was growing fast, but not faster than the capacity to service the debt. Since 1980, on the other hand, several developments have occurred that make the debt look excessive of which I cite three:

1) exports of the developing countries have virtually stagnated, mainly because of the world recession;
2) at the same time, interest rates in world markets have risen beyond expectations; and
3) domestic economic policies in some of the important debtor countries were temporarily inadequate, contributing to the poor balance of payments performance.

Against this background of the growth in developing country debt in the past decade, let me now turn to the question of where we go from here. What is a manageable plan for growth in the debt during the remainder of the 1980s? While recognizing all the pitfalls in planning for the future in an uncertain world, I think that almost everyone now agrees that the growth in debt must be slowed down to a much more moderate level. We need to be planning for at least a five-year period in which the growth in debt is slower, perhaps 2–3 percent a year slower, than the growth in capacity to service the debt as measured by the exports of goods and services.

With the present prospects for world inflation and growth, it would not be unreasonable to expect export earnings of developing countries to rise by 10 percent a year during the next few years, or about one half the rate of the 1970s. It is essential in this case to limit the growth in debt to 7 percent a year. An increase of 7 percent on total debt of $600 billion would represent an increase of about $42 billion in 1983 (Chart 3).

Some countries, particularly in Latin America and Africa, need an even slower rise in debt than 7 percent unless they are able to contract an increased portion on concessional terms, which does not seem likely. For example, in Brazil, economists have been talking of making sure that the debt does not

**Chart 3. Non-Oil Developing Countries:
External Debt, Exports, and Interest Payments**

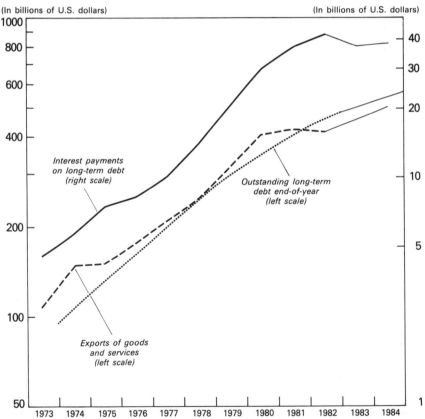

Source: Table 4.

grow in real terms during the next few years; and in Mexico a program has been adopted for 1983 and beyond that would result in a rise in total debt of less than 7 percent, even after allowing for some extra borrowing to increase the depleted international reserves. On the other hand, in Asia, there clearly are several countries that still could tolerate a rise in debt by more than 7 percent a year.

If during the next few years, the growth of external debt could be held at 7 percent a year then we would enter the late 1980s with a sustained period in which the debt of the developing countries would have grown more slowly than export earnings. Even more important, it would be a period that would show that the growth of debt can be controlled.

2. BALANCE OF PAYMENTS OF THE NON-OIL DEVELOPING COUNTRIES

This section discusses the balance of payments deficits in the non-oil developing countries during the past decade, how these deficits were financed, and the relationship between this and the growth of debt that was summarized in the preceding chapter. In particular, the role of commercial banks in financing the deficits and in promoting adjustment is discussed.

The annual current account deficit for the 110 non-oil developing countries is shown in the first line of Table 1. After reaching a peak of $102 billion in 1981, the deficit is estimated to have declined to $85 billion in 1982 and is projected to decline further to about $65 billion this year. If the projection turns out to be correct, it would represent a $35–40 billion adjustment in the balance of payments in two years; but because exports and imports of these countries are now more than twice as large as in the mid-1970s, this adjustment would be no larger in relation to the trade flows of those countries than the $19 billion reduction shown in the table between 1975 and 1977, following the first oil shock.

What are the prospects of achieving a reduction of the combined deficits of these countries to $65 billion in 1983? Not only is the reduction possible, but an adjustment of approximately this size is almost inevitable. In fact, the process is well on its way toward completion. Two countries alone, Mexico and Brazil, have adopted financial programs for 1983 calling for reduced current account deficits—$3 billion for Mexico and $7 billion for Brazil. The combined deficit of these two countries in 1981 was $24 billion. These two countries, which account for almost one quarter of the total debt and over one third of the debt for this group of countries, will therefore be achieving over one third of the required downward adjustment in current account deficits between 1981 and 1983. Similar adjustments are occurring in other large members of the group, such as Argentina, Chile, Korea, Yugoslavia, and South Africa. Furthermore, in some of these countries a previous outflow of domestic captital has also been slowed down or reversed, and while this

Table 1. Non-Oil Developing Countries: Current Account Deficit and Financing

(In billions of U.S. dollars)

	1973	1974	1975	1976	1977	1978	1979	1980	1981	Prel. 1982	Proj. 1983
A. Current account deficit	12	37	47	32	28	39	59	86	102	85	65
B. Addition to reserves	10	2	-2	14	12	16	12	5	2	-10	8
C. Financing required (A + B)	22	39	45	46	40	55	71	91	104	75	73
Financing that does not create debt	10	13	12	12	15	17	23	24	26	26	26
Net unrequited transfers, SDR allocations, etc.	(6)	(8)	(7)	(7)	(10)	(10)	(14)	(14)	(13)	...	...
Direct investment	(4)	(5)	(5)	(5)	(5)	(7)	(9)	(10)	(13)	...	...
Commercial banks in BIS reporting areas	10	15	15	21	15	25	40	49	50	22	20
Long-term borrowing from official sources	5	9	11	11	13	14	15	21	20	22	22
IMF and other reserve-related credit	—	2	3	4	—	1	-1	2	5	8	8
Other (net)	-3	—	4	-2	-3	-2	-6	-5	3	-3	-3

Source: International Monetary Fund, *World Economic Outlook: A Survey by the Staff of the International Monetary Fund,* IMF Occasional Paper No. 9 (Washington, April 1982), p. 166; *International Capital Markets: Developments and Prospects, 1982,* IMF Occasional Paper No. 14 (Washington, July 1982).

outflow was not a part of the current account deficit, it was similar in that it required financing by recourse to foreign borrowing.

A current account deficit of $65 billion in 1983 is approximately the size which is consistent with holding the growth in foreign debt to $42 billion, or 7 percent of the outstanding debt at the beginning of the year. To understand this relationship between the current account deficit and the growth of debt, it is useful to look for a moment at one of the years in Table I. Take the year 1977 as an example. In that year, the deficit on current account was $28 billion; in addition, the countries increased their international reserves by $12 billion, requiring total financing of $40 billion.

Of the $40 billion of financing in 1977, $15 billion came from sources that did not create debt. These sources are direct investment by multinational corporations or official grants of aid, the latter mainly from industrial and oil exporting countries. The remaining financing in 1977 came from $15 billion of net lending by commercial banks and $13 billion of net long-term lending from official sources, such as the World Bank, the regional development banks, and the industrial country export-import banks. Net lending, of course, means the amount by which new loans exceed repayments on old loans, so that the indebtedness of the non-oil countries increases by the amount of net lending. The IMF and central banks did not engage in net lending in 1977, which is not unusual in a year when reserves increased rapidly. (Such indebtedness is not, at any rate, regarded as a part of foreign debt, but rather is netted out of gross reserves.) The final line in the table is a catchall, that is, a net figure of all other inflows and outflows of capital, particularly short-term borrowing from nonbank sources, minus any loans that the countries themselves make abroad through their own export promotion schemes or any recorded capital outflows from private citizens, plus errors and omissions; there was a small net outflow of funds in these categories in 1977. From these numbers, one would estimate that the foreign debt of the non-oil developing countries rose by about $30 billion in 1977 ($15 billion to banks, $13 billion long-term to official agencies, and perhaps a small amount of other debt—the latter is concealed in the net figures in the table by a corresponding capital outflow.)

For our purposes, the most interesting line in Table I is the financing provided to the developing countries by the commercial banks, and particularly the volatility of that financing. Although lending from other sources was relatively stable, loans from commercial banks rose sharply beginning in 1979, peaked at $50 billion in 1981, and were reduced again abruptly in 1982. Much of the criticism currently directed at banks is due to these wide swings in financing. Specifically, the criticism is that commercial banks expanded loans excessively from 1979 through 1981, thereby permitting countries to run deficits that were larger than could be sustained. Then, discovering their error during the course of 1982, the banks abruptly stopped lending altogether. (In fact, almost all of the estimated $22 billion of bank financing to these countries in 1982 occurred in the first half of the year, whereas in the second half of the year net lending appears to have been near zero.)

Mexico has been cited as the clearest example of this wide fluctuation in bank lending (Table 2). There can be little doubt that Mexico's $13 billion deficit in 1981 was too large and that banks were indirectly responsible—in that the deficit closely parallels bank lending and that Mexico could not have incurred the deficit unless commercial banks had been willing to finance it. In fact, it was the sharp cutback in commercial bank financing in 1982, and Mexico's resulting inability to import, which initiated the delayed adjustment and brought the deficit back down again to $6 billion in 1982.

How could Mexico's excessive deficit in 1981 have been prevented and the necessary adjustment achieved more promptly? No doubt the ideal way would have been for the Mexican authorities to have recognized the emerging crisis and to have restrained the deficit through timely adjustments in the exchange rate and strengthening of monetary, fiscal and wage policies. Alternatively, creditors could have restrained lending in 1981, forcing imports down, as happened belatedly in 1982. Adjustment by one route or another was inevitable; and while timely adjustment forced by the creditors is certainly better than no adjustment at all, I think that we would all agree that it is a poor substitute for adjustment through the adoption of a comprehensive economic program.

Table 2. Current Account Deficit and Commercial Bank Financing, 1977–83

(In billions of U.S. dollars)

	1977	1978	1979	1980	1981	Est. 1982	Proj. 1983
Exports of goods and services	9.2	11.6	16.3	25.0	30.6	29.4	34.5
Imports of goods and services	10.8	14.3	21.2	31.8	43.6	35.3	37.2
Current account deficit	−1.6	−2.7	−4.9	−6.8	−13.0	−5.9	−2.7
Financing of deficit	1.6	2.7	4.9	6.8	13.0	5.9	2.7
Commercial banks	—	—	7.5	9.3	14.3	4.7	5.0
Other (net)	—	—	−2.6	−2.5	−1.3	1.2	−2.3

Source: Interbank Working Group on Mexico.

When should commercial banks have cut back lending to Mexico and thereby have taken the initiative in forcing adjustment? Those who argue that this should have occurred in 1979 or 1980 are asking for something that is not realistic to expect even in the future. While Mexico's policies clearly were somewhat too expansionary in 1979–80, so were those of two thirds of the other countries in the world. Commercial banks are not likely to force an adjustment, by withholding lending when policies in a country are only moderately unsatisfactory. Only the monetary authorities of the country are able to do this type of fine tuning.

By mid-1981, it was evident that Mexico's external accounts had become so far out of line that prompt adjustment was needed to avoid lasting damage to the economy. Still, commercial banks lent Mexico $14 billion net that year, an amount equal to almost 30 percent of their total net loans to all non-oil developing countries. Why? It has been suggested that banks lack the full information and expertise required to make timely decisions. That is, no doubt, part of the problem. Despite considerable improvement in recent years, many commercial banks still have a limited capacity to spot balance of payments ailments at the initial sign of bad policies and only recognize the ailment 6–12 months later when the symptoms appear—in the form of outdated statistics. The newly formed Institute of International Finance, which is being established in Washington, D.C., will help banks to see trends developing more quickly, by improving the information available to banks.

It would be a mistake, however, to think that it was only blindness to the facts that caused banks to lend Mexico so much money in 1981. Most banks were aware that the financial situation was deteriorating, although no one, of course, inside banks or outside, expected the extreme turn of events which occurred and made the situation much worse during 1982. The main reason that banks continued lending was that they had a long-standing relationship with borrowers in Mexico. Mexican government agencies and banks look to their creditors to tide them over short-run difficulties, and they arrange in advance credit lines that can be drawn on as needed. This practice is particularly prevalent in countries which do not keep large foreign exchange reserves, but rather depend on lines with banks to provide a cushion against unexpected developments, such as the temporary collapse of the world oil market in June 1981. These existing bank lines were specifically designed to allow a period in which to adjust, just as the large international reserves of Venezuela provided such a period. This is a reasonable and prudent arrangement, provided the borrower does, in fact, use the period to adjust. The utilization of such lines "delays" adjustment only in the same way that high international reserves delay adjustment. The crucial question is, Do the countries adjust? Most bankers were impressed in mid-1981 with the number of Mexican officials and technicians, particularly in the central bank, who recognized that adjustment was needed and who seemed confident that some important steps toward adjustment would be undertaken even in the pre-election period. Of course, this assessment proved to be wrong, and serious adjustment measures were not initiated until 1982. The central bank by then had exhausted both reserves and bank credit.

While the behavior of banks in Mexico in 1981 is not as extreme as is sometimes suggested, the banks as a group should nevertheless have been more restrained in granting credit in that year. How can banks do a better job in the future to promote timely adjustment?

Unfortunately, there are no miracle cures or obvious potential remedies. The solution is for banks to do a better job at what they are already doing, namely, trying to distinguish between, on the one hand, creditworthy countries who are encountering short-term problems but who are taking the necessary steps to correct the situation in the medium term, and, on the other hand, countries who are not coping successfully with their problems and whose situation is, therefore, continuing to deteriorate. Credit to the latter group must be restrained, not only in the lenders' interest, but also in the borrowers'; borrowing countries are not helped by a continued flow of capital to finance inadequate policies that in the end leave them further in debt, with little to show for it.

For banks to do a better job in allocating credit around the world, two main improvements are needed. First, we need a better flow of accurate and timely information on country developments to all banks involved in lending. This can be arranged with the cooperation of borrowing countries, the IMF, the new Institute of International Finance, and the bank regulators in the major lending countries. Second, individual banks need to continue to develop their internal capacity to understand and interpret the information available on countries. This seems to be more of a problem, and for many small banks the development of this capacity may be so difficult that they would be better-advised to stay out of international lending altogether. The remaining banks will want to work closely with the IMF and to continue taking into consideration whether a country is vigorously implementing a program that has been endorsed by the IMF.

There has been considerable talk recently about the need for direct government control over commercial bank lending to developing countries. No one can argue with the idea that the governments have the responsibility to inspect banks and to set minimum prudential standards; this should and does include inspection of an individual bank's lending procedures and its capacity to analyze developments in borrowing countries. However, the proposals that bank regulators in lending countries might actually decide how credit should be allocated around the world seems to have little merit. There is no foundation for the idea that public officials would make fewer mistakes than the banks themselves, and this would be particularly true if political considerations were allowed to play a role in the credit allocation. Poland is a good example of a deteriorating country situation where U.S. commercial banks were more alert than U.S. Government agencies to the approaching problems. Between 1977 and 1980, a time of rapid increase in international lending, the unguaranteed loans of U.S. banks rose from $1.21 billion to $1.46 billion, or about 21 percent. In the same period, on the other hand, loans and guarantees by U.S. Government agencies, mainly to facilitate U.S. farm exports which would not otherwise have found financing in the private banking community, increased sharply from $0.5 billion to $1.7 billion (a 240 percent increase). Public sector and private sector funds frequently have quite different justifications, but statements which characterize the U.S. banking system as blindly pouring large sums of money into countries whose external accounts are deteriorating do not seem to be supported by the data on Poland.

During the past year or two, commercial banks have received a new type of criticism, not for lending too aggressively but rather for being too cautious in renewing their lending to countries that were emerging from difficulties. This is a relatively new turn of events. In fact, in almost all of the programs adopted by countries with IMF support in those years, commercial banks renewed their lending so quickly that countries after a few months were gaining reserves so rapidly that central banks often were concerned about the resulting monetary expansion. Until 1982 most of the stabilization programs that failed to receive bank support were, in my view, programs that themselves were not fully credible. Unfortunately, there were a few such programs in the late 1970s—programs which banks were not convinced would produce sufficient adjustment to re-establish a viable balance of payments position even in the medium term.

During 1982, some commercial banks became so cautious that there was no assurance that banks as a group would renew lending to a developing country in difficulty even after the country had adopted a feasible medium-term balance of payments program. Mexico is a good example. The new authorities in Mexico, before and after assuming office, adopted an economic program with IMF support that represented a sharp reversal of the previous inadequate policies. This program was designed to reduce the balance of payments deficit on current account from $13 billion in 1981 to about $3 billion in 1983. Approximately $5 billion of new bank money was needed in 1983 to finance this deficit, clean up arrears, and restore the country's depleted reserves to a minimum working level. Provided one believes the program is going to work, this $5 billion would be one of the investments that commercial banks have made in Mexico both from their own narrow interests and from their broader interest of preserving the health of the world economy. The international pessimism in late 1982 was so great, however, that there was no assurance that the commercial banks, which had lent Mexico $14 billion in 1981 when the country's balance of payments was deteriorating, would provide the $5 billion needed in 1983 to support a strong program designed to ensure a viable balance of payments in the medium term.

The initiative of the IMF in arranging the $5 billion of commercial bank financing for Mexico in 1983 was essential in the circumstances. Even after Mexico had worked out a strong adjustment program, there was a danger that commercial bank support for the program would have been so weak that Mexico would have run out of international reserves again in mid-1983. A financial program in which a country runs arrears on payments can hardly be regarded as satisfactory. The Managing Director of the IMF, therefore, informed the banks in December that Mexico had adopted for 1983 what he regarded as a workable program—provided that the banks were prepared to put in new funds of $5 billion. Otherwise, the program would not be workable, and he would be unable to recommend it to the Executive Board.

Some newspaper accounts have reported that commercial banks regarded this initiative by the Managing Director as a form of arm-twisting, of dictating to banks how much they had to lend to Mexico. I do not view it in that way. Banks retained their freedom of action, but at the same time, they had to recognize that one consequence of not arranging for the $5 billion of financing would be to make the Mexican program for 1983 unworkable. Not only do I think that banks retained their freedom of action, but I also anticipate that there may be cases where the IMF endorses programs that the banks are not convinced provide adequate adjustment even in the medium term; in these instances banks have no choice but to restrain their financing and take the consequences of the program not being submitted to the IMF Executive Board. The crucial test will be for countries to have adequate programs that are recognized to be so.

As you may know, the way that the $5 billion for Mexico has been arranged is for each bank with outstanding loans in the country to agree to increase them by 7 percent, and this seemingly simple formula has in fact taken weeks of work to organize. Why, if it was in the banks' interest to support the Mexican program, has it been necessary to arrange the funding in such a tortuous way? The answer is that it was in the interest of banks as a group to do this, but the numbers involved were too large for a few of the banks to undertake it on their own. For all banks to go up 7 percent is reasonable, but it would be imprudent for a third of the banks to go up by 21 percent or more, while the other two thirds did not increase lending at all or even withdrew funds. It was essential, therefore, that all Mexico's bank creditors participate.

3. COMMERCIAL BANK CLAIMS ON NON-OIL DEVELOPING COUNTRIES

The view has been expressed that the world banking system is now dangerously overextended in lending to developing countries and that it would be imprudent for banks to increase loans further even if the countries appear to be creditworthy. Proponents of this idea sometimes seem to be saying that even if the developing countries can safely increase their debt by moderate amounts in the next few years, it will have to come from sources other than commercial banks. In this section, I want to discuss this idea that banks are overcommitted to developing countries, by looking at the data from the point of view of the commercial banks themselves, and particularly the large commercial banks that provide most of the lending.

First, let me say that everyone agrees that commercial banks cannot return to lending at the rate that existed prior to 1982. In 1981, commercial banks increased their outstanding claims on non-oil developing countries by $50 billion, sufficient to provide almost one half of the financing needs of the countries in that year (Table 1 and Chart 4). This unusually large financing was recognized to be temporary while the countries adjusted to the unfavorable shocks of the late 1970s and early 1980s. In earlier years, commercial banks had to provide around one third of the financing, another one third came from official sources, and the final one third from direct investment, grants, and other sources that do not create debt. By 1982, this earlier balance was re-established. In fact, reacting to the overextension of the previous years, banks appear to have provided only about $22 billion in 1982, which was slightly less than one third of the $75 billion of total financing received by the developing countries in that year. It is reasonable to project that banks will continue to finance only one third or somewhat less of the requirements during the next few years. Fortunately, if the aggregate current account deficit of the non-oil developing countries is in the process of being reduced to about $65 billion in 1983, as I believe it is, this deficit can be adequately financed with approximately $20–22 billion of new money from commercial banks, or an increase of less than 7 percent on the claims of $325 billion that the commercial banks currently have outstanding in these countries. This is the kind of growth rate which can be prudently undertaken and sustained in present circumstances. The total portfolio of commercial banks probably will grow by a few percentage points more than this, which means that this type of lending will decline slightly in relation to portfolio, after rising strongly in recent years.

Sometimes it is suggested that banks are so overextended to developing countries that even a 7 percent annual growth rate in the next few years is excessive and that a more dramatic cutback in international lending is required; but the facts do not support this idea. On June 30, 1982, the last date for which data are available, the nine largest banks in the United States had total foreign currency claims (loans, placements, bankers' acceptances, and other claims) on the non-oil developing countries of about $78 billion [2] (Table 3). These nine banks account for almost two thirds of the lending done by all U.S. banks to developing countries, and the concern that U.S. banks are over extended is generally directed at them. The total assets of the nine

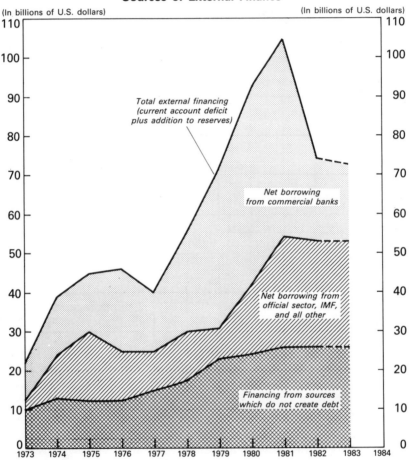

**Chart 4. Non-Oil Developing Countries:
Sources of External Finance**

Source: Table 1.

---

[2]This is after eliminating interbank deposits in booking centers, the inclusion of which would involve double counting. For example, if Chase places short-term funds in the Bank of America branch in Hong Kong, and the latter makes a loan to the Philippines, the placement in Hong Kong is removed from the statistics to avoid double counting of exposure.

**Table 3.   Nine Largest U.S. Banks: Total Foreign
Currency Claims on Non-Oil Developing Countries
and Areas, June 30, 1982**

	In Billions of U.S. Dollars	As a Percent of the Banks' Total Assets
All non-oil developing countries and areas	78.0	13.1
Mexico	13.4	2.3
Brazil	11.8	2.0
Argentina	5.3	0.9
Korea	5.1	0.9
Philippines	3.9	0.7
Chile	3.4	0.6
Hong Kong	2.7	0.4

Source: Semi-Annual Statistical Release of the Federal Financial Institutions Examination Council, Board of Governors of the Federal Reserve System (Washington).

banks last June 30 was approximately $600 billion, which means that their foreign currency claims on non-oil developing countries were equivalent to 13 percent of their total assets. In addition to these nine banks, 158 other U.S. banks have foreign portfolios which are of sufficient importance that they are required to report their foreign currency exposure to U.S bank regulators semi-annually. These 158 other banks have total assets of about $850 billion, of which about $45 billion represents foreign currency claims on non-oil developing countries. Such claims, therefore, account for approximately 5 percent of the total assets of these banks. For the U.S. banking system as a whole, the portion of such claims in the total portfolio is perhaps 7 percent. Does this represent a worrisome concentration of portfolio for the U.S. banks to have 5–13 percent of total assets in the form of foreign currency loans to developing countries? (Sometimes this is referred to as having one-to-three times equity in such loans, since equity usually represents something over 4 percent of assets.)

Diversification of assets clearly is an essential part of any system of risk control for a financial institution. No system of analysis of creditworthiness can ever foresee all the difficulties that might arise, and not putting all one's "eggs in the same basket" is therefore an important consideration. That is to say, diversification of assets has a place in risk control even if the borrowers are judged to be creditworthy.

Leaving aside for the moment the question of whether the 110 non-oil developing countries are judged to be creditworthy, it is hard to see how the U.S. banking system, with 7 percent of its total assets in the form of foreign currency claims on these countries, could be regarded as overly concentrated in this direction. These countries account for perhaps 12–15 percent of the world's GNP, and from a pure diversification standpoint, banks' portfolios do not seem to be abnormally tilted toward these countries. (The economies of the countries of the Council for Mutual Economic Assistance (CMEA) are about equal in size to those of the 110 non-oil developing countries, and U.S. banks' nonguaranteed claims on these countries total less that 0.3 percent of their total assets; so the suggestion that U.S. banks have poured money into these countries indiscriminately and are now heavily overextended is even more farfetched.)

There is also a prevailing idea that even if U.S. banks are not overconcentrated in lending to the non-oil developing countries as a group, they are too heavily involved in a few of the large developing countries, such as Mexico and Brazil. Five large developing countries, Mexico, Brazil, Argentina, Korea, and the Philippines, account for 50 percent of U.S. bank lending to the non-oil developing countries. Of course, the main reason for this is simply that these countries are much larger than most of the other countries. Brazil, for example, accounts for slightly over 15 percent of the total credit extended by U.S. banks to non-oil developing countries, but it also accounts for almost 15 percent of the GNP of the group. For the nine large U.S. banks, foreign currency claims on Brazil account for about 2 percent of their total portfolio, which is slightly less than Brazil's share of world GNP. When size is taken into account, a large part, but not all, of the apparent abnormal concentration of credits in a few countries is explained.

In the final analysis, it seems to me that most people who are saying that the world banking system is too heavily involved in lending to developing countries are not really talking about asset diversification at all. They are simply making a judgment that developing countries as a group are not creditworthy, and obviously, for a group of banks to have 13 percent of its claims, or even 5 percent, on borrowers who are not creditworthy is too much. The fundamental question, therefore, remains, are the developing countries creditworthy?

Some of those who believe that developing countries are uncreditworthy seem to base their belief on the simplistic notion that people or countries with low incomes do not or cannot pay their debts, while those with high incomes do. This, of course, is too superficial a basis for bank lending. Most of the developing countries have had a good record in the past decade. In the case of my own bank, during the 1970s, loan losses as a percentage of total loans were less than one half as high in international lending as in the United States. While the data on developing countries are not available separately, the bank's claims on that group were large enough that substantial losses on these loans would not have been consistent with the relatively good performance on international loans as a whole.

The world economy is now recovering from two years of slow growth, declining inflation, and relatively high interest rates. The adjustment to this new situation has been painful not only for developing countries, but also for most industrial countries. In my view, however, most of the developing countries are now well along in the process of adjusting to this new situation. Based on the above considerations, I believe that commercial bank lending can and will continue to play an important role in the economic development of these countries, by providing a further moderate growth of credit, as long as lenders and borrowers work closely together to maintain the health of the world economy and the creditworthiness of individual countries.

APPENDIX
Table 4.   Non-Oil Developing Countries:
External Debt, Exports, and Interest Payments
(In billions of U.S. dollars)

	Outstanding Long-Term Debt, End-of-Year	Exports of Goods and Services	Interest Payments on Long-Term External Debt
1973	97	109	4.6
1974	120	149	5.7
1975	147	150	7.5
1976	181	177	8.3
1977	222	211	10.1
1978	276	249	14.2
1979	324	318	20.7
1980	375	404	30.1
1981	437	423	37.5
1982	485	416	42.0
1983	525	454	37.0
1984	562	500	38.0
1985	601	550	39.0

Source: International Monetary Fund, *World Economic Outlook: A Survey by the Staff of the International Monetary Fund*, IMF Occasional Paper No. 9 (Washington, April 1982), pp. 170, 171 and 173, and author's estimates and projections for 1982 and beyond.

Commentary*

CARLOS MASSAD

The paper by Jack Guenther discusses three main aspects: the growth in external debt in the non-oil exporting developing countries since 1973; the necessary financing, after adjustment, and how much of it can be expected from commercial banks in the next few years; and the exposure of commercial banks active in international lending in non-oil exporting developing countries.

The discussion of the first of these aspects starts by showing that the rate of growth of long-term external debt of non-oil exporting developing countries grows pari passu with the dollar value of exports of goods and services between 1973 and 1980. Guenther argues that the growth of debt during this period played a very useful role in the world economy since it occurred as a by-product of the recycling of liquid funds accumulated by a few oil-rich countries. However, the rate of growth of exports slowed sharply in 1981–82, and this is the main cause of the external sector problems of non-oil exporting developing countries. Furthermore, interest rates rose substantially in recent years, which complicated the problem further. Also, domestic economic policies in some debtor countries were temporarily inadequate. He finds that it would be necessary to plan for at least a five-year period in which the growth in debt falls 2 or 3 percentage points below the rate of increase in exports which is expected to be about 10 percent a year. He concludes this section pointing to a 7 percent a year increase in debt as a limit for the next five years or so. Some Latin American and African countries should expect their debt to grow at rates somewhat lower than this while some countries in Asia "could tolerate" a rise in debt of more than 7 percent a year.

In discussing the second aspect, that is, how much of the imbalance should be adjusted and how much of it could be financed from different sources, Guenther reports that most developing countries have already adopted financial programs leading to a substantial reduction in their current account deficits. Such deficits are estimated to decline from a peak of $102 billion in 1981 to about two thirds of that figure in 1983—an adjustment which would be no larger than the one achieved between 1975 and 1977, after the first oil shock, in relation to trade flows.

Taking into consideration other forms of financing, Guenther finds that the estimated current account deficit for 1983 is consistent with the 7 percent growth of the outstanding stock of debt. He calls attention to the fact that

---

*The original version of this paper was written in Spanish.

commercial bank financing is substantially less stable than the financing from other sources and that this lack of stability explains the problems experienced by some countries. He assigns this lack of stability to the fact that banks lack the full information and expertise required to make opportune decisions. He warns that the problem will not be solved, but rather aggravated, if the decision on how credit should be allocated around the world were to be left to bank regulators in lending countries arguing that "there is no foundation for the idea that public officials would make fewer mistakes than the banks themselves" (pages 198–99). Commercial banks have been criticized as lending too aggressively in the 1970s, and of becoming too cautious in the 1980s to the point where the Fund had to intervene and actively prod the banks to provide additional financing to some debtor countries with credible programs.

The last section of the paper is devoted to a discussion of the idea that banks may be overcommitted to developing countries. Guenther agrees with the opinion that commercial banks cannot return to lending at the rate that existed prior to 1982, but they can provide about one third of the total financing required by the expected current account deficit of non-oil exporting developing countries in 1983, which again would be about a 7 percent increase of outstanding claims. As the total portfolio of commercial banks is expected to grow faster than that, lending to non-oil exporting developing countries will decrease in relation to portfolio. Guenther justifies continuous growth of lending on the grounds of asset portfolio diversification while pointing out that developing countries have a good record as borrowers in the past decade.

The paper ends with a call to lenders and borrowers to work together and keep the world economy healthy and individual countries creditworthy.

I tend to agree with the general line of argument and, with some caveats, with the moderately optimistic view of Guenther's paper. I would like to emphasize, however, a few aspects of the problem which seem to me are important for the full understanding of its implications. Such aspects are particularly relevant for the actions that ought to be taken both to smooth out the adjustment process and give credibility to an optimistic view.

Guenther recognizes at an early stage that the "size of the debt is worrisome, particularly under present world conditions" (page 186). Under different world conditions the size of the debt ought not to be worrisome at all. As a matter of fact, if for 18 non-oil exporting developing countries in Latin America, terms of trade in 1982 had been those prevailing on the average between 1965 and 1969, the deficit in current account of this group of countries would have been $17 billion smaller than the actual figures. If, in addition, interest rates had been those prevailing in the years 1978–79, the deficit in current account would have been $1.0 billion as compared with the actual figure of $25.2 billion. The results shown raise important questions: Are these shocks permanent or transitory? Should they bring about adjustment of financing?

The calculations are, of course, hypothetical. A change in the terms of trade or interest rates would probably have triggered other changes in policy and results. But the calculation is useful to give an idea of the explanatory power of these two variables, terms of trade and interest rates, in explaining the deficit in current account of the balance of payments. This calculation is not intended to diminish the domestic responsibility in debt and balance of payments management since both the debt and the deficit in current account are now with us. In this context, an exploratory study of nine countries in Latin America gives indications that foreign savings substituted for domestic savings in the period 1975–81 in five cases out of the total.

By the way, the relationships and mutual influences between the capital account and the current account in the balance of payments have been explored only recently in the literature; probably this explains why in different sections of Guenther's paper the order of causality between capital inflow and deficit in current account is changed. It looks as though there are two types of cases in Latin America: those where excessive domestic spending based on an expansion of domestic credit led to a deficit in current account, which induced further borrowing abroad; and those where banks' aggressiveness and an increased degree of openness of the domestic capital markets to foreign competition resulted in an inflow of foreign capital in the form of debt, which, through an overvaluation of the domestic currency despite negative effects of terms of trade, was transformed into an increased deficit in current account that facilitated absorption of the additional resources obtained.

These two types of cases, which seem to coincide with the oil exporting or non-oil exporting character of countries, ought to be distinguished because the recipes to produce adjustment should also be different. In the first case, excessive domestic spending through domestic credit creation should be curtailed as part of the adjustment process. In the second type of case, however, one might find that fiscal balance is well under control and that domestic credit is not expanding at any dangerous rate. This "good behavior" translates into relatively high real domestic interest rates as compared with foreign interest rates and in a substantive opening-up of the capital account which facilitates excessive *private* spending financed with foreign borrowing. This latter case is a nontraditional case and is difficult to recognize as a source of future problems except through the overvaluation of the currency and the imbalance in current account that accompany the process.

I would argue, as I have done in the last couple of years or so, that private overspending is as dangerous as public overspending in its effects on the external and internal balance of the economy. And perhaps private over-spending demands a more painful adjustment process than public excesses.

General conditions in the world economy and domestic policies are thus crucial to determine whether the 7 percent rate of growth of the stock of debt advocated by Guenther is feasible. Let me note that a 7 percent growth of outstanding claims would be equivalent to financing interest payments, or slightly less than that. That is, no net foreign savings would be flowing to non-oil exporting developing countries through bank financing in the next few years. For Latin America this means transfer of real resources to the rest of the world, since countries in the area are not among those whose debt is expected to grow faster than the average. As a matter of fact, countries in Latin America are being "graduated" from the World Bank and even from the Inter-American Development Bank (IDB) on the grounds that they have easy access to private bank financing!

Here I believe it may be useful to give a few figures to gauge the adjustment effort being made in the continent. For the first time since the Great Depression all countries in the area, without exception, have registered a drop in gross domestic product (GDP) per capita in 1982, and the region as a whole has shown a decrease in the level of total GDP in that year. Total unemployment reached 40 million, and the trade balance has swung from a deficit of $12 billion in 1981 to a surplus of $1.0 billion in 1982, while traditionally this is a foreign saving recipient region.

It is clear to me that, over and above what banks could do, international action is urgently required to avoid a prolonged, politically intolerable, period of stagnation.

(a) The official international financial institutions should be strengthened to make the private financial institutions viable. The resources of the World Bank and the IDB and other regional banks should be increased substantially. Those of the Fund should ideally be expanded to SDR 120 billion, which roughly implies only SDR 60 billion in usable currencies, a figure comparable to a one-year deficit in the current account of non-oil exporting developing countries, after adjustment.

(b) A new allocation of SDRs should be agreed upon soon, to bring up international foreign exchange reserves at least to the level they had at the end of 1981. The well-known asymmetries of the power of the Fund on debtors and creditors give a recessive character to global policies at present. A new allocation of SDRs would provide a better distribution of efforts throughout the world, helping to reactivate the world economy. Banks would not expand their lending as they did in the past.

(c) Institutionality for debt refinancing or reprogramming should be created to replace the outmoded "club" organizations. A debt reprogramming facility or a joint undertaking of the Fund and the World Bank, with access decided on the basis of objective indicators, but with terms and amounts of assistance studied case by case, would in a way only formalize, and give some stability, to present informal and hence erratic, arrangements. Financing for the facility could come from the interested banks themselves.

(d) A debt reprogramming facility would probably reduce the costs to borrowers of reprogramming, which are now quite substantial. In fact, before World War II creditors used to take part of the cost in the form of a reduced market value of their bonds: most debt was bonded. Debtor countries or institutions could buy back those bonds at a fraction of their face value. Now, bank portfolios are not easily transacted in the market, except *in articulo mortis*. So, debtors take up the whole burden of debt and at substantially increased spreads and flats. Is this a by-product of creditors' cartelization?

(e) Trade and financing are closely linked. If exports of non-oil exporting, developing countries grew at 15 percent a year instead of the 10 percent considered by Guenther, external debt of non-oil exporting developing countries could grow at a rate of 12 percent, faster than interest payments, and still decrease relative to exports. But figures like these require a more dynamic world economy and trade, and no protectionist measures against the exports of developing countries. Perhaps these latter countries should consider getting together to make sure that their full bargaining power is brought to bear in trade matters.

(f) Given the stock of debt already accumulated, changes in interest rates become a crucial element in external equilibrium of many debtor countries, so that smoothing out the effect of their changes on debtors could make a substantial contribution towards external stability. Mexico has made an interesting suggestion on this matter, and perhaps now is the time to give it serious consideration.

The new active catalytic role of the Fund is a sign of hope. Without it, the situation of many debtors would have already become unbearable. But this role, I believe, can continue to be effective only if it is (i) institutionalized, and (ii) accompanied by substantial additional resources, both conditional and unconditional. Without this, we will probably see an increasingly erratic behavior of countries and institutions in the adjustment process, a long, protracted period of slow recovery, and a growth of banks' claims on non-oil exporting developing countries, particularly those of Latin America, perhaps substantially below the modest 7 percent coming out of Guenther's calculations.

I would like to conclude my comments with Guenther's words: Lenders and borrowers, and, I would add, international institutions, should "work closely together to maintain the health of the world economy and the creditworthiness of individual countries" (page 204).

Commentary*

ALBERTO BENSIÓN

These remarks will deal with several of the topics raised in Jack Guenther's excellent paper.

Indebtedness Level

In the paper, external debt is defined in terms of medium- and long-term government-guaranteed liabilities and an estimate of private indebtedness with no government guarantee. It also includes an estimate of the short-term debt, with more detailed references to the private sector debt and, at the other extreme, to countries' external assets being omitted from the analysis.

The short-term debt of the non-oil developing countries is estimated to have amounted recently to about $100 billion, as against a medium- and long-term debt of $485 billion. Other related estimates show that the short-term portion of the debt has grown more rapidly than medium- and long-term debt. This not only reinforces the general conclusion of the paper with regard to the excessive rate of external debt expansion in the recent past, but also makes the need for international banks to support adjustment programs even more urgent.

Private borrowing without government guarantee is, as you know, difficult to assess. On the one hand, some systems of exchange arrangements do not require systematic recording of such liabilities to foreign countries; on the other, there are exchange systems with an opposite focus, which encourage accounting entries not reflecting true external liabilities. Quite apart from the case of foreign branches of developing countries' banks, which is examined in the paper, some countries have a banking system within their own boundaries which gathers foreign currency deposits of nonresidents. This could be considered a form of external indebtedness, indeed a highly volatile one, which has not been uniformly treated in the various countries' statistics. Finally, some countries may hold foreign currency assets of nonresidents as one means of partially offsetting the debt. In this case, to determine the country's net position as compared with the rest of the world, these assets should be subtracted from the debt.

Various Forms of Bank Assistance

Because of the debt incurred in the past and current liquidity problems, the first contribution the international banking community can make involves

---

*The original version of this paper was written in Spanish.

loans now maturing and the need to refinance them. At the same time, in view of the simultaneous need to bolster countries' liquid reserves and the resources to be used to support the activities of certain economic sectors, it is also essential to provide new loans, at least temporarily.

Neither form of financial support can be confined to relationships with government-guaranteed debtors, but instead should be extended to the private sector in general and the banking system in particular. It is known that the majority of adjustment programs impose some degree of temporary contraction in certain economic sectors, which of course has an impact on their ability to pay off their existing external liabilities. In these circumstances, and taking into account the fact that there has also been some recurrence in recent years of excessive expansion of domestic bank credit as well, some of those who owe money to the banks will require refinancing arrangements similar to those now being made available to governments and their central banks. For this to be fully possible, the private banking systems of the countries concerned require financial support from the international banks.

Finally, there is a third form of assistance; it is indirect in nature but is extremely important to the economic functioning of countries and the success of their adjustment programs.

The various financial reforms introduced in these countries in recent years have tended to produce a more direct relationship than in the past between the interest rate, the position of the external sector, and the consumption and investment plans of economic agents. These variables in turn are highly dependent on the expectations of the private sector and its confidence in the ultimate success of the adjustment programs under way.

In these conditions, the private sector looks upon the financial support of the international banking community as a vote of confidence in the policy pursued by the authorities, which improves the general climate for business and makes it possible to overcome more easily the difficulties inherent in the initial period of adjustment.

Debt Projections

In response to the diversity of recently expressed views, the paper reaffirms the traditional concept that exports are the best indicator of a country's external debt in the long term. Surely, under particular economic circumstances such as the present ones, the degree of external liquidity can be more important; however, it is no less certain that, fundamentally, export results continue to be the most significant element for evaluating a given growth policy and the ability of a country routinely to fulfill its external commitments.

Second, the paper reaches yet another conclusion which merits support, at least in general terms. Given the combination of the accelerated growth of debt in the past and the foreseeable persistence of high real interest rates in the future, it is advisable for increases in external debt in the next few years to be held below the level of the growth of exports.

Third, the paper includes specific projections of exports, debt, current account imbalances, and the supply of funds from various sources of financing. It is difficult to comment on this projected scenario without the information and global perspective which can be acquired only by constant work with the topic. It is known, for example, that various sources have ventured extreme predictions on topics such as future exports from the developing countries, these countries' capacity to fulfill existing adjustment programs, and the supply of funds from the international financial markets. The latter point, at least, merits some comment.

Obviously, for the debt to increase in the future, under normal circumstances it must be assumed that new loans will more than cover the amortization payments on earlier loans. This gives rise to two thoughts.

From a strictly financial point of view, it would be desirable to concentrate such new commercial banks' lending more than in the past on dealing with the countries' problems of liquidity, cutting back in relative terms on the financing of investment projects for the time being. The latter form of credit assistance is normally tied to the import requirements of the investment, and hence cannot be used to deal with the purely financial expenditure required for loan amortization.

From another standpoint, it bears noting that, in times more normal than the present, it was customary banking practice not to have debts repaid but instead to roll them over so long as interest continued to be paid as due. To some extent, the increase in external debt projected for the future could be considered an application of the same idea, with the added factor that a new increase in debt is anticipated.

It is this latter argument which is the most difficult to accept fully, given the magnitude of the problems recently experienced by the financial system and, in particular, their great exposure to the public eye. Therefore, while the need for simultaneously refinancing the debt and providing new loans in the immediate future must be stressed, it appears more realistic to assume that once this phase is over, the next few years will have to be characterized by a level of debt that remains stationary or even declines slightly in real terms. This, moreover, is the scenario set forth for Brazil and Mexico in the paper.

Following this more restrictive hypothesis with respect to financing, the most important consequence could/be that current adjustment efforts in individual countries should be prolonged somewhat in response to this new reality on international financial markets.

The Banks and the IMF

The relationship between the international banking community and the Fund appears, as we know, to have changed substantially as a result of recent financial events. Thus, while in the 1970s banks channeled their loans to the developing countries without regard to the Fund, credit agreements between the Fund and individual countries have now become a necessary condition for obtaining financial support from the international banks. This new functional arrangement appears to provide greater assurance than before that countries will have a more stable financing framework for their development plans.

We must therefore express our concern about the possibility referred to in the paper that banks may not consider programs worked out between individual countries and the Fund to be adequate, perhaps even to the extent that the banks would be prompted to cut back their future financial assistance.

Clearly international banks, like any other public or private institutions, cannot be bound by decisions of third parties. Be that as it may, there are a number of arguments in favor of banks' giving priority attention to countries' agreements with the Fund, at least under current economic circumstances.

As the paper notes, banks still do not have the information and capabilities required to understand and interpret fully the economies of individual countries or the viability of their adjustment programs. Furthermore, if deprived of their standing in the eyes of the international banking community, agreements with the Fund would lose a considerable proportion of the advantages which can mobilize public opinion in favor of their acceptance. Finally, it could well be now that direct relationships between the banks and individual countries would create a greater bias in favor of the aspirations of the larger debtors, to the detriment of the position of countries with smaller economies.